Upgrade or Repair Your PC & Save a Bundle

3rd Edition

Aubrey Pilgrim

Windcrest®/McGraw-Hill

New York San Francisco Washington, D.C. Auckland Bogotá
Caracas Lisbon London Madrid Mexico City Milan
Montreal New Delhi San Juan Singapore
Sydney Tokyo Toronto

THIRD EDITION
FOURTH PRINTING

© 1993 by **Windcrest**.
Windcrest is a division of McGraw-Hill, Inc.

This book was previously published as Upgrade your IBM Compatible
and Save a Bundle.

Library of Congress Cataloging-in-Publication Data

Pilgrim, Aubrey.
    Upgrade or repair your PC and save a bundle / by Aubrey Pilgrim.
        p.   cm.
    Rev. ed. of: Upgrade your IBM compatible and save a bundle.
    Includes index.
    ISBN 0-8306-4215-3   ISBN 0-8306-4214-5 (pbk.)
    1. IBM-compatible computers—Upgrading.   2. Microcomputers-
    -Upgrading.   3. IBM microcomputers—Repairing.   I. Pilgrim, Aubrey.
    Upgrade your IBM compatible and save a bundle.   II. Title.
    TK7887.5.G57   1992
    621.39' 16—dc20   92-46786
                                                                       CIP

Acquistions Editor: Roland Phelps
Editor: Laura Bader
Supervising Editor: Lori Flaherty
Director of Production: Katherine G. Brown
Book Design: Jaclyn J. Boone   EL1
Cover design and illustration : Rick Holdberg   4269

Contents

Foreword

I WAS SITTING AT THE CHILI COOKOFF AT COMDEX TRYING TO DECIDE WHAT TO DO. I had spent the day on the show floor looking at fast 486 systems, and I was still using an old 386/16. Worse yet, it seemed like everyone in my user group knew that I had an outdated system. Even my brother-in-law had a faster computer. It was embarrassing. I knew it was time to move to a 486. I thought about buying something new, but I'm cheap. The old system's case, power supply, video adapter, disk drives, and about everything else was still good, except for the slow motherboard.

As luck would have it, sitting next to me, a bottle of beer in front of him, was Aubrey Pilgrim, a longtime member of the Pasadena IBM Users Group and world famous author. So I thought, what better opportunity to get some expert advice.

Aubrey suggested I just replace the motherboard. "It's easy," he said. "I'll send you a copy of my *Upgrade Your IBM Compatible and Save a Bundle* book. It probably won't take more than an hour to upgrade." What he didn't know is I am a klutz.

But the neat thing about Pilgrim's Save a Bundle series of books is they are written for people who aren't engineers or tinkerers. Even if you're not very handy with tools, don't worry; Aubrey's books are geared toward both the novice and the expert user. He takes you through the process step-by-step. He helps you learn more about your system and discover new ways to fine-tune it.

Aubrey Pilgrim is a preeminent guru on the inner workings of computers. Aubrey's years of careful and painstaking research into upgrading and building computers has resulted in a clear, concise, and easy-to-understand teaching style. At a recent PIBMUG meeting, Aubrey demonstrated to 400 eager attendees how easy it was to upgrade their systems. It took him less than half an hour.

In *Upgrade or Repair Your PC and Save a Bundle—3rd Edition.* Aubrey gives you the benefit of his many years of experience as he prepares you for an exciting journey of upgrading your system. You'll learn many of the tricks and traps known only to bench technicians. Using his upgrade book saved me a bundle. By the way, my 486 upgraded system is still cooking, patiently awaiting a Pentium upgrade.

Steve Bass
President, of the 1400-member Pasadena IBM Users Group
Contributing Editor, *PC World magazine*
Founding member of the worldwide APC Users Group

Introduction

IF YOU ARE FAMILIAR WITH THE EARLIER EDITIONS OF THIS BOOK YOU MIGHT notice that the title has changed. It now includes the word "repair." In many cases, repair and upgrade might be one and the same. It is very easy to upgrade, replace, or repair.

Upgrade or repair a PS/1 or PS/2

This edition includes the PS/2. At one time, the only way you could upgrade or repair a PS/2 was to have an authorized IBM dealer do it. The parts had to be genuine IBM components installed by an authorized IBM dealer.

But times have changed. It is now possible to purchase many PS/1 and PS/2 components on the open market, and you don't need an IBM dealer to install them. In many ways, the PS/1s and PS/2s are easier to upgrade and repair than the compatible clones. And you can really save a bundle if you do it yourself. This book includes lots of photos and easy instructions to show you how. Anyone can do it.

You can use this book to upgrade or repair an IBM PS/1 or any IBM PS/2 model 25, 30, 35, or 40. These models are industry standard architecture (ISA) machines. The ISA machines are those that used to be called IBM and IBM compatible machines.

The PS/1 and PS/2 models 25 through 40 can use much of the $10 billion worth of hardware that is available. However, PS/1s and PS/2s have only one to three slots, so you are limited in what you can install. Of course, IBM supplies upgrade hardware for these machines, but at a much higher price than what you can buy it for on the open market.

It is a bit more difficult to find upgrade or replacement parts for the Micro Channel Architecture (MCA) models 50 and up. However, several components and upgrades that are available include larger hard disks, memory upgrades, and tape backup.

Troubleshooting a PS/1 or PS/2 system is no different than troubleshooting any other PC system. Chapter 18 offers many suggestions for finding and solving problems.

How much can you save?

Because the titles of all my books include the phrase "And Save A Bundle," I am often asked just how much can one save. The answer depends on many different things, including where the person shops, how well they shop, whether they buy brand names or clone products, and the type of upgrade or repairs they want.

Here is just one example of how you can save. A 386 computer costs from $1200 to $2000. You might have an old XT or 286. If you tried to sell these computers, you might get $200 or $300 for them. But you can replace the motherboard for $300 to $500 and your computer will be every bit as good as the $1200 to $2000 machine. It takes less than an hour to replace a motherboard. In that time, you can save from $900 to $1500.

Do you need to upgrade?

Some people drive around in 10-year-old cars. The old car gets them where they want to go, and it is usually paid for. There are other people who wouldn't be caught dead in an old car. They must have a brand new car every year.

When it comes to computers, many people are the same way. There are many people using computers that are 10 years old, and they are still using programs such as dBASE II and WordStar 3.0. These computers and programs are quite adequate. But there are other people who must have the biggest, most powerful, and fastest computer available, even if they are only doing word processing.

The B-B gene

I am convinced that there is a gene, as yet undiscovered, that influences and controls those people who must have the biggest, the best, and the most expensive of everything available. This includes cars, homes, clothes, and even computers. When this gene is finally discovered and documented, I suggest that it be called the "Biggest and Best" gene, or the B-B gene. There is little doubt in my mind that this gene exists in all of us, but it exerts a far greater influence over some.

Many of the people who are influenced by the B-B gene are quite willing to pay exorbitant prices for goods they perceive to be better than others simply because of a brand name. I have never had much money, so I try to make sure I get all the value I can for my few dollars. That is why it is difficult for me to understand why a person would pay three or four times more for an item simply because it has a well-advertised brand name. The same goes for computers. I can't understand why a person would buy a computer just because it has an IBM or Apple logo. For the price of an IBM or Apple, you can buy two or three equivalent compatible, no-name computers.

Please don't misunderstand me. I think the B-B gene is a good thing. I am influenced by it myself. Without it, there would be very little progress and innovation. Without the B-B gene we might all still be living in caves and using stone tools. Without the B-B gene we probably wouldn't have the many computer goodies that are available to us.

Some reasons you need to upgrade

The B-B gene might not be exerting much influence on you, and your old computer might be doing everything you want it to do. Still there are a few reasons why you should consider upgrading.

Time

One of the foremost reasons to upgrade is time. The XT lumbers along at a speed of only 4.77 MHz. It can run most DOS programs, but some of them take hours to complete. The 486 runs at speeds of up to 66 MHz, which is about 14 times faster than the XT. Because of new technologies and processing developments, a 486 can process data hundreds of times faster than an XT.

Time is important to all of us; we have so little of it. If you are wasting time while your old computer is struggling to run a simple program, you should consider upgrading.

New programs

Some of the newer programs simply will not run on older machines such as the XT. Some will not even run on the 286. Some excellent programs are available, such as Windows 3.1 and OS/2 2.0, that can make computing much easier and faster, and allow you to do many more things. There are thousands of new applications being developed every day. You might be missing out on a lot of goodies.

More friendly

Many software programs cost from $500 to $1000. Then you have to spend an additional $500 to $1000 for classes and instructions to learn to use them. Some software programs are much friendlier and easier to learn and use. But there is a price to pay. The programs are much larger and require more memory and disk space. To install and run OS/2 2.0 requires about 30 megabytes (Mb) of disk space. You also need a minimum of 4Mb of random-access memory (RAM).

The cost to upgrade or repair

If you send your computer to a shop to have it upgraded or repaired, it might cost you $50 to $100 an hour, plus the cost of the parts. I can understand why you might hesitate to upgrade. But you don't have to send your computer out to have the work done. You can do the work yourself. It is very easy to upgrade or repair your old computer. This book shows you how easy it is with lots of photos and easy-to-understand instructions.

Used computers

This book shows you how to upgrade or repair your old computer to bring it up to date with the newest technologies. If you don't have an old computer to upgrade, don't let that stop you. Buy a used one and upgrade it. The problem with buying a used computer is that you might have trouble finding one. I live in the Los Angeles area, and I seldom see more than two or three IBMs or compatibles listed when I check the classified ads.

About 100 million computers have been sold, and evidently everybody is holding onto them. They might be upgrading them, or they might be passing their old ones to their kids or relatives and buying new ones. Many large companies are buying newer, bigger, better, and faster systems. But these companies don't get rid of their old computers. They just pass the old computers down the line to the personnel and departments who were doing without computers. Of course, an older XT or 286 is better than no computer at all. Besides, most people probably don't need the power and speed of a 386 or 486.

Perhaps one reason you don't see too many used computers for sale is that computers are built primarily from semiconductors. If a system is designed properly, it should last for several lifetimes. Of course, the disk drives, keyboard, and other components will eventually wear out, but most of them can be replaced.

Buying a used IBM

A used computer with an IBM logo on it will probably cost more than two new clones. This is pure snob appeal. There is no basic difference between the IBMs and the clones. You can take anything out of the clone and plug it into the IBM, and vice versa.

Some might argue that IBM is an American company so the quality is better. If you look inside an IBM, you will find almost as many circuits and components with foreign names as you will find in any clone. As for quality, I have had quite a lot of experience with both IBM computers and clones, and I am convinced that the main difference between them is the IBM logo.

Beware of used mechanical items

It is perfectly okay to buy anything electronic that is working. But I strongly advise against buying used printers, disk drives, or anything mechanical. As I said earlier, semiconductors do not wear out, but mechanical components have a finite lifetime and do eventually fail. According to Murphy's law, they usually fail at the most inopportune time.

Of course, if you find a mechanical component that is almost new, and you get a good buy on it, don't pass it up. Several companies buy old hard disks and printers and rebuild them. If you can get a good warranty and a resonable price on these products, they should be all right.

Buying a bare-bones unit

You might consider buying a bare-bones system and configuring it yourself. A bare-bones unit usually consists of a case, a motherboard, and a power supply. In order to have a functioning computer, you need disk drives, a keyboard, a monitor, and several other goodies. You can buy them from different sources for the best price, you don't have to buy them all at once. You can build your system gradually as you can afford it. You will still save money, and you will put together your own computer.

Compatibility

Some computers and some software are more IBM compatible than others. In the early days of computers, there weren't many hardware and software choices, so compatibility wasn't much of a problem. Now, about 7 billion dollars worth of software and about the same amount of hardware is available. One of the most basic principles of sales is to make your product different and better than the competition. Many of the clone products are made better than similar IBM products. Certainly, a lot more clone products are available.

What you put into your computer or add to it should depend on what you want it to do. In most cases, it will be at least 99 percent compatible. But if it does what you want it to do, it doesn't really matter if it is only 50 percent compatible.

Organization of this book

One of the problems encountered in writing a book is you don't know how much your readers already know. If you make it too simple, you discourage the old pros. If you make it too technical, you write over the heads of the newcomers. I try to take the middle ground throughout this book.

This book is primarily about hardware and components you can add to your system to make it bigger and better. I discuss the options and choices at the beginning of each chapter, and then go into more detail for those who want more information. I use plain English throughout this book, and try to avoid using computer jargon unless it is absolutely necessary. In some cases, there is no other way. A comprehensive glossary is included at the back of the book. If you come across something that is unfamiliar, check for a definition in the glossary.

The future

Figure I-1 shows a 486 central processing unit (CPU). There are 1.2 million transistors in this small chip. The chip measures 0.414 inch by 0.619 inch. (I can remember when a single transistor was bigger than this chip.) In contrast, Fig. I-2 is a 386 chip with only 275,000 transistors. It measures approximately 0.38 inch by 0.38 inch.

I-1 The 486 chip with 1.2 million transistors. The chip measures 0.414 inch by 0.619 inch.

I-2   A 386 chip with 275,000 transistors. The chip measures about 0.375 inch by 0.375 inch.

But the 486 is not the "ultimate chip." Intel's 586 has about 3 million transistors and is even faster and better than the 486. Several manufacturers have developed products using the Pentium CPU. The CPU is called Pentium because Intel was unable to copyright the 386 and 486 names, and other manufacturers have applied 386 and 486 designations to their clone products. Intel is unhappy about this and might apply a new name or designation to the P5 that can be copyrighted and protected as a brand name.

Intel says it will have CPUs with over 100 million transistors by the year 2000. The technology of the computer industry is one of the fastest changing technologies. I discuss many new and improved products in this book, but I can't possibly list them all. Such a book could never be complete because thousands of new products are introduced every day.

You can be sure that faster, more-powerful, and more-useful computers will be on the market by the time you read this, but that doesn't mean you should wait for the latest development. Remember, there will always be something new out tomorrow. Besides, maybe you don't really need the newest, the fastest, and the most powerful computer. Perhaps you can get by with one that is almost the fastest and most powerful.

You can do it

Despite all my assurances, some of you might still have doubts or fears about upgrading or repairing your computer. Don't worry. It does not require a lot of expertise. It requires no soldering or board assembly. Please believe me, you can do it.

1
Upgrading, enhancing, or repairing your PC or PS/2

COMPUTER TECHNOLOGY IS ADVANCING AND CHANGING FASTER THAN ANY OTHER technology. The technology is changing so fast that if you walk out of a store with a brand new computer, by the time you get it home, it is practically obsolete. New programs and products are developed every day that cannot be used on some older systems. These new products can make life a lot easier and simpler. If your computer is three or four years old, it belongs to the dinosaur age. But not to worry. Your computer, no matter how old, can be upgraded to take advantage of all the latest technology.

If you are unfamiliar with the insides of your computer, chapter 2 provides a brief explanation of the components. Figure 1-1 shows some of the components needed to assemble a computer. Except for the motherboard, the parts in a PC, XT, 286, 386, or 486 are all basically the same. There are in-depth discussions of the major components in later chapters.

Internal upgrades

Here are a few major upgrades that can make your computer faster, more powerful, and more effective. They are also cost effective.

Plug-in boards

About $10 billion worth of hardware has been developed for ISA machines. The ISA machines are what used to be called *IBM PCs and compatibles*. The PS/1 and several PS/2 models are ISA-type machines.

Because of the open architecture of ISA computers, they can be configured to perform thousands of applications. In fact, many boards have been designed for these applications. A board can be plugged into one of the slots in the motherboard for a very easy upgrade.

1-1 The parts needed to assemble a computer. The major parts are the monitor, the case, the large motherboard with the plug-in boards (left center), the chrome-plated power supply (right center), a floppy drive sitting on edge (center), the keyboard, and various cables. These basic parts are found in all PCs.

Accelerator boards

Several companies have developed accelerator boards that can be plugged into older motherboards. The more popular of these boards have newer CPUs such as the 386 and 486. Just plug these accelerator boards into your computer to give your old XT or 286 many of the features of a powerful 386 or 486 machine. See chapter 3 for more information on accelerator boards.

Processors

Several companies have developed 386SX processor modules. When plugged into a 286 or a PS/2, these modules turn the computer into a 386SX or 486. This allows you to use all the latest software. The upgrade is very easy and quick. Minor upgrades and 386SX processor upgrades are discussed in chapter 3.

Motherboards

The motherboard is the main board in your computer. The motherboard is the primary difference between the systems. Except for the motherboard, the XT, 286, 386, and 486 all use the same basic components, such as disk drives, monitors, modems, and other components.

The motherboard contains the CPU, the memory, the basic input/output system (BIOS), the bus, and many other components. It has slots so other boards can be plugged into it. If you have an XT or an older PC, you can remove the motherboard and replace it with a late-model 386 or 486. Figure 1-2 shows a standard-size 486 motherboard.

1-2 A standard-size 486 motherboard. The white section near the top left is for SIMMs. The chip sockets in the lower right corner are for SRAM cache chips.

A new 386SX, 386DX, or 486 motherboard can be one of the most beneficial upgrades you can make. These motherboards allow you to run any software or use any hardware available. Best of all, it is very easy to pull out your old motherboard and install a new one.

CPUs

If you have a 386 or 486, you might be able to install a faster or more-powerful CPU. However, this can only be done with those motherboards that are designed for the upgrade. Chapter 4 goes into more detail about motherboards.

Upgrades for the PS/2

In the past, there weren't many parts and components available for upgrading PS/2 machines, except those from IBM. But there are now quite a number of sources for components and parts. It is no more difficult to upgrade or repair a PS/2 than any other PC. Chapter 5 is devoted to a more detailed description of the PS/1 and PS/2.

More memory

My first computer, a little Morrow CP/M machine, had a whopping 64K of memory. That was plenty for the few applications that were available, but programs soon required many times more memory than this. OS/2 requires 4Mb in order to run smoothly. Depending on the application, it might require much more.

Today, most major software programs require a minimum of 2Mb. In fact, many new software programs require at least 4Mb of memory to run. Fortunately, the cost of memory has come way down. Memory is very easy and simple to install. For more information about memory, see chapter 6.

ROM BIOS

If you really want to keep your old computer, you might need a new read-only memory (ROM) BIOS. The BIOS is on plug-in chips on the motherboard. As the name suggests, it controls the input and output of data to the computer. In the early days, the BIOS was fairly simple because not many applications were available. The original IBM PC didn't even support hard disk drives. If you have an older machine, you probably need a new BIOS. I have an ancient 286 that was designed and built in 1984. I had problems with several new programs and applications until I installed a new BIOS.

Several companies specialize in selling replacement BIOS chips. They advertise regularly in *Computer Shopper* and other computer magazines. Be aware, however, that new BIOS chips could cost more than a new motherboard that has a new BIOS and all the other chips. Their cost ranges from $40 to $60. I have seen new complete XT motherboards for less than $50, and a 286 motherboard for about $60. See chapter 7 for more information on the BIOS.

Floppy drives

The old 360K floppy drive has served us well, but it is obsolete. Several newer drives are available that are inexpensive and easy to install. The 1.2Mb floppy drives can read, write, and format both 360K disks and 1.2Mb disks. These drives cost about the same as a 360K drive, but can store three times more data.

The 1.44Mb, 3½-inch drives can read, write, and format both 720K disks and 1.44Mb disks. A 1.44Mb drive will cost about the same as a 720K drive, but it allows you to store twice as much data.

I don't know why anyone would buy a 360K or 720K drive, but many vendors still advertise and sell them. Further, 2.88Mb floppy drives are now reasonably priced. At least two companies, Brier Technology and Insite, have developed 21Mb floppy drives that are now very reasonably priced, and Iomega has a 90Mb floppy drive. Floppy drives are discussed in more detail in chapter 8.

Hard drives

I assume you already have a hard drive. If not, then by all means you should get one. It is almost impossible to do any productive computing without at least a 100Mb hard drive. The prices have come way down. Hard drives are also very easy to install. Even if you have an older hard disk that is less than 100Mb, you should probably get a second one or a larger one.

Several companies have developed external hard drives that can be plugged into the computer's parallel port. These hard drives can be used on almost any computer—laptops, desktops, and all models of the PS/1 and PS/2. It is a very easy way to upgrade your hard drive system. More information about hard drives is provided in chapter 9.

Backup

If your data is worth anything at all, it is worth backing up. It is very easy to lose or erase files that took many hours to create. Data can disappear in a fraction of a second. Make sure your hard disk is backed up *at all times*. You never know when it might fail, or when you might accidentally erase a critical file.

There are several good backup programs available. One of them is not very sophisticated, but it comes free with your copy of DOS—the BACKUP and RESTORE commands. Commercial backup programs cost a bit of money, but their speed, versatility, and convenience make them worthwhile. Many hardware systems, such as tape and other disk systems can be very good backup methods. Chapter 10 covers some of the many ways to back up your data.

Monitors

Small monochrome monitors are very inexpensive. So are the old color graphics adapter (CGA) types. But life is too short not to have good color. Today's new monitors have much greater resolution than earlier CGAs, and the prices have come way down. A good, high-resolution Super VGA (SVGA) color monitor costs about the same as a monochrome monitor did a few years ago. Super VGA is becoming the new standard, with many options and choices available.

Monochrome monitors can be very inexpensive and give excellent resolution, but I like color. Even if I do nothing but word processing, I am willing to pay a few dollars more for color. In many applications color is essential. See chapter 11 for more information about monitors.

Input devices

If you use your computer very much, you know the importance of the keyboard. It is the primary method of data input. If the keys are too soft or they don't suit your typing style, consider upgrading. Keyboards are very inexpensive.

The PC and XT keyboards look exactly like the 286 and 386 keyboards, and even have the same connector, but if you plug a PC or XT keyboard into a 286 or 386 computer, it will not work. Some later model keyboards have a switch that allows them to work with both systems.

Mice and trackballs

One of the biggest selling points of the Apple Macintosh is the fact that it is so easy to learn and use. With a mouse, you just point and click. Now there's Windows and thousands of software programs that make a PC as easy to learn and use as the Macintosh. There are also thousands more programs and hardware devices available for the PC than for the Macintosh. The cost of a mouse has come way down. As I write this, I am using a mouse that cost $10. A mouse can make life in the computing lane a lot easier.

Trackballs operate much like a mouse, but they require much less desk space. Some companies have developed keyboards with a built-in trackball.

Scanners

A scanner is essential if you plan to do any type of desktop publishing. You can often save a lot of time by simply scanning a printed page and drawing into your computer. Scanners are now fairly inexpensive and they are easy to install. See chapter 12 for more details about input devices.

Communications

With a modem, your computer can communicate with thousands of bulletin boards, online services, and other computers. Your computer can use the telephone line almost as easily as you do. Most bulletin boards are crammed full with public domain and shareware programs. Many of these programs are as good as the high-cost commercial programs. Downloading just one of these programs might even pay for the cost of a modem.

Very few offices or businesses can exist today without a fax machine. You can easily install a fax board in your computer and have all the benefits of this great tool without buying a separate machine. Chapter 13 covers some of the ways to communicate.

Printers

Printers are a very important part of your computer system. If you have an old dot matrix printer, you might be unhappy with the quality. New printers can deliver near letter quality type. Most of them are fast and comparatively inexpensive. Even the prices of new laser printers are coming down to where they are afford-able. I recently bought a Panasonic KX-P4410 laser printer for $589. My HP Laser-Jet III cost almost three times that much. Chapter 14 discusses the many types of printers.

Software

Without software you could not run your computer. Software is as essential to a computer as gasoline is to an automobile. Billions of dollars worth of software has been developed for the IBM PC and compatibles. New programs and improvements are introduced daily. This software can give you great versatility, utility, and capability.

Depending on your applications and needs, you will probably want to move up to DOS 5.0 or DR DOS 6.0. Windows can make life much easier too. OS/2 2.0 is now very inexpensive and it includes Windows, DOS 5.0, and Adobe Type. It is a real bargain. Chapter 15 lists some of the essential software you should have.

Ways to benefit from your computer

You can use your computer for thousands of tasks, such as desktop publishing, networking, and other business uses. It can also be a great recreation tool for playing games such as solitaire, chess, and others. It is impossible to list them all. One reason is that new devices, hardware, and software are being developed and introduced every day.

Multimedia

It is now possible to turn your computer into a full orchestra or a learning classroom. You can add sound and musical instrument digital interfaces (MIDI). There are even software and hardware programs that can make your computer respond interactively, much like a human being.

CD-ROM

The cost of CD-ROM drives has come way down. I bought a CD-ROM drive in 1987 that cost more than $1000. I recently bought one that cost $345. The cost of CD-ROM disks has also come way down. There are now hundreds of programs that are quite reasonable. The programs include everything from games to very complex science and technology subjects. They can be an excellent educational tool. Chapter 16 discusses some of the many ways you can get the most from your computer.

Sources

One of the better sources for information about computers and components is computer magazines. There are at least 100 being published today. Most are filled with ads because ad revenue is what makes them possible. Several magazines are listed in chapter 17.

Mail order is discussed in chapter 17 also. It might be one of your better alternatives for components and supplies. Another good source is computer shows and swaps. If you live near a large city, there is probably a computer show or swap going on every weekend. I enjoy going to them even if I don't need anything. The atmophere is almost like a circus.

Of course, you should patronize your local computer dealer whenever possible. His prices might be slightly higher than the mail-order houses or the prices at computer swaps, but he might be able to give you help and support and answer questions if you have problems.

You should also join a user group and attend meetings. Members can help you and exchange ideas with you. Most groups are also able to acquire public domain software and other goodies at a discount. If you have a modem, you can access bulletin boards to download public domain software and get help for any of the problems you might encounter. Chapter 17 lists some sources for components, such as computer swaps, retail outlets, and mail order.

Troubleshooting and repairing

You have to know what is wrong in order to repair your computer. Chapter 18 tells you how to find most common problems and how to fix them. But in most cases you will want to replace, rather than repair. For instance, over the years, several of my floppy drives have become defective. In 1983, an IBM 360K floppy drive cost over $400. When one became defective, it was worth it to send it out and have it repaired. A floppy drive today costs about $50. Most repair shops charge from $50 to $100 an hour plus parts. It is much better to throw the old drive away and replace it with a new one.

The same goes for most motherboards. It is possible that a circuit trace on a motherboard might break or one of the IC chips might become defective. It can take hours of time and some very sophisticated equipment to find the fault. Even when the fault is detected, it might require some highly technical skills to repair it or to remove and resolder the component. An XT motherboard can be purchased for less than $50. It costs only slightly more for a 286 motherboard. A 386SX motherboard costs a little over $100. Some of the high-end 386 and 486 motherboards are still a bit expensive, but in most cases, it is cost effective to scrap the motherboard and replace it with a new one. The same goes for most of the other components in your computer. In most cases, repairing means replacing the component.

Why you should do it yourself

There are shops and several mail-order stores that will upgrade your computer for you. Of course, these stores cannot stay in business unless they make a profit, so they tend to be a bit expensive. They can also take a lot of time and be rather inconvenient.

First, you have to find someone to do the work for you at a reasonable price. Then, you have to lug the computer to the shop, usually during business hours, fight the traffic, and find a place to park. Or you can package it up and send it off to a mail-order store. If you send it to a mail-order store for an upgrade, communication can be a problem. Just what do you want done to your computer? How much do you want to spend? How busy is the shop or mail-order store? How reliable is the shop? Can you get a firm price for the total cost and a date as to when they can get your computer back to you? How long can you wait for it? If the shop is very busy, it might take longer than promised to get it out.

Is it too old to upgrade?

Your computer is never too old to be enhanced or upgraded in some manner. But considering all the trouble and expense, you might think that it's better to sell your old computer for scrap and buy a new one. Depending on what you have, and what you want, scrapping it or selling it might be a viable alternative.

Another alternative is to donate it to a church or to a charitable organization. You might not be able to sell the computer for what you think it is worth. The computer that you paid $2500 for a few years ago might not be worth $500 today. Also, you might not want to go through the hassle of advertising and selling it. Depending on your tax situation, you might come out ahead by donating it and deducting it as a gift on your income tax return.

Buying a used computer

If you are lucky, you might be able to buy a used computer and upgrade it. You might look around your area and check the classified ads. A used XT should cost about $200; a 286 about $400. Depending on what you need a computer for, this might be all you need. An XT is very good for word processing and other applications such as some small databases. If you buy a used computer and find that you need more speed and power, you can upgrade it yourself. It is very easy to do.

If you work for a large company, chances are they are in the process of buying new more-powerful systems to meet their added business needs. Find out what the manager of the computer procurement department is doing with the old computers. Some companies pass them down to secretaries and other people who are low on the totem pole. Many companies sell them to their employees for a good price.

Enhancing a new computer

Even if you have a new computer, there are all kinds of things you can do to upgrade and enhance it, and you can do it yourself. If you are not familiar with the innards of your computer, you might be afraid to tackle a project like this, but it is very simple. I show you how you can do it yourself and save a bundle.

A new business opportunity

After you finish this book, I think you will agree that it is very easy to upgrade a computer. Once you see how easy it is, you might even want to go into business for yourself. Worldwide there are about 100 million computers in use. About half of them are older computers that can be upgraded. Many of these computers might be sitting in corners, not being used, because they have a defective floppy drive or some other minor problem that could easily be fixed. Many companies buy new computers because they don't realize how easy and inexpensive it is to upgrade or repair their older ones. That is a terrible waste of money and resources.

2
What's inside

IF YOU ARE NOT FAMILIAR WITH THE COMPONENTS INSIDE YOUR COMPUTER, IT WILL be difficult for you to upgrade or replace them. This chapter tells you how to remove the cover, how to identify the major components, and how to remove and replace them.

Tools needed

A few inexpensive basic tools are all you need. Even if you don't expect to do much computer upgrading and repairing, these tools are good for other uses around the home. Figure 2-1 shows some of the tools that you need.

2-1 Some helpful tools for upgrading and repairing your PC.

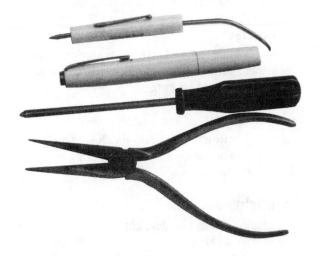

Screwdrivers

You should have a couple of different size flat-blade screwdrivers and Phillips screw-drivers. Most computer systems use Phillips-type screws. Some use a Phillips-type head with a slot so you can use either a Phillips or a flat-blade screwdriver. Some systems use screws that have a hexagonal head. A ¼-inch nut driver can be used on these screws.

A few systems, such as Compaq, use Torx screws. Torx screws are similar to Phillips screws, but they have six slots. You might be able to remove them with a Phillips screwdriver, but it is much easier with a proper size Torx screwdriver. The two sizes most often used are T-10 and T-15.

Pliers

You need standard pliers and long-nose pliers. The long-nose pliers are very handy for retrieving dropped screws. The flat portion of the long-nose blades are also excellent for straightening the pins on integrated circuit (IC) chips or the pins on connectors.

Volt-ohmmeter

A volt-ohmmeter is used to check for the presence or absence of voltages in your computer. A volt-ohmmeter can also be handy around the home for checking out small appliances that might be defective. They are available at any Radio Shack or electronics store.

Many problems can be traced to cables. One of the wires in a cable might break, especially if it is subject to a lot of use and frequent flexing. I once spent a lot of time on a bad cable. It had a broken wire that made contact until the cable was moved. A volt-ohmmeter can be used to check the continuity of cables and power cords.

Wire strippers

There might be times when you need to build a special cable or repair one. You should have wire strippers and cutters for just such occasions.

Bench vise

You need a small bench vise to hold cable connectors and other small parts while you check them or work on them. A small vise is also very handy to have around the house for dozens of other uses.

Soldering iron

You probably won't need to do much soldering, but just in case, you should have a soldering iron and some solder. A soldering iron is essential if you have to build or re-pair any of your cables.

Flashlight

A flashlight or a good bench light is essential for troubleshooting and exploring your computer. A good magnifying glass might also come in handy for reading the small type and part numbers on some chips.

Chip pullers

CAUTION! Before removing any chip, make a diagram with the socket number you find on the motherboard and the orientation of the chip. It is very easy to forget just where a chip belongs or how it should be oriented.

Standard chip pullers or extractors are available if you need to remove or replace any of the chips, such as when installing a new BIOS. These are necessary if you expect to do a lot of removing and installing of chips.

Ordinarily you won't be removing and changing chips very often. I use a small bent screwdriver that works very well. I also use the metal fillers used on the back panel to cover slots that have no boards installed. Just place the bent portion of the filler under one end of the IC, prying up one end and then the other until it is free (see Fig. 2-2).

2-2 The metal fillers from the back panel that cover the unused slots make a great tool for lifting out chips.

It takes a special tool to remove the large square chips. They usually have one corner cut off. This cut corner matches the socket and ensures that the chip is plugged in properly. To remove one of these chips, you need a tool similar to an ice pick. It is a thin hardened metal probe. The probe is used to pry the chip up from the cutoff corner. You might be able to use an ice pick or a very small screwdriver.

Removing the cover

The first thing to do before removing the cover is to remove the power from the unit. Unplug the monitor, the keyboard, and any other cables from the unit. Before unplugging any cable, make sure the connectors and cables are plainly marked so that you can plug them back together properly. If the cables are not marked, take some masking tape and a marking pen and label each cable and connector. If there is a chance that the connector could be plugged in improperly, place a mark across both connectors so that the mark lines up when they are reconnected.

In the early days, there were only one or two different types of cases. Most of them were similar to the IBM-type XT or standard AT type. The covers of these cases are held in place by five screws on the back panel. There is one in each corner and one at the top center (see Fig. 2-3). When the screws are loosened, the cover can be slipped off toward the front. There might be several other screws on the back panel. These are for the power supply and various connectors. These screws should not be removed.

2-3   The back of a standard case. Five screws hold the cover on. They are located at each of the four corners and one in the top center.

Many cases today are similar to the XT and AT types, but there are also many new styles available. Some are the low-profile and small-footprint types. These use different methods to secure the cover.

Case and power supply

The desktop-type case is still the most popular type. Most desktop cases are limited to three or four bays for mounting disk drives. If you want to install two hard drives, a 1.2Mb floppy, and a 1.44Mb floppy, you need a case with at least four bays.

Some low-profile cases are similar to the IBM PS/2 type. They are not even high enough to mount a vertical plug-in board. They usually have a single slot on the motherboard and a daughterboard plugs into this slot. The daughterboard has three to five slots for plug-in boards that are mounted horizontally. Low-profile cases limit the number of plug-in slots and also the number of drive bays available. Most of them only have room for two drives—a single floppy drive and a hard drive. Because of these limitations, I don't recommend the low-profile systems.

You might want to buy a tower case. The tower case sits on the floor, and the larger ones have space for eight drive bays. This provides room for two hard drives, two floppies, a tape backup, a CD-ROM, a write-once read-many (WORM) drive, and others. Figure 2-4 shows some various types of tower cases.

Tower cases are a bit more expensive than standard or baby-size cases. Tower cases come in three sizes: a mini tower, a medium size, and a large size. The smaller sizes do not have as many bays for mounting drives. Most tower cases include a power supply and sell for $80 to $150. Make sure that the power supply is at least 200 watts.

Static electricity warning

CAUTION! Before touching any of the components inside your computer, make sure you discharge yourself of any static electricity. It is possible for a person's body to build up 4000 volts of static electricity. If you touch any of the sensitive electronic components in your computer, static electricity can be discharged through them. This static electricity can destroy or severely damage some circuits.

Discharging yourself

When you touch a metal door knob, you discharge static electricity. A much better discharge occurs if you touch something that goes directly to ground, such as a water pipe. Because you probably don't have a water pipe near your computer, the next best thing to touch is a bare metal part of your computer.

The power switch on your computer should be turned off. Plug the power cable into the wall outlet. Even with the computer switch off, the third wire (the ground wire) of the power plug is still connected to the power outlet. If you trace this ground wire back to your main circuit breaker or fuse box, you will find that this ground wire is connected to a water pipe or to a metal rod that goes to earth ground. The metal chassis of your computer should be connected to this earth ground by the third wire of the 110-volt power outlet.

Most boards and components have a static electricity warning label on the packaging. In most cases, you have to break the warning label in order to open the package. It is a good idea to discharge yourself before handling any electronic component or board, especially if you have walked across a carpeted room.

Motherboards

Once the cover is removed, you will see several boards plugged into the large motherboard that sits on the floor of the chassis. There are usually eight slots on the

2-4 Various types of tower cases.

motherboard for various types of plug-in boards. You might have a board for your monitor, one for your printer, one for your mouse, one for your modem, one or more for your disk drive controllers, and perhaps several others.

Motherboard slots

Most computers have eight slots on the motherboard, whether it be an IBM XT or AT, or a clone XT, 286, 386, or 486. Some baby 286 and 386 motherboards have only seven slots. The early IBM PC had only five slots. Some high-end systems have motherboards with 12 slots.

The IBM PS/2 systems and the clone low-profile systems have a single slot on the motherboard for a plug-in daughterboard. This daughterboard has from two to five slots for plug-in boards that are mounted horizontally. If it has five slots, there are usually three slots on one side and two on the other. Figure 2-5 shows a low-profile system with a single daughterboard.

2-5 A low-profile system. Note the three slots for mounting horizontal plug-in boards.

The motherboard slots are for the various plug-in boards you might want to use. Plug-in boards have an edge connector with etched copper fingers that contact the spring-loaded contacts of the motherboard slot connectors.

Motherboard differences

One of the major differences between the XT, the 286, the 386, and the 486 is the motherboard. Figure 2-6 shows an XT motherboard on the left, a 286 motherboard in the center, and a 386 motherboard on the right. The plug-in slots are at the bottom in the photo. Notice that the 286 has six extra 36-pin slots above the eight standard 62-pin slots. The 386 motherboard shown in the photo has four extra 36-pin slots and two extra 62-pin slots. The extra 36-pin slots are for 16-bit system boards. The two extra 62-pin slots on the 386 motherboard are for special proprietary 32-bit memory boards. Instead of an extra 62-pin slot for memory, most modern motherboards use single in-line memory modules (SIMMs).

2-6 Comparison of an XT (left), a 286 (center), and a 386 motherboard (right).

The standard 62-pin slots on all motherboards are eight-bit slots. Boards developed to utilize the extra 36-pin slot are 16-bit boards. Notice that all of the eight-bit 62-pin slot connectors are separate from the extra 16-bit and 32-bit connector slots. As you have probably deduced, an eight-bit board designed for the XT can also be used in a 286, 386, or 486 computer. But a 16-bit board designed for a 286 cannot be plugged into an XT; however, it can be used in a 386. And of course, a 32-bit board designed for a double 62-pin slot cannot be used in a 286 or an XT.

If you have an older PC, your motherboard might be mounted on nine standoffs. It will have nine screws or nuts on the bottom of the chassis and on top of the motherboard holding it in place. Most of the newer systems use raised channels on the floor of the chassis. The channel has wide slots that become narrow. The motherboard has white plastic standoffs, and these standoffs are dropped into the wide portion of the slot on the raised channel. The motherboard is then pushed to the narrow portion of the channel slot. A screw in the front center and one in the rear center are sufficient to hold the motherboard secure. To remove the motherboard, remove the two screws and pull the motherboard toward you until the standoffs are disengaged. There is more information about motherboards in chapter 4.

Power supply

If you have a desktop-type case, the power supply is located in the right rear corner of the chassis. It has a chrome-plated cover around it. It has a cooling fan that generates the only noise you hear, except for the disk drives, when your computer is running. The power supply usually has four screws on the back panel that hold it in place. The power supply might also have a couple of cutouts on the bottom that interlock with the raised tabs on the floor of the chassis. To remove the power supply, remove the four screws on the back panel, and slide the power supply toward the front of the chassis to disengage the tabs.

Computer systems use direct current (dc). The dc voltages needed are 12 volts and 5 volts. The voltage that is provided by a wall socket is usually 110-volts alternating current (ac). The computer power supply uses rectifiers and transformers to convert the ac voltage to the proper dc voltages.

The 110 volts in the power supply is the only voltage in your computer that might harm you. That is one reason for the cover over it. Another reason for the cover is to reduce any stray radiation that might emanate from the conversion process.

Disk drives

The disk drives are usually mounted in the right front quadrant of the chassis. Depending on the type of case you have, you might have bays for two floppy drives and one or two hard drives. The bays for the floppy drives are accessible from the front. The hard drive bays might not be accessible once the cover is installed.

The drive bays have slots and holes for mounting the drives, and the drives have several screw holes on their sides that match up with the holes in the bays. Some cases have slots for using plastic or metal slides. The slides are attached to the drives, and the drives are inserted in the slots and pushed to the rear of the bay. A couple of screws or small flanges are used to hold the drives in place.

Cost of components

All of the PCs use the same basic components. The main difference between the various systems is the motherboard and the CPU. Because the common components are all interchangeable, you can shop around for the best buys. Look at the ads in computer magazines such as *Computer Shopper, PC Sources, InfoWorld Direct, Computer Monthly,* and others for an idea of what is available. These ads will also give you an idea of the cost of the various components and options. You can order the components through the mail, or if you live near a large city, go to a swap meet or to a local store.

Motherboard costs

Here are some approximate costs for the various types of motherboards. There are hundreds of different manufacturers and many, many options, so the prices will vary.

XT	$ 40 – 60
286	70 – 150
386SX	100 – 350
386DX	300 – 600
486SX	350 – 650
486DX	500 – 900
486EISA	800 – 1500

Component costs

Here are some approximate costs for the various components that are common to all PCs.

Case	$ 35 – 105
Power supply	40 – 70
Monitor	65 – 900
Monitor adapter	40 – 200
Memory, 4Mb	140 – 180
Multifunction board	50 – 200
Floppy drive, 1.4Mb	55 – 75
Floppy drive, 1.2Mb	55 – 75
Floppy drive, 2.8Mb	300 – 400
Hard drive, 80–300Mb	250 – 995
Disk controller	20 – 150
Keyboard	40 – 150

As you can see, there can be quite a large variation in price. The price depends on available options and whether the component has a well-known brand name. There is also a large variation in price from dealer to dealer. Some high-volume dealers might charge less than the smaller ones, so it pays to shop around and compare prices. These figures are only rough approximations. The market is so volatile that prices change overnight. If you are buying through the mail, you should call about the advertised price before ordering. Often the advertisements are made up one or two months before the magazine is published, and the prices can change considerably.

The variation in the cost of motherboards depends to a large extent on the frequency of the CPU. The higher the operating frequency, or the faster the PC can operate, the higher the cost. At one time Intel was the only manufacturer of 386 and 486 chips. But Cyrix, AMD, Chips and Technology, and several other companies now have 386 and 486 CPU clones on the market. This added competition has forced CPU prices down, and when CPU prices go down, motherboard prices go down.

Options

I listed several components in the common components list that are not absolutely necessary for a system. If you don't need a lot of goodies at this time, you can buy the minimum components and add to your system later. For instance, you don't absolutely need two floppy drives.

Memory

On older systems, the memory chips were usually located in the front left quadrant of the motherboard. They used dual in-line pin (DIP) chips. Almost all systems today use SIMM-type memory. These are small boards that have miniature chips on them. The board has an edge connector that plugs into a special socket on the motherboard. SIMM technology provides a much greater chip density than could be achieved with DIP chips. A few systems use the single in-line pin (SIP) type of memory. These are miniature chips mounted on a board and are very similar to SIMMS except the boards have pins that plug into special sockets.

When a computer runs a program, the program is loaded into memory and is processed there. When the processing is completed, the information is loaded back on the hard disk, printed out, or sent to wherever you want it to go. You can get by with just 2 Mb of memory but as programs become increasingly more complex and user-friendly, your computer will need more memory. There are many different types of memory, and chapter 6 goes into detail about these many types.

Floppy drives

You can get by with a single 360K floppy drive, but I recommend that you buy a 1.2Mb drive. It will read and write to both 360K and 1.2Mb disks. You can store more than 3 times as much data on a 1.2Mb disk as a 360K disk. The 360K drives cost about $50, while the 1.2Mb drives cost about $55.

I also recommend that you buy a 1.44Mb, 3½-inch drive. These devices can read and write to 720K disks as well as 1.44Mb disks. The 1.44Mb drives also cost about $55, about $5 more than the 720K drives. Both the 360K and 720K drives are obsolete. I don't recommend them.

You might also have to buy a floppy drive controller (FDC) board for your floppy drives. If you have a hard drive, it might have a hard/floppy drive controller (H/FDC) built in. If not, you can buy a floppy drive controller for about $20. You might not need a controller if your motherboard has a built-in integrated drive electronics (IDE) interface. See chapter 8 for more details on floppy drives.

Hard drives

It is possible to operate a computer without a hard drive, but it is difficult to do much productive work. If your time is worth anything at all, a hard drive can pay for itself in a very short time.

There are several hard drive manufacturers with hundreds of different models, sizes, and types of hard drives. IDE drives have all of the controller electronics on the drive itself, but they still need an interface to the system. This might be built in on the motherboard, or you might have to buy a low-cost interface that plugs into one of the motherboard's slots. Other hard drives need a controller on a plug-in board. In many cases the controller is made by some company other than the one that made the hard drive. Because the controllers for IDE drives are made and matched by the same manufacturer, they operate a bit better. They also cost a bit less than buying a drive and a separate controller. It all depends on what you want and how much you want to spend. Chapter 9 contains more details on hard drives.

Backup

It is very important that you keep copies or backups of all of your software and important data. You never know when your hard disk might crash or have a failure. There are thousands of ways to lose your very important data. You should always have a current backup. There are many methods of backup, some using hardware and some that require special software. See chapter 10 for more details on backing up.

Monitors

A wide variety of monitors are available. You can buy a monochrome monitor for about $65. I like color, even if I am just doing word processing, so I am willing to pay a little more for color. You can buy a good enhanced graphics adapter (EGA) color monitor for about $200. A better video graphics adapter (VGA) costs about $300. Or you can spend $3000 or more for a large screen, very high-resolution monitor.

Monitor adapters

You need a plug-in adapter board to drive your monitor. Some motherboards have a built-in adapter. A monochrome adapter might cost as little as $20. You should be able to buy a standard VGA color adapter for about $100. For very high-resolution color, an adapter might cost up to $600. See chapter 11 for more details on monitors and adapters.

Keyboards

The keyboard is a very important part of your computer. It is the main device for communicating with the computer. There are many manufacturers, and each of them have slight differences in the placement of the keys, the tactility, and special adjuncts such as trackballs, calculators, and keypads.

To run Windows and other graphical user interface (GUI) programs, it is essential that you have a mouse, a trackball, or some other pointing device. Chapter 12 contains information about keyboards and other input devices.

Modems, faxes, and communications

You can use your computer to communicate with millions of other computers, with online services, and with a host of other services. You can download software from bulletin boards, and you can send low-cost faxes to millions of other fax sites. You definitely need communications hardware and software if you want to get the most from your computer. I discuss communications in greater detail in chapter 13.

Printers

You have lots of options when it comes to buying a printer. There are many manufacturers and hundreds of different types and models including dot matrix, laser, ink-jet, daisy wheel, and many others. Some types are better for particular applications than others, so it depends on what you want to do with your computer and how much you want to spend. Chapter 14 contains information about the various types of printers.

Software

You need software for your computer. Before you even turn it on, you need operating software such as MS-DOS, DR DOS, or OS/2. Billions of dollars worth of off-the-shelf software are available. Some of the commercial programs are a bit expensive, but there are inexpensive public domain and shareware programs that can do just about everything the commercial programs do. See chapter 15 for some software recommendations.

More utility

Chapter 16 contains a discussion of the ways you can get more out of your computer. Just a few of the thousands of things that you can do with your computer are discussed.

Sources

You need to know where to buy all of the components you need to upgrade or repair your PC. If you live near a large city, there are probably local stores that sell the parts. Local vendors and computer stores will be most happy to help you. They might charge a bit more than a mail-order house, but if anything goes wrong, they are usually very quick to help you or make it right.

Computer swaps are held frequently in most large cities. A computer swap is just a gathering of local vendors at a fairgrounds, a stadium, or some other area. The vendors set up booths and tables and present their wares. You can usually find all that you need at these meets. Go from booth to booth and compare the components and prices. The prices are usually very competitive, and you might even be able to haggle a bit with the vendors.

The other good source for components is through mail order. Just look at the ads in any of the computer magazines. At one time mail order was a bit risky, but it is very safe today.

If a price seems too good to be true, then the vendor has probably cut a few corners somewhere. There are some very good bargains out there, but you should be careful. Your best protection is to be fairly knowledgeable about the computer business. Computer magazines and books are some of the better sources for this knowledge. Another excellent source of knowledge and help is a local computer user group. If you live near a large city, there are probably several groups. Most of the people in these groups are very friendly and are anxious to help you with any problem.

If you are fairly new to computing, be sure to read the chapters on floppy drives, hard drives, monitors, keyboards, and the major components before you buy your parts. Billions of dollars worth of products are available, and many of them are very similar in function and quality. What you buy depends on what you want your computer to do and how much you can afford to spend.

3
About upgrading

IF YOU HAVE AN IBM COMPUTER OR A COMPATIBLE CLONE, YOU HAVE A MACHINE
that is quite versatile. About $10 billion worth of boards and peripheral hardware are
available for use with your computer. With this hardware, an IBM or clone can be upgraded or configured to do almost anything you can imagine. There is also about $10
billion worth of software that can be used with your PC. But some of the newer software packages will only run on the later model machines such as the 386 and 486.

You don't have to buy one of the newer and more-powerful machines in order to
take advantage of the newest software. You can easily upgrade an older PC. One feature that makes the PC so versatile and useful is the plug-in slots on the motherboard. There are hundreds of different boards that you can plug into these slots to
configure a PC to do almost anything you want.

If you have put off adding or replacing a board in your computer because you
were afraid you might mess something up, don't wait any longer. There is really not
much you can do to harm your computer or yourself. If you know how to use a screwdriver, you will have no trouble upgrading your computer, and you can save a bundle.

Installing a new board

Adding a new board is one of the most common and easiest ways to upgrade. Maybe
you need to install an adapter board for a new color or graphics monitor. Or maybe
you want a multi-I/O (input/output) board to give you extra ports for your printer or
an external modem. Installing these is a very simple task.

Maybe you need a modem so you can access some of the bulletin board services.
Most of them are crammed full of public domain software and other goodies. You can
buy a board with an internal 2400 baud modem for less than $50. For less than $75, you
can get a board with a 2400 baud modem and a 9600 baud fax. Just a few years ago, I
bought a combination 2400 baud modem and 9600 baud fax board for a little over $900.
One reason they are now so inexpensive is that several newer and faster systems have

been developed. Some of the new modems can transmit at a speed of 57.6K. Of course, a high-speed modem costs much more than $50, but if you plan to do a lot of telecommunicating, it is well worth it. Chapter 13 has more information about modems and faxes.

Inside your computer

The inside of your computer is safe. Except for the power supply, which is completely enclosed, the highest voltage in your computer is only 12 volts. But of course, if you open your computer and add or change anything, there won't even be 12 volts, because the very first thing you should do, even before you take the cover off, is unplug it. CAUTION! Never plug in or unplug a board, cable, or any component while the power is on. The fragile transistors and semiconductors on these boards and components can be easily destroyed. It only takes a second to turn the power off or remove the power.

Make a diagram

I mentioned this earlier, but it is worth repeating. If you remove any boards or change any cables or switch settings, make a drawing or diagram of the original setup. It is very easy to forget how a chip or cable was plugged in. Many cables and connectors can be plugged in backwards or into the wrong receptacle. I am ashamed to admit it, but I once ruined an expensive BIOS chip because I plugged it into the wrong socket. It takes only a minute to make a rough diagram, and it might save you money and hours of agony and frustration trying to solve a problem that was caused because something was plugged in backwards or into the wrong receptacle.

You can also use a marking pen or fingernail polish to put stripes on all the cable connectors and board connectors before they are unplugged. Vary the location of the stripes on the connectors so that when they are plugged together the stripes line up. This way you can tell immediately if it is the right connector and if it is plugged in properly.

Set switches and jumpers

When you buy a board or any component, always make sure you get some kind of manual or documentation with it. Check the manual or documentation for installation instructions. The component might have switches or shorting bars that must be set to configure it to your system or to whatever it has to do. Your computer has certain addresses and interrupt request (IRQ) assignments. If two devices are set for the same IRQ, it causes a conflict.

After you set any necessary switches, look for an empty slot and plug in your board. It doesn't matter which slot. The slots are all connected to the standard bus. If you look closely at the motherboard, you will see etched lines that go across the board to the same pin on each slot connector. The contacts on one side of the eight-bit connectors are numbered A1 to A31. On the other side they are numbered B1 to B31. For example, contact B1 on every connector is ground; B9 on every connector is +12 volts. The connections on the A side are I/O and address lines. A complete listing of the function of each contact is contained in chapter 18.

Multilayered motherboards

In most cases, it is physically impossible to plug a board into a slot backwards, but you should make sure it is plugged in all the way. You should be very careful when you plug in boards. Some slot connectors are very tight, and it can be difficult to get the board to seat properly. If you press down too hard you can flex and damage the motherboard. The copper circuit traces on the motherboard that carry the signals to all of the various components are very complex. Some traces might cross over other traces. These are usually placed on separate thin layers of plastic. The traces on the separate layers are then connected. There might be 10 or more layers, and these layers of plastic are fused together into a solid board. The traces in the various layers are then connected to each other at various points and to the components without interfering with other circuit traces. Using layers for the various traces is similar to a highway system with overpasses and cloverleafs. If a motherboard is flexed, it is possible to break some of these traces and ruin the motherboard.

After you are satisfied that the board is seated properly, install a screw in the bracket to hold it in place. It helps if you have a magnetized screwdriver to hold screws while you get them started. If you don't have a magnetized screwdriver, you can magnetize one by rubbing it against any strong magnet. You should be careful not to place the magnetized screwdriver, or any magnet, near your floppy disks because it can partially erase them.

XT dipswitches

The XT is obsolete, but there are still millions of them in existence. For many applications, they are still a very good tool. For simple word processing, they are as good as the most powerful 486.

Several things can be added to an XT to make it even better. You can add a color monitor, more memory, a new floppy drive, a hard drive, a coprocessor, a modem, a fax, a scanner, a CD-ROM, and almost anything that can be added to the more-powerful systems. If you need instructions on adding any of these items, refer to the various chapters that discuss those items.

If you are upgrading an XT or PC, you might have to reset the dipswitches on the motherboard. The PC has two switches and the XT has one that are set for various configurations. Here are the settings for the XT at various configurations:

- 1—OFF
- 2—OFF without an 8087, ON with an 8087
- 3—OFF; 4—ON if the motherboard has 128K memory
- 3—OFF; 4—OFF if the motherboard has 256K or more memory
- 5—ON; 6—OFF for a color monitor
- 5—OFF; 6—OFF for a monochrome monitor
- 7—ON; 8—ON for one floppy drive
- 7—OFF; 8—ON for two floppy drives

The motherboards of other systems are considerably different than the XT. Most of these have dipswitches or jumpers that need to be set. You should get some sort of documentation with your components. Be sure to check and follow directions.

Installing more memory on an XT

If you have an XT you can have up to 640K of memory. The later models have DIP sockets for this much memory in the left front quadrant of the motherboard. Some of the early models only had sockets for up to 256K. In order to add another 384K, you have to buy a memory board and plug it into one of the eight slots.

There are four banks of memory, with nine chips in each bank. The systems that came with 256K of memory used 64K chips in each bank. For 640K, they used 64K chips in two banks and 256K chips in the other two banks. If you need to add memory, check the type that is already installed and buy the same type.

When you plug the memory chips in, make sure they are oriented properly. Pin 1 usually has a small dot or some sort of marking. All of the chips should be oriented the same way. Also make sure that all of the legs are plugged in properly. It is very easy to have a leg bend underneath the chip or go outside of the chip socket. After you install the memory, check your documentation. You have to set DIP switches 3 and 4 to match the amount of memory that you now have.

Coprocessors

Another very easy upgrade is installing a coprocessor. If you do a lot of heavy number crunching or large spreadsheet work, then you could probably benefit from a coprocessor. Depending on the program that you are running, a coprocessor can make your computer operate from 5 to 100 times faster.

Almost all motherboards are designed with an empty socket alongside the CPU for a coprocessor. Most computers are sold without this chip because not all programs make use of them. At one time, coprocessors were rather expensive, but several companies are now manufacturing them and the competition has forced the prices down.

Coprocessor chips all have an 87 at the end of their chip designation; for the 8088 family it is 8087, for the 286 it is 80287, and for the 386 it is 80387. The Intel 486DX CPU has a coprocessor built into the chip somewhere among its 1.2 million transistors. The 486SX does not have a coprocessor. You need a 487SX to add one.

Sources

Coprocessor chips are priced according to the speed at which they are designed to operate. The higher the frequency, the greater the cost. They are priced from $50 up to $300. Look in the computer magazines for coprocessor ads.

Here are some typical prices. Note that the XT is obsolete, so there are not many vendors that still carry the 8087. Those that do might charge more for the XT coprocessor than for the 287 or 387. The prices of coprocessors depend on the manufacturer. Intel was the original developer of the chips, but now several companies make them, such as AMD, Cyrix, ULSI, Integrated Information Technology (IIT), Chips and Technology, and Weitek. Intel is usually the most expensive.

8087-5	$ 70
8087-10	135
80287-10	58
387SX-16	120
387SX-20	130
387DX-25	180
387DX-33	190

387DX-40	230
487SX-20	490

Here are just a few of the hundreds of vendors. Look through any computer magazine for others. Call them for their latest prices.

Access Computer Components	(800) 332-3778
Asean Computer Technologies	(714) 598-2828
Bulldog Computer Products	(800) 438-6039
California Microchip	(818) 884-3660
Chips For Less	(214) 416-0508
CompuSave	(800) 544-8302
Computer Discount Warehouse	(800) 800-2892
Dynamax Products	(800) 886-2882
Focus Computer Center	(800) 223-3411
H. Co. Computer Products	(800) 726-2477
H&J International	(800) 275-2447
Leo Electronics	(800) 421-9565
Main Street Computers	(800) 456-6246
Memory Plus	(800) 388-7587
OS Computer City	(800) 926-6722
Treasure Chest Computers	(800) 723-8282
Ulta Computers	(800) 755-7518
Upgrades International	(800) 877-6652
USA Electronics	(800) 332-8434
USA FLEX	(800) 872-3539
Worldwide Technologies	(800) 457-6937

Installing a coprocessor

Step 1—remove the cover of the computer If you have a PC or XT, look for the 8088 CPU. It is a long, narrow chip with 40 pins. It is probably located near the motherboard power supply connector at the back of the board. There should be an empty socket alongside the 8088.

If you are installing an 80287 or 80387, look for the 286 or 386 CPU, a square chip of about 1½ inches. It is probably located near the center of the board. There should be an empty socket nearby.

You might have to disconnect the power supply cables or remove some of the plug-in boards. Make a diagram of the boards and cables before you disconnect them.

Step 2—note the orientation of the chip There should be a small U-shaped notch at one end of the CPU indicating pin 1. The empty slot should have some sort of indication or outline on the board that shows you the orientation of the chip.

The 286 CPU chip is square, but the 80287 coprocessor has the same long shape and 40 pins of the 8087. The 80387 coprocessor has 128 pins and fits in the square socket near the 386 CPU. It can only be plugged in one way.

Step 3—a final check Once you install your new board, coprocessor, or whatever, check it again to make sure that everything is connected properly. Connect the keyboard, the monitor, and reinstall any boards or cables that were removed. If you are satisfied that everything is correct, connect the power and try the system before you replace the cover. There have been times when I have installed new parts, replaced the cover, turned on the power, and it didn't work. It is usually some small thing that I have not done or have done improperly. So I end up having to remove the cover again.

It won't hurt your computer to run it without a cover. I have several computers, and I am constantly running tests and evaluations and trying out new boards and products. Most of the time I don't even bother to replace the covers.

One reason to have a cover on your computer is to shield it and prevent it from radiating TV and radio interference. The FCC gets very concerned about this, but in most cases, the interference from a computer will not affect a TV set unless it is within a few feet of it.

The 487 coprocessor

If you have a 486DX system, the CPU has a built-in coprocessor; however, the 486SX does not. This lack of a coprocessor, and slower speed, are the primary differences between the 486DX and the 486SX. You can install a 487 coprocessor on a 486SX system to give you all the benefits of a 486DX. In fact, the 487 is an actual 486DX CPU. It costs about the same as a 486DX, which can be a bit expensive. Figure 3-1 shows a 486SX motherboard with a 487SX coprocessor. If you think you might need

3-1 A 486SX motherboard with a 487SX coprocessor. This converts the 486SX into a 486DX. It has 8Mb of SIMM memory at the top center.

a coprocessor later, you should consider buying a 486DX rather than a 486SX. More about the 486 CPUs later.

Cooling system

The little electrons that represent bits of data get hot as they go racing around through the semiconductors in your computer, and heat is an enemy of all semiconductors. What you hear when you turn on your computer is the sound of the cooling fan located in the power supply.

The power supply fan draws air from the front of the computer, pulls it over the boards and components, and forces it out through the rear opening of the power supply. To work efficiently, all of the openings in the rear panel should have covers installed, and there should be no obstructions around your computer that will interfere with the flow of air through the power supply.

Accelerator boards

Several companies have developed accelerator boards that are plugged into your old motherboard. The more popular of these boards have newer CPUs, such as the 386 and 486. Just plug one of these boards into your computer, and it gives your old XT or 286 many of the advantages of a 386 or 486 machine. But there are also many limitations. You still have to cope with an eight-bit system bus for communications with the plug-in boards. The eight-bit system is limited to 4.77 MHz, although this can be increased to 10 MHz. You cannot use any of the many 16- or 32-bit system boards that are available.

Earlier editions of this book devoted a complete chapter to accelerator boards because it was an easy and cost-effective upgrade. In many cases, it is now much easier and less expensive to replace the motherboard. The IBM PS/2 machines are the exception to this. These motherboards are still very expensive and IBM is the sole source, so an accelerator board is one of the better ways to upgrade a PS/2. The AOX Corp. ((617) 890-4402) makes several accelerator boards for both PS/2 and ISA machines. Figure 3-2 shows an AOX accelerator board that can convert a 286 into a

3-2 An accelerator board from AOX that can convert a 286 into a 386.

3-3   The Evergreen 286 to 386SX processor upgrade. It can also be used in the ISA-type PS/2 models. Evergreen Technologies Inc.

3-4   The Evergreen 286 to 486SX processor upgrade. This can also be used in ISA-type PS/2 models. Evergreen Technologies Inc.

386. Other companies that still make accelerator boards are SOTA ((408) 955-1900) and Orchid Technology ((510) 683-0300). These companies also make other enhancement products for upgrading your computer.

It is very easy to install an accelerator board. Just remove the cover of your computer and plug in the board. In some cases, you might have to remove the existing CPU and plug in a cable. The vendor usually sends some kind of documentation that covers any unusual circumstances.

Installing a processor upgrade

Several companies have developed processor modules that can transform a 286 into a 386SX. The 386SX allows you to use all of the newest software such as OS/2, Windows NT, and other 32-bit software. Evergreen Technologies ((800) 733-0934) has processor modules and replacement chips that can transform a 286 into a 386 or 486. These chips can be installed in most ISA-type machines and in the 286-based PS/2s. They use an Intel chip for the 386 and a Cyrix chip for the 486 conversion (see Figs. 3-3 and 3-4). It is a very easy upgrade. Just pull off the cover, locate the 286 CPU, and plug in the new module.

The original 286 chip was made in several different styles that used different types of sockets. Some of them have pins or a pin grid array (PGA), some have plastic leaded chip carriers (PLCCs), and others have leadless chip carriers (LCCs). Figure 3-5 shows the various types of sockets used for the 286 CPU. Evergreen sends copies of these drawings to their customers so they can determine which type of

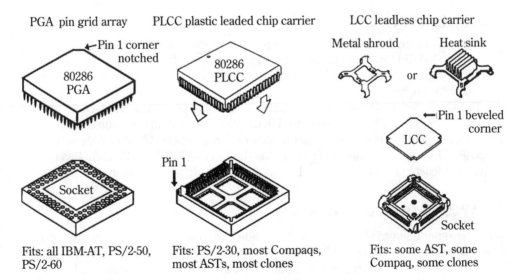

3-5 Evergreen's drawings of the different types of 286 CPUs. You must know which type you have before ordering a processor upgrade. Evergreen Technologies Inc.

chip to order. The following other companies make processor modules for the 286 upgrade. Most of the modules are quite similar. Figure 3-6 shows a Kingston SX Now. Compare it with Figs. 3-3 and 3-4.

AOX Corp., StaX/SX	(617) 890-4402
Cumulus Corp., 386SX Card	(216) 464-2211
Intel Snap-In	(503) 629-7402
Kingston SX Now	(714) 435-2600

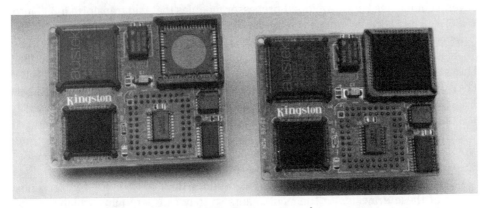

3-6   Kingston Technology's 286 to 386SX processor upgrade. Kingston Technology.

The Cyrix 486 CPU

The Cyrix Company has a 486 CPU that is pin compatible with the 386DX chip. Just remove the 386 CPU and plug in the Cyrix CPU. This chip also comes with a coprocessor that plugs into the 387 socket. This gives you the coprocessing ability of the true 486DX systems.

The Cyrix 486 CPU operates internally at 40 MHz but it can be used in any 386DX system. This CPU can also be used in the PS/2 386 systems. This upgrade provides almost all of the power and functionality of a true 486DX 33- MHz system. The Cyrix 486 CPU costs less than half as much as the Intel 486DX 33- MHz chip. It is the easiest and least expensive way that I know of to upgrade to 486 power.

Power precautions

If you have not done so already, a small upgrade that you should make is to install a power strip. This allows you to plug all of your equipment into one source. You might have five or six power cords from your computer, monitor, printer, lamps, and other devices plugged into various outlets and extensions. This is messy and potentially dangerous.

Some older or less-expensive equipment has only two-wire cords. It is possible to plug these devices in so that there is a voltage potential between them. This can cause grounding problems. Check the prongs on the plug. One prong should be wider than the other. This is the ground side, and it should be plugged into the wider slot in the receptacle. If at all possible, buy only those components that have a three-wire power cord and plug.

A power strip with six outlets costs $10 to $15. Each outlet should accommodate three-wire plugs. Some companies advertise very expensive power outlets with filtering. In most cases, these have a cheap capacitor and a varistor that filter some spikes from the voltage source. But ordinarily there is not that much need for filtering. If you do need a filter, make sure the unit has a good electronic filter that includes coils and more electronics than just a capacitor and varistor.

Uninterruptible power supply

You might live in an area with frequent storms and power outages. If so, you might consider buying an uninterruptible power supply (UPS). This is essential if you do any critical work on your computer. A UPS takes over any time the power goes off, and keeps your computer going.

Several UPS techniques provide uninterruptible power. Most use rechargeable batteries; some even use automobile batteries. The cost of the various systems depends primarily on the amount of wattage required.

Emerson ((714) 380-1005) makes the AccuCard. It is a small plug-in board with a rechargeable battery. You plug it into any slot on your motherboard, and if there is a power outage, the board immediately takes over and keeps the computer running long enough for you to save your data. A large number of companies make UPS devices. Most advertise in the computer magazines. Here are just a few:

Alpha Technologies	(206) 647-2360
American Power Conversion	(401) 789-5735
Best Power Technology	(800) 356-5794
Brooks Power Systems	(215) 244-0624
Clary Corporation	(818) 287-6111
Computer Power Products	(213) 323-1231
Sola Corporation	(312) 439-2800
Tripp Lite Corporation	(312) 329-1777
UPSystems	(213) 634-0621

Pentium upgrade

At the time of this writing, Intel had not yet released much information about the Pentium. Because Intel was unable to copyright and protect their 386 and 486 names, they named their new CPU the Pentium. The CPU has about 3 million transistors, over twice as many as the 486. This makes it much more powerful and faster than the 486.

Several manufacturers are already designing motherboards for the Pentium. The procedure for upgrading to a Pentium is the same as for any of the other upgrades. Just remove your old motherboard and install a new Pentium.

4
Motherboards

A NEW MOTHERBOARD CAN GIVE YOU ALL OF THE BENEFITS OF A NEW SYSTEM AT a fairly reasonable cost. Just pull out your old motherboard and install a new 286, 386SX, 386DX, 486SX, 486DX, or 586. If you have an XT or 286 and you try to sell it, you probably won't get more than $200 to $300 for it. But if you spend $200 to $300 for a new motherboard, it can be worth as much as a new $1500 machine. You definitely can save money by spending a little to upgrade.

Using old components

Even if you are moving up from a PC or XT, you can still use some of your old XT components, such as the plug-in boards and disk drives, in your new system. All of the components in PCs are basically the same except for the motherboards.

Of course, if you decide to install a fast and powerful 386 or 486 motherboard, you might not want to use some parts, such as an old monochrome or CGA monitor. You also might want a larger capacity hard drive and new floppies. But if you are on a tight budget, you can always use your old components until you can afford the new goodies.

Keyboard differences

You might not be able to use your old keyboard when you upgrade. Although the XT- and AT-type keyboards look exactly alike and have the same connector, the XT keyboard will not work on anything except the XT. The keyboards for the AT-type machines, which include the 286, 386, and 486, have a different scanner frequency.

Some keyboards have a switch on the back that allows them to be switched from one type to the other. Some of the newer keyboards can automatically sense what system they are plugged into and automatically switch. The XT is now obsolete, but most keyboard manufacturers still provide the XT/AT switch. If you buy a new keyboard, make sure the switch is set to the proper position.

What is a motherboard?

The motherboard is the largest and most important board in your system. It has the CPU and all of the chips and electronics that make computing possible. In the beginning there were only two different types and sizes of personal computers, the XT and the AT or 286. The standard-size AT or 286 is a bit larger than the XT. The XT is 5 inches high, 19½ inches wide, and 16½ inches deep. The AT is 6 inches high, 21½ inches wide, and 16½ inches deep. By combining several chips into very large-scale integrated (VLSI) chips, the clone builders developed a "baby" 286 motherboard that is about 1 inch longer than the XT motherboard, but it still fits in the XT case. Figure 4-1 shows a baby 286 motherboard. Figure 4-2 shows a baby 386 motherboard alongside an XT motherboard.

4-1   A baby 286 motherboard.

Slots

The motherboard usually sits on the floor of the chassis. Most motherboards have eight slots for plug-in boards, but some models like the PS/2 and low-profile systems might have only a single slot for a daughterboard. The daughterboard has from two to five slots (see Fig. 2-5).

There are so many different plug-in boards available that you will never seem to have enough slots. Because of this problem, some special motherboards have 12 slots. Figure 4-3 shows a 12-slot motherboard with a 486DX2 CPU.

4-2 A baby 386 motherboard (left) and an XT motherboard (right). Note that the 386 is about 1 inch longer, but it will fit in the XT-type case.

4-3 A 12-slot 486 motherboard.

The CPU

The motherboards are named and differentiated according to the CPU chip installed on them. The 286 has an 80286 CPU, the 386 has an 80386 CPU, and the 486 has an 80486 CPU. Within these designations are several other CPU variations such as the 386SX and 486SX. There are also variations according to the speed and frequency of the CPU, for instance, 16-MHz, 20-MHz, 25-MHz, 33-MHz, and 40-MHz variations of the 386 CPU. There are even more variations of the 486 CPU.

Intel invented the 8088, 80286, 80386, and 80486. For some time they were the one and only source for these CPUs. Because they had no competition, the prices were high, especially during the period after an initial release. The price of the CPU determines to a large extent the price of the motherboard. I paid $1825 for my first 386 motherboard. It operated at only 16 MHz. Today I can buy a 386 motherboard that operates at 40 MHz for about $300. I paid $4450 for my first 486 motherboard that operated at 20 MHz. Today I can buy a 486SX motherboard that operates at 20 MHz for about $400, and I can buy a 486DX that operates at 50 MHz for about $800.

One reason the prices have come down is that AMD, Chips and Technology, Cyrix, IIT, and several other companies have developed clone CPUs. Intel now has some competition. These companies have also contributed to the growing number of CPU variations. Table 4-1 lists the various CPUs and some of their characteristics:

Table 4-1. CPU differences

CPU	Freq (MHz)	Mmbs	Proc	I/OBs	I/OSp (MHz)	MbLns	Cch	Copro
8088	4.77–10	8	8	8	4.77–10	1 Mb–20	No	No
286	6–25	16	16	16	8	16–24	No	No
386SX	15–25	16	32	16	8	16–24	No	No
386DX	16–40	32	32	16	8	32–25	No	No
486SX	16–25	32	32	16	8	32–25	8K	No
486DX	16–50	32	32	16	8	32–25	8K	Yes
486DX2	40–66	32	32	16	8	32–25	8K	Yes
Pentium	66–	64	64	32	8	64–26	16K	Yes

Notes:
Abbreviations: CPU=central processing unit; Freq = frequency or operating speed of the CPU; Mmbs=width of memory bus in bits; Proc=internal processing width in bits; I/OBs=width of I/O bus in bits; I/OSp=speed of I/O; MbLns=direct address capability and number of address lines; Cch=internal cache; Copro=internal coprocessor.

The 386SX has a 16-bit external bus to memory, but it processes data in 32-bit chunks. The 486DX2 CPU operates externally at a speed of 25 MHz or 33 MHz, but the internal processing speed is double the external frequency.

Compatibility with early systems

Most PCs, even the 386 and 486, operate at an I/O speed of 8 MHz to 10 MHz. This is done so they are downward compatible with early software and hardware. The fact that they are compatible allows us to use the early software and hardware, but it can be a real bottleneck for some operations and applications where speed is important. The width of the I/O bus is another bottleneck for some systems. All of the ISA systems, even the 32-bit 386s and 486s, are limited by the 16-bit I/O bus. The extended ISA (EISA) and high-end MCA systems have a 32-bit I/O bus system.

Benefits of competition

Competition has forced CPU prices down. Competition has also forced the companies to improve their products. Intel seemed to be perfectly happy with their 386 that operated at 33 MHz until AMD introduced their 386 that operates at 40 MHz. AMD also reduced the required voltage of the CPU from 5 volts to 3 volts. This reduces the amount of heat produced in the CPU. Cyrix has developed a 486-type CPU that is the same size as a 386. The competition is great for consumers.

Deciding what to buy

One of the most useful upgrades you can make is to replace your old motherboard. One of the first things you have to do is decide what you want, or, if you're like me, decide what you want at a price you can afford. I subscribe to many computer magazines, and most of them have articles and reviews of software and hardware. Of course, they also have lots of ads from stores that sell by mail. These ads give me a fairly good idea of prices, so I know what I can afford. Mail order is one of the better ways to purchase your parts, especially if you don't live near a large city.

Usually, larger cities have lots of computer stores. The San Francisco Bay and Los Angeles areas have hundreds. There are also computer swap meets every weekend. If I need something, I go to one of these swap meets and compare the prices at the various booths. I often take a pad along, write the prices down, then go back and make the best deal I can. Sometimes you can haggle with the vendors for a better price, especially if it is near closing time.

Upgrading a PC or XT to an XT turbo

When it was first introduced, the XT was the hottest thing around. It was the best desktop computer you could buy. But that was over 10 years ago, and the XT is now obsolete. A lot of people ignore this fact and still use them. For some applications, such as word processing, they are just as good as the faster and more powerful 386 or 486. XT systems can also be used as low-cost terminals on a local area network (LAN).

The original PC and XT used the 8088 CPU. This CPU has about 29,000 transistors and operates at 4.77 MHz. Computers perform their operations by moving blocks of data in precise blocks of time. The PC and XT can cycle eight-bit blocks of data at 4.77 million times per second. That sounds fast, but it takes eight-bits to make a single byte. It also takes eight bits to create a single character of the alphabet. And it takes a whole lot of bytes if you are using graphics. This speed is painfully slow if you are running a CAD program or a large spreadsheet. But soon after IBM introduced the XT, compatible clone makers introduced the turbo XTs. These were sped up to speeds of 8 MHz, 10 MHz, or 12 MHz.

The XT is now obsolete, but a few companies still manufacture the motherboards. If you have an old 4.77-MHz XT that you are in love with, you can replace the motherboard for about $50. Not only will this new motherboard run twice as fast as the old one, but it has a new BIOS that allows you to use 1.2Mb and 3½-inch floppy drives. If you can afford it, I recommend that you spend a little extra and upgrade your XT to a 286, or better yet, a 386SX or 386DX.

If you have an original IBM PC, it has only five slots, so the case has five openings on the back panel. The XT has eight slots with eight openings on the back panel. Almost all motherboards now have eight slots, so your old PC case with the five openings will not accommodate an eight-slot motherboard. Your best bet is to scrap the old case and buy a new one. New cases sell for about $30. If you are in love with the IBM logo, rip it off and glue it to the new case.

If you are upgrading an IBM PC, you should buy a new power supply. The original PC has a puny 63-watt power supply. The XT and later models have 135-watt to 150-watt power supplies. A 150-watt power supply costs from $40 to $60.

Upgrading a PC or XT to a 286

The IBM AT (advanced technology) uses the 80286 CPU. It has 125,000 transistors and is a 16-bit system. The original IBM AT operated at a very conservative speed of 6 MHz, but many of the 286 clones boosted this speed to 12 MHz, 16 MHz, and even 20 MHz. A 286 CPU handles data in 16-bit chunks, twice that of the 8088. A 286 operating at 10 MHz would be more than four times faster than an XT operating at 4.77 MHz. And because it handles twice as much data per cycle, the 286 is still twice as fast as an XT operating at the same 10 MHz.

If you are upgrading an XT to a 286, look for a baby 286 motherboard. The cost of a baby 286 motherboard depends on several options. Most of the boards have built-in clocks, calendars, and serial and parallel ports. Some even have built-in VGA monitor drivers. The speed of the CPU is a cost factor, and so is the amount of memory. If you choose a system that runs at 12 MHz or less, you might be able to use your old memory chips. Depending on the options you choose, a baby 286 motherboard can cost from $70 to $125. You also might be able to get by with your old power supply if it is at least 150 watts. But if you expect to install a couple of hard drives and fill all eight slots with boards, then you should buy a 200-watt supply.

Because it is a 16-bit system, the 286 cannot run some high-end 32-bit software, such as that developed for the 386 enhanced mode, OS/2 2.0, or Windows NT. However, it can run in protected mode and directly access up to 16Mb of extended memory with the proper software.

Upgrading a PC or XT to a 386SX

The 386SX is a low-cost hybrid of the 386DX. It handles data in 16-bit chunks externally, but it processes data internally at a 32-bit rate. It can run all of the software that the 386DX or 486 can run. However, it is considerably slower than the 386DX or 486.

Most 386SX motherboards are baby size, and most have several built-in functions, such as printer ports, COM ports, IDE hard and floppy disk controllers, and other options. Depending on the options, a 386SX motherboard can cost from $100 up to $300. It is the least expensive way to move up to the wonderful world of the 386.

Upgrading a PC or XT to a 386DX

The 386 systems use the Intel 80386 CPU. It has 275,000 transistors and handles data in 32-bit chunks. The original 386 motherboard was the same size as the original 286 motherboard. But, by using VLSI chips, baby 386 motherboards were developed that are about 1 inch longer than the original 386, but they still fit in the XT case (see Fig. 4-2 for an XT and 386 motherboard comparison). Almost all 386 motherboards manufactured today are the baby size.

Several options are available on the 386 motherboards, including various speed CPUs, on-board RAM, cache memory, built-in serial and parallel ports, VGA monitor drivers, and other options. Of course, the more goodies you get already built into the motherboard, the more open slots you will have. Besides, a utility that is built-in, such as a VGA driver costs less than buying a VGA board. You should still be able to use all of your old plug-in boards and peripherals, but you might need to buy a power supply with greater wattage.

The 386 systems are much more complex than XT or 286 systems, so the motherboards are more expensive. Depending on the options you choose, a 386 motherboard can cost from $300 to $700.

Upgrading a 286 to a 386

If you have a standard-size 286, it is very easy to move up to a faster and more-powerful 386. The baby-size motherboards line up and fit in the larger size case, and you should have no trouble using your old plug-in boards. There are also hundreds of options such as speed or frequency, cache, amount of memory, built-in options, and many more goodies. What you plan to do with your computer and how much you can afford are determining factors in what you choose.

Upgrading an XT, 286, or 386 to a 486

Most of the original 486 motherboards were the same size as the standard AT boards. But now almost all of the 486 motherboards are baby size. Most of them have the same built-in options as the 386 motherboards, including built-in serial and parallel ports, monitor adapters, and floppy and hard disk controllers. In addition, the 486 motherboards have sockets for a static random-access memory (SRAM) cache. Static RAM is very fast, and depending on the software being used, SRAM can greatly improve the performance of your computer.

At one time the cost of a 486 CPU was more than $1000. Now depending on the speed of the CPU, they range in cost from $200 to $500.

ISA or EISA

The industry standard architecture (ISA) is what used to be known as the IBM standard. When IBM introduced their Micro Channel Architecture (MCA) PS/2 line, they abandoned the standard they created. Their MCA uses a different connector with several new pins for the plug-in boards. This means that the billions of dollars worth of hardware that was compatible with XT and AT systems can no longer be used with MCA systems. The MCA systems are the PS/2 models 50 and up. The PS/2 models 25 to 40 use the ISA-type connectors and boards. The PS/1 is also an ISA-type system.

One reason IBM created the new system was because the old AT system was limited. It has 98 pins, but this simply is not enough to add new features and functions. Everyone agrees that the MCA system has several advantages, but many believe the disadvantage of not being able to use existing hardware outweighs the advantages.

A group of clone manufacturers, called the gang of nine, got together and created some new standards. One thing they did was rename the IBM AT standard the ISA. They then created the extended industry standard architecture (EISA). The EISA system adds a second row of pins, below the standard 98 pins of an AT or 16-bit board. The connections for these pins are etched lines on the board that run between the standard edge connector contacts to the set of EISA contacts. Figure 4-4 shows an EISA plug-in board. Note the pin arrangement. The EISA motherboard connector or slot accepts 32-bit boards, as well as 8-bit and 16-bit boards. The connector has crossbars so that the 8-bit and 16-bit boards cannot be inserted deep enough to contact the bottom set of contacts. EISA boards have cutouts to match the crossbars so they can be inserted to their full depth.

4-4 An EISA plug-in board. Note the pin arrangement.

The system works great. All of the billions of dollars worth of present and past hardware can be used on an EISA motherboard system. You can use the oldest 8-bit boards, as well as the very latest 32-bit boards. Also, by using the extra contacts now available, many new features can be added to the plug-in boards.

EISA/ISA combos

Some manufacturers have developed EISA/ISA combination motherboards. These motherboards have from two to six EISA slots, with the remaining slots used for the

ISA bus. These motherboards cost from $800 to $1200, or about $200 to $400 more than the ISA ones.

The combination EISA/ISA motherboards are a good idea because you can use the older 8-bit and 16-bit hardware, as well as the new 32-bit hardware. In many cases, you don't need the full 32-bit power of EISA, and there are not that many 32-bit products available at this time. However, when IBM introduced OS/2 2.0 in April 1992, over 800 companies committed to producing 32-bit hardware and software.

Do you need an EISA system?

Whether you need an EISA system depends on what you want to do with your computer and how much you want to spend. Several features have been created for EISA systems. They are much faster and more powerful than ISA systems, can detect and automatically set up a board that is plugged in, and have several other sophisticated functions.

At the present time, EISA motherboards cost from $900 to $1500. The cost will eventually come down, and in the very near future, the majority of all computers will be the EISA type. If you are running applications such as large spreadsheets, CAD programs, or any high-end type of application, then I recommend an EISA type of system. If you can afford it, you might want to go ahead and buy an EISA system, even if you are not running the high-end types of applications.

Local bus

The 386DX, 486SX, and 486DX systems process data 32 bits at a time and communicate with memory over a 32-bit bus. But all ISA systems communicate with their plug-in boards and other I/O peripherals over a 16-bit bus. Some companies have developed what they call *local bus* ISA motherboards that have one or more slots with a 32-bit bus. One or more of the motherboard's standard 16-bit slots have an additional special slot for the 32-bit bus. There aren't many boards available for this system at this time, and most of the boards that do use the 32-bit local bus are enhanced VGA cards.

Microlink ((818) 330-9599) offers a motherboard with one local bus slot and one EISA slot. The motherboard with a 33-MHz CPU lists for $595. The enhanced VGA card for the local bus costs $340. Syncomp ((800) 875-9799) has several different local bus motherboards. Several other companies manufacture local bus motherboards. Look for ads in the computer magazines.

The Video Electronics Standards Association (VESA) has developed a set of standards for the local bus, and companies are now manufacturing these systems. The local bus adds $25 to $50 to the manufacturing cost. But it adds a tremendous amount of utility to the system. Almost all 386 and 486 motherboards will soon have the local bus.

486 CPUs

I have seen ads for 486 motherboards for as little $150, but in small print it says "w/o CPU." The CPU costs from $350 to more than $500. You have to pay close attention to the ads. One reason some vendors don't list a price for the 486 motherboard with a CPU is because there are several different CPUs and other options available. Intel manufactures over 30 different CPUs. You can choose the 20-MHz or 25-MHz 486SX for about $250. There are 25-MHz and 33-MHz 486DX CPUs available for about $400. And the 50-MHz 486DX will cost about $600.

The 486DX2

The 486DX2 is similar to the 386SX in one respect: the 386SX handles data externally in 16-bit chunks, but processes it internally 32 bits at a time. The 486DX2/50 handles data externally, at a speed of 25 MHz, but it processes data internally at a speed of 50 MHz. The 486DX2/66 handles data externally at 33 MHz, but processes it internally at a rate of 66 MHz. The doubling of the internal rate of processing does not double the overall speed. For instance, a 486DX2 increases the overall speed of a 25-MHz system to about 40 MHz. At the present time, the 50-MHz and 66-MHz 486DX2 costs from $600 to $1000.

The 486SX

The 486SX is the same as the 486DX, except that it operates at a slower frequency and its built-in math coprocessor is nonfunctional.

Coprocessors

A considerable number of the 1.2 million transistors on the 486 are devoted to its built-in coprocessor. This makes the 486 very fast for applications such as spreadsheets and CAD programs that can utilize a coprocessor. But there are many software applications that do not require a coprocessor. The coprocessor is useless unless the software application is designed to use it. Except for the 486DX systems, almost all motherboards and computers are sold without a math coprocessor. An empty socket is provided on the motherboard so that a coprocessor can be added if it is needed.

The 486DX CPU has 168 pins. Intel has insisted that manufacturers of 486SX motherboards provide a 169-pin socket for a coprocessor. Intel has developed a 487SX coprocessor for the 486SX. It is actually a 486DX with an extra pin. When plugged in, it disables the 486SX and takes over all of the CPU and math coprocessor functions. The 487SX operates at the same frequencies as the 486SX—16 MHz, 20 MHz, or 25 MHz.

The overdrive

The overdrive 486 CPU can be plugged into the coprocessor socket of a 486SX to double the internal processing speed. It does essentially the same thing that the 486DX2 does.

The manufacturing process

The 486 CPUs are etched onto a thin slab of silicon about six inches in diameter. Several CPUs are etched onto a single slab. The chips then go through several stages of processing, and at the end of the processing, the individual CPUs are cut and separated. They are then tested and selected.

When a batch of chips is processed, some chips have defective transistors or circuits. The chips that are not completely dead are tested for several specifications and parameters. Some of them operate at higher voltages, higher frequencies, or higher temperatures than the others. They are also tested for several other important specifications and criteria. The CPU chips are then separated and selected according to the tests they pass successfully. In a single batch there might be a few that operate at 50 MHz, a few that operate at 33 MHz, and some that operate at 25 MHz, while some will only operate reliably at 20 MHz. Intel denies it, but a chip that might be limited to 20 MHz is sold as a 486SX.

Because the coprocessor section represents a fairly large portion of the 486 chip, there are probably some defective transistors in this area. If the chip is otherwise okay, it can be used as a 486SX.

The Fading 486SX

When the 486SX first came out, a large number of vendors developed 486SX systems. They were a very hot item. But I recently attended a swap meet in Los Angeles with about 300 vendors present, and found only two vendors who were offering the 486SX motherboard. I talked to several of the vendors, and they said that most people who build their own computers want a 486DX with a coprocessor. The overdrive chip won't help much either. Why would a person pay $300 to $400 for a 486SX, then pay another $400 to $600 for an overdrive chip, when they can save $300 to $400 if they buy the 486DX in the first place.

If you look through the computer magazines you will see very few ads for 486SX systems. If you can afford the extra $150, I recommend that you bypass the 486SX and buy the 486DX.

486 Memory

A 486 motherboard should have sockets for the installation of at least 8 Mb of RAM. Most of them have provisions for 16Mb up to 128Mb. The majority of the motherboards use SIMM-type sockets. These allow the most memory to be installed in the least amount of space. You might find a few 486 boards that use SIP-type sockets. But the SIP-type memory is not as popular as the SIMM type. Very few, if any, 486 boards use the older DIP-type memory chips. They require too much board space. You can install about 32Mb of SIMM memory in the space that 1Mb of DIP memory requires.

Your motherboard will probably be sold without memory. Make sure that you order the type and speed of memory that is required for your board. You can probably get by with 80 nanoseconds (ns) for a 20-MHz 486SX. For 25 MHz, you want 60 ns to 70 ns, and at least 60 ns for 33-MHz and faster systems.

SIMMs are very easy to install. Just follow the documentation you receive with your motherboard and make sure you orient the SIMMs properly when you plug them in. If you are not filling all the sockets, check your documentation; you might have to install memory in multiples of two, that is, 2Mb, 4Mb, or 8Mb. The sockets are usually numbered. If you are only installing 2Mb or 4Mb, it has to be plugged into the proper sockets. Also there are probably some switches or jumpers on the mother-board that have to be set to tell the system how much memory is installed. Again, your motherboard documentation should tell you how to do this.

Cache

When processing data, quite often the same data is used over and over again. Having to traverse the bus to retrieve the data can slow the system down considerably. The 486 has a small built-in 8K cache that contributes to its speed. But 8K is not nearly large enough for some programs, so many motherboards have sockets for adding a very fast cache. This cache is usually made from SRAM. It can be added in 32K increments, usually up to 256K.

Write through and write back

After the data is processed it is returned to RAM. The older write-through systems simply sent the data back to RAM. System operations are delayed while the data is written to RAM. The delay might be only microseconds, but if you are processing a lot of data, it can add up. The newer write-back systems keep the data in the cache until there is a break in operations, then they write the data to RAM.

Sources

Computer magazines are the best place to look for motherboards and components. They are full of ads for computers and components, and you can get a good idea about what they will cost. If you live in a large city, there are probably several computer stores nearby, and the larger cities have computer swaps. If you can't get to a store or a computer swap, then order through the mail from the ads in the computer magazines. Read the ads closely. Many motherboards are advertized without a CPU. Almost all of the boards are advertised without memory. See chapter 17 for more about mail order.

Installing a motherboard

Now that you have a new motherboard, you can install it in a few simple steps. The following basic procedures can be used for installing any motherboard.

   Step 1—remove the cover   The first thing to do is remove the cover from your computer. Unplug the power and remove the screws that hold the cover on. If you have one of the older XT- or AT-type cases, there is a screw at each corner on the rear panel and one at the top center (refer to Fig. 2-3). Slide the cover off.

   Step 2—remove plug-ins   Make a rough diagram of the cables and boards and how they are connected. You might even take pieces of tape or a marking pen and mark each board and cable with a number. Notice that the ribbon cables have one wire that is a different color. This indicates pin 1. Pay close attention to how the connectors are oriented. On most boards that have vertical connections, pin 1 is toward the top. If the connection is horizontal, pin 1 is usually toward the front of the computer, but this is not always true. Check the boards for a small number or some indication as to which pin is pin 1. Note the colored wires on the ribbon cables, and record their positions on your diagram. If possible, leave the cables from the disk drives connected to the plug-in boards when you remove them.

Note that the connectors from the power supply are connected so that the four black wires are in the center. When reconnecting the cables, it is possible to replace the cable connectors upside down, backwards, or in the wrong connector. Be sure that your diagram is complete before disconnecting anything.

Remove all of the plug-in boards, the keyboard cable, and any other wires and cables that are connected to the motherboard. If at all possible, leave the cables connected to the disk controller boards. Just pull the boards out and lay them across the power supply. It should not be necessary to remove the disk drives or the power supply.

Step 3—remove the motherboard Depending on the type of computer you have, you might have nine standoffs holding the motherboard off the case. If so, there are nine small nuts on the bottom of the case. Some standoffs are made of plastic. If they are plastic, they are held in place by the flared portions of the body of the standoff. Use pliers to press the flares together so the standoff can be removed. With the XT motherboard removed, the case will look like Fig. 4-5.

4-5 The case with the motherboard removed.

Step 4—install the memory chips If you got a board without memory, you have to install some. Check the documentation you got with your board. It should tell you what type and kind of memory to install. This depends primarily on how fast your new board operates. For the older 4.77-MHz PCs and XTs, 200 ns was plenty fast enough. You should also buy only the type of memory that can be used on your board, such as DIP, SIMM, or SIP.

The memory is set up in banks. If you don't buy enough memory to fill all the sockets on your motherboard, check your documentation to determine which sockets or banks should be filled. For more information on memory, see chapter 6.

Step 5—install the new motherboard   Most of the newer boards use a standoff system that is different that used in old PCs and XTs. The new ones use raised channels on the floor of the case. These channels have holes with elongated slots. Plastic standoffs with rounded tops and a thin groove fit in the holes. These standoffs are pressed into the holes in the motherboard (see Fig. 4-6).

4-6   The white plastic standoffs on the bottom of the motherboard.

The board is placed so that the standoffs fit into the holes in the raised channels. The board is moved to the right so that the grooves slide into and are locked in the narrow elongated slots (see Fig. 4-7). One screw at the back center of the board and one at the front center locks the board in place.

Step 6—replace the boards and cables   You are now ready to replace your components. Reconnect the power supply. Make sure that the connector is oriented so that the four black wires are in the center as shown in Fig. 4-8. Replace your plug-in boards and any cables that were disconnected (see Fig. 4-9). Make sure they are connected properly. If you made a diagram before you removed them, you shouldn't have any problems.

4-7 Position the motherboard so the standoffs drop into the holes in the raised channels, then slide it until it locks in. A screw is installed in the front and the rear center of the board.

4-8 Plug in the power to the motherboard. Note that the four black wires are in the center. P8 goes toward the rear of the socket.

4-9   Reinstall the plug-in boards.

Step 7—the smoke test   You are now ready to turn on your computer and try it before you replace the cover. If everything was done properly, you shouldn't have any problems. If you have problems, check your documentation, and recheck all of the cables, switches, and boards. If the problem remains, turn to chapter 18 for troubleshooting hints.

If you have no problems, replace the cover on your computer. You are now entitled to pat yourself on the back for doing a good job and saving a bundle.

5
Upgrading an
IBM PS/1 or PS/2

PS/1S AND PS/2S HAVE A LOT OF BUILT-IN GOODIES ON THEIR MOTHERBOARDS, IN-cluding floppy and hard disk controllers, monitor adapters, parallel and serial ports for printers, ports and connectors for mice, and other peripherals. The integration of these utilities on the motherboard makes it possible for IBM to manufacture the PS/1 and PS/2 systems almost entirely with automated equipment. This automation vastly reduces labor costs. Unfortunately, IBM doesn't pass these savings along to the consumer. It is estimated that it costs IBM less than $150 to manufacture a complete PS/2. That same computer sells for about $2500.

Advantages and disadvantages of built-ins

Integration reduces or eliminates the need for some cables. Cables are the source of many problems. Integration also reduces problems by reducing the number of solder joints and components. The more solder joints and components there are, the more chance for errors and failures.

But there are some disadvantages. If one of these utilities fails, the entire motherboard usually has to be replaced. On the clone ISA systems, utilities are on plug-in boards, and if one of these boards fails, it is usually fairly inexpensive to replace it. Another disadvantage is new and better products are being developed every day. New monitor adapter boards are available that are much better than the built-in systems on the older PS/2s. With clone ISA systems, you can easily replace and upgrade your older boards with new boards.

PS/1 and PS/2 differences

IBM has created a very large number of variations in their PS/1 and PS/2 models. Basically, the PS/1 is an ISA-type system. So are the PS/2 models 25 through 40. These systems can use many of the $10 billion worth of ISA boards that are available.

The PS/2 models 50 and up are Micro Channel Architecture (MCA) systems. They can only accept MCA-type boards. Models 56 and 57 are 16-bit systems, while models 70 through 95 are 32-bit systems.

Differences in ISA and MCA

When IBM introduced the 16-bit AT, it was designed so that it could address 16 Mb of memory. A total of 24 lines (2^{24}) were needed. Several other new bus functions were added to the AT bus. They needed the 62 pins already in use on the bus, plus several more for the new functions. A larger connector was needed but a new connector would make all of the hardware that was available at that time obsolete. Someone at IBM came up with a brilliant design. They simply added a second 36-pin connector in front of the standard 62-pin connector. The new connector readily accepts both 8-bit and 16-bit boards.

Later when the 386 and 486 were developed, the standard AT bus was still used. Many of the early 386 and 486 ISA machines had a special 32-bit connector for plug-in memory boards. Almost all of today's motherboards have sockets for 32-bit memory chips. Other than the 32-bit bus for the memory, all the other I/O functions use the standard 16-bit AT bus.

In 1987, IBM introduced their new PS/2 line with MCA. This new system added many new functions to the computer, and it used a new bus system that was completely incompatible with the older hardware. Figure 5-1 shows the edge connectors of a 16-bit ISA plug-in board (top) and an MCA board (bottom).

5-1 A comparison of a 16-bit board edge connector (top) with the smaller MCA connector (bottom).

MCA offers some real advantages over the original IBM standard. One of the excellent features of the MCA system is the programmed option select (POS). MCA plug-in boards have a unique identification (ID). When a board is plugged in, the bus recognizes it by its ID and automatically configures the board for use with system interrupts, ports, and other system configurations. If there are any switches on the board, it tells you how they should be set.

I recently spent almost a whole day trying to install a board that had three dip-switches and three different jumpers. The switches and jumpers had to be set so the board would not conflict with the rest of the system. The three dipswitches alone meant that there were eight different configurations (2^3), then include the three different jumpers for another eight different configurations, and you have a total of 64 possible combinations. By the time you turn the computer off, set the switches, turn it back on, and wait for it to reboot, it can be awfully time-consuming and frustrating. I had a manual, but like most manuals, it was practically worthless. A PS/2 with MCA POS could have saved me a lot of time and frustration.

MCA offers other very good features such as bus arbitration. This is a system that evaluates bus requests and allocates time on a priority basis. This relieves the CPU of some of its burdens. The MCA bus is also much faster than the old AT bus. There are several other excellent benefits to MCA, but IBM is still the single source. A few clones and a few third-party MCA boards are available, but they are rather expensive.

Upgrade difficulties

Some of the PS/1 models have no slots for adding extra boards, and some of the later models have only one or two slots. Most of the PS/2s have two or three slots. Again, there is $10 billion worth of boards that can be used on these machines, but the small number of slots puts a severe limit on you. You have to make some tough decisions as to what to buy.

Except for a few third-party boards, IBM is the only authorized source for upgrades, replacements, or repairs. Because they have no competition, the parts and supplies are rather expensive. Another reason IBM products are more expensive than clone products is the large number of distributors between the manufacturing plant and the showrooms. Many of the clone products go directly from the manufacturer to the dealer.

Upgrade components from IBM

IBM has a large number of upgrade components. For instance, you can buy the following PS/2 MCA 486 components, but they are expensive.

- 487SX math coprocessor.
- 486-25/50 processor upgrade (for SX models only).
- 486DX2/50 processor upgrade (25-MHz SX models only).
- Enhanced 486DX 50-MHz processor upgrade.

You can order upgrade parts for any of the PS/1 or PS/2 models, but first you have to know what the part numbers are. IBM sells reference manuals for all of their systems. These manuals are quite detailed and highly technical. They probably give you more information than you need. There are separate manuals for each model they manufacture called *Guide to Operations and Quick Reference Manual Part Numbers and Prices*. There are different prices for each manual. The manual for the model 25, part number 75x1051, sells for $28.75. The manual for the model 25 286, part number 15F2179, sells for $42.50. The manual for the model 60, part number 68X2213, sells for $54.25. The manual for the model 80, part number 15F2186, sells for $63.75. They also have manuals for the XT, the AT, and other systems. They even have manuals for the PCjr, part number 1502292, for $23.25.

IBM also has manuals of *Hardware Maintenance Manual Part Numbers and Prices*. Complete libraries of manuals for various systems are available. These libraries cost from $150 to $268. If you would like to contact IBM for more information call:

Authorized dealer locator	(800) 447-4700
IBM general information	(800) 426-3333
IBM part number ID and lookup	(303) 924-4015
Technical and service publications	(800) 426-7282

You can use a credit card when ordering by telephone.

PS/1 and PS/2 parts and components

Several small companies now offer parts and components for PS/1 and PS/2 machines. Many of these components are parts that were purchased on the "gray" market. IBM has very strict rules as to which distributors and dealers get their products, and these distributors and dealers are supposed to abide by their strict pricing policies. But there are thousands of dealers, and despite IBM's rigid rules, some of the units and components find their way into the hands of "unauthorized" dealers.

Some dealers also buy used PS/2s. Used systems are then repaired, refurbished, and resold. The systems that cannot be repaired are stripped down, and the parts are sold to anyone who needs them. They are usually sold for much less than what IBM would charge. The parts are usually tested before shipping and a warranty is provided. I have no problem with buying a used electronic part, but I do not recommend buying a used mechanical part, such as a disk drive.

Sources

Several magazines now carry ads from these "unauthorized" dealers. One of them is *The Processor*. It is sent free to qualified subscribers. To get a subscription request form, write to:

The Processor
P.O. Box 85518
Lincoln, NE 68501-9856

Here are just a few of the companies that advertised PS/2 components in a recent issue of *The Processor*:

Century Computer Marketing	(310) 827-0999
Computer Reset	(214) 276-8072
DakTech Company	(800) 325-3238
Federal Computer Exchange	(404) 642-2400
Gemini Parts	(407) 998-8735
Hartford Computer Group	(708) 934-3380
Selecterm	(800) 676-4944
Shreve Systems	(800) 227-3971

Theses companies have almost any component or part you might need to repair or upgrade a PS/2. Call them for a list of their products.

Hard drive upgrades

Many companies offer large hard drives. Manufacturers have vastly increased the capacity of hard drives without increasing their physical size. In some cases, the capacities have more than doubled. Many of the early PS/2s were sold with 20Mb to 30Mb hard drives. It is very difficult to do any productive computing now without at least 100Mb. In some instances, even 200Mb is not enough.

The drives used in the PS/2s do not use cables. The IBM drives are plugged directly into a motherboard connector. The drives are mounted on a special "sled" that positions them so that they mate correctly with the motherboard connector. The power lines and all data lines are in this one connector. Most hard drives have three different connectors and cables—a 34-wire flat ribbon cable, a 20-wire ribbon cable, and a power cable. Many companies offer direct replacement hard drives for the PS/2 and PS/1. To mount other drives some companies offer special kits and controllers.

The list price for a 20Mb hard drive from IBM is $787. You can buy a 200Mb hard drive for about the same amount from one of the clone companies. Here is a list of a few of the companies that advertise in *Computer Shopper, Byte, PC World, Computer Reseller, and PC Week*:

Compu.D	(800) 783-5783	Many PS/2 components
Computer Techniques	(407) 453-8783	PS/2 hard drives
Data Solutions	(714) 637-5060	PS/2 hard drives
Dynamic Electronics	(800) 845-8228	Many PS/2 components
General Technics	(800) 487-2538	PS/2 hard drives
InterSolutions	(800) 666-0566	Many PS/2 components
jb Technologies	(800) 688-0908	PS/2 hard drives
MegaHaus	(800) 426-0560	PS/1 and PS/2 drives
Page Computer	(800) 886-0055	Many PS/2 components
Universal Memory	(800) 899-8518	PS/2 drives, memory

Memory upgrades

Many of the larger magazines carry ads for PS/1 and PS/2 memory upgrades. Almost every company that provides memory chips for other computers provides them for the IBM systems as well. Here is a list of just a few of the companies that provide PS/1 and PS/2 memory upgrades:

Altex Electronics	(800) 531-5369
AMT International	(408) 942-9695
BPS International	(800) 444-1341
CitiTronics	(818) 855-5688
CyberTron Components	(408) 294-8700
I.C. Express	(800) 877-8188
L.A. Trade	(800) 433-3726
Microchip Company	(800) 848-9102
NECS	(800) 922-6327
PMP	(800) 424-1968
RSVPeripherals	(800) 554-7787
Source	(800) 535-5892
TDSI	(408) 287-4410
Worldwide Technology	(800) 457-6937

BIOS upgrades

If you have one of the early PS/2 models 30 through 40, you probably need to upgrade your BIOS. Everything discussed in chapter 7 regarding the BIOS system applies to the PS/2 ISA machines. Because they are ISA machines, they should be compatible with all other ISA machines, but they are not. I list several BIOS suppliers in chapter 7, but only Unicore Software ((800) 800-2467) said they had chips for the model 30. All the other companies said their chips would not work in a PS/2 system. It is a bit expensive, but your only source seems to be IBM.

External drives

PS/2 systems are made so small that there is not enough room to mount more than two drives. You can have two floppy drives, or one floppy drive and one hard drive. These systems come with a 3½-inch floppy drive, but there are times when you might need a 5¼-inch floppy. You also probably need a larger capacity hard drive, or a second hard drive. You might also want to install a CD-ROM and a tape backup system, but there just isn't room in the desktop systems. Several companies have developed external drives for the PS/2. Many of these use a cable that is plugged into the motherboard with a special connector. Another cable is then run to the outside for the drive.

Parallel port drives

Several companies have developed hard drives that work off the printer's parallel port. The printer cable is unplugged and the cable from the drive is plugged into the port. If you intend to install the external drive permanently, most of these drives have a connector for the printer. When the printer is plugged into this connector, it operates as usual.

One company that offers these drives is Pacific Rim Systems ((510) 782-1013). They have 20Mb and 40Mb systems that can run off batteries or, with a small power supply, from 110 volts. I bought one to use with my Toshiba laptop, but I use it more on my desktops than on my laptops. By using the STAC compression software, I can store 40Mb on this small 20Mb drive (see Fig. 5-2).

5-2 A portable parallel port hard drive from Pacific Rim. Pacific Rim Systems.

Another company that provides external drives is MicroSolutions ((815) 756-3411). They have 3½-inch and 5¼-inch floppies and various hard drives that can be plugged into the parallel printer port. Axonix ((800) 866-9797) has small portable hard drives in 20Mb, 40Mb, 100Mb, and 200Mb capacities. Sysgen ((800) 821-2151)has portable hard drives that use the parallel port in capacities ranging from 40Mb to 210Mb.

Kingston Technology ((714) 435-2600) has several external hard drives that can be plugged into the parallel connector. They have capacities ranging from 52Mb to 240Mb (see Fig. 5-3). Kingston has also developed several other upgrade components.

SyQuest ((800) 437-9367) manufactures several hard drives with 88Mb removable cartridges. They also have a model that attaches to the parallel port. These systems are great for backup, for security, or for transporting data.

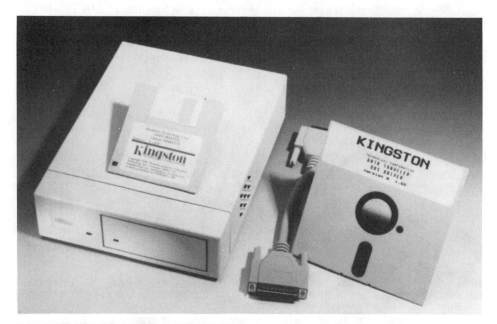

5-3 A parallel hard drive system from Kingston. Kingston Technology.

External tape backup

Several companies provide tape backup systems that can be plugged into the parallel port, just like the hard drives mentioned earlier. Sigen ((408) 737-3904) has several different tape drives that are operated from the parallel port. Another company that provides portable tape backup systems is ADPI ((513) 339-2241).

Accelerator boards

An accelerator board is a card with a 386 or 486 CPU and other associated circuitry on it. It can be plugged into a model 25, 30, or 40 to transform the system into a much more powerful and faster machine. These boards cannot give you all of the benefits of an actual 386 or 486 machine, but they can give you most of them.

At one time, the accelerator boards were one of the better ways to upgrade the compatible clone systems. But now you can buy a complete 386 or 486 clone motherboard for less than the cost of an accelerator. Motherboards for the PS/2 systems still must come from IBM, and they are still very expensive. So accelerator boards are a very good alternative.

One of the companies that provides PS/2 accelerator cards is AOX ((617) 890-4402). They have MicroMASTER 386 and MicroMASTER 486 cards. These are designed to convert a 286 MCA PS/2 system into a 386DX or a 486 (see Fig. 5-4).

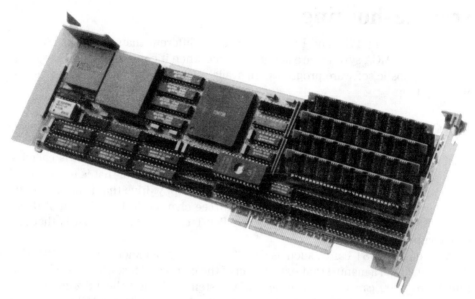

5-4   The AOX MicroMASTER accelerator card that can convert a 286 MCA PS/2 into a 386. Note that this board has 4Mb of SIMM memory on the right end. Because the memory is on the card, it can communicate with the 386 CPU over a 32-bit path. AOX Incorporated.

Processor upgrade modules

Several companies have developed processor modules that can transform a 286 into a 386 or 486. These modules operate in any of the ISA-type 286 PS/2 or PS/1 machines. The chips can be installed in most ISA clone machines and in the 286-based PS/2s. An Intel chip is used for the 386 conversion, and a Cyrix chip is used for the 486 conversion (see Figs. 3-3 and 3-4). This is a very easy upgrade. Just pull off the cover, locate the 286 CPU, and plug in the new module.

Here is list of a few of the other companies that make processor modules for the 286 upgrade:

AOX Corp., StaX/SX	(617) 890-4402
Cumulus Corp., 386SX card	(216) 464-2211
Evergreen Technologies	(800) 733-0934
Intel, Snap-In	(503) 629-7402
Kingston, SX Now	(714) 435-2600

Most of the modules are quite similar. Refer to chapter 3 and Figs. 3-3, 3-4, and 3-6.

Installing a component in a PS/2

The PS/2 systems require very few tools to work on them. The plastic cases snap together, so the systems can be completely broken down and taken apart without any tools. By pressing plastic catches and latches, the whole system can be taken apart.

Troubleshooting

Troubleshooting the PS/1 and PS/2 systems is no different than the other ISA systems. Even the MCA systems are about the same when it comes to troubleshooting. Several diagnostic software programs are available that work on the PS/2 as well as on ISA systems.

POST cards

When a computer is first turned on, the BIOS checks the system. This is called a power on self-test (POST). If it finds a component or peripheral that is not working properly, such as a stuck key on the keyboard or a floppy drive that is not responding, it gives you an error code on the screen (see chapter 18 for a listing of these codes). Several companies have developed POST card diagnostic boards that are quite comprehensive.

Most of the POST cards, such as the POST-Probe from Micro 2000 ((818) 547-0125), come with a manual that explains all of the codes and tests. The POST-Probe from Micro 2000 can be used on any ISA system including the PS/2 models 25 through 40. It also comes with an adapter so it can be used with the MCA models 50 and up. If you have a problem, turn to chapter 18 and follow all of the suggestions offered there for diagnosing and solving problems.

6
Memory

MEMORY IS ONE OF THE MOST CRITICAL ELEMENTS OF THE COMPUTER. COMPUTING as we know it would not be possible without memory. The PC uses two primary types of memory—ROM and RAM.

ROM

Read-only memory (ROM) is memory that cannot be altered or changed. The principal use of ROM in PCs is for the BIOS. The BIOS contains routines that set up the computer when you first turn it on, and it facilitates the transfer of data between peripherals. The ROM programs are usually burned into electrically programmable ROM chips. The ROM BIOS for an early XT could be programmed onto a 128K chip. The 486 ROM BIOS needs 512K. To give you some idea of how much 512K is, the text for this whole book takes less than 512K.

RAM

If you open a file from a hard drive or a floppy, the files and data are read from the disk and placed in random-access memory (RAM). *Random access* means you can find, address, change, or erase any single byte among several million bytes. When you load a program, be it word processing, a spreadsheet, a database, or whatever, you work in the system RAM. If you are writing, programming, or creating another program, you work in RAM. Actually it is dynamic RAM (DRAM).

You can randomly access any particular byte on a floppy or hard disk, but you cannot randomly access data on a magnetic tape system. The data is stored on tape sequentially. In order to find a particular byte, you have to run the tape forward or backward to the proper area. Being able to randomly access memory allows you to read and write to it. It is somewhat like an electronic blackboard. You can manipulate data, do calculations, enter more data, edit, search databases, or do any of the thousands of things software allows you to do.

RAM volatility

An important difference between ROM and RAM is, RAM is volatile. That is, it disappears if the machine is rebooted or if you exit the program without saving your data. If there is a power interruption to the computer, even for a brief instant, any data in RAM will be gone forever.

You should get in the habit of frequently saving your files to disk, especially if you live in an area prone to power failures. If your data is critical, you might consider using an uninterruptible power supply.

A brief explanation of memory

Computers operate on binary systems of 0s and 1s, or off and on. A transistor is turned off and on to represent these 0s and 1s. Two transistors can represent four different combinations: both off; both on; #1 on, #2 off; #1 off, #2 on. A bank of four transistors can represent 16 different combinations. With eight transistors, there are 256 different combinations. It takes eight bits to make one byte. These can be used to represent each letter of the alphabet, each number, and each symbol of the extended American Standard Code for Information Interchange (ASCII) code. With eight lines, plus a ground, the eight transistors are turned on or off in combination to represent any of the 256 characters of the ASCII code.

Programs that stay in RAM

Besides the application programs that must be loaded into the 640K of RAM, there are certain DOS programs that must be in RAM at all times. These are programs such as command.com and the internal commands. There are over 20 internal commands such as copy, cd, cls, date, del, md, path, time, type, and others. These commands are always in RAM and are available immediately. The config.sys file and any drivers you have for your system are also loaded into RAM.

Terminate and stay resident (TSR) files are also loaded into the 640K of RAM. They are memory resident programs, such as SideKick Plus and others, that can pop up anytime you press a key. Portions of RAM can also be used for a very fast RAM disk, for buffers, and for print spooling.

All of these things contribute to the utility and functionality of the computer and make it easier to use. But unfortunately, they take big bites out of your precious 640K of RAM. After loading all these memory resident programs, there might be less than 400K left for running applications. Many programs will not run if you have less than 600K of free RAM, and some are so large they need up to 4Mb in order to run properly. These programs are designed to run in extended or expanded memory.

DR DOS 6.0 from Digital Research and MS-DOS 5.0 from Microsoft load much of the operating system and the TSR files in upper memory. Several other memory management programs have been developed to help alleviate this problem. One excellent program is DESQview from Quarterdeck Office Systems ((213) 392-9701).

Motherboard memory

The XT motherboard can accept 640K of memory. The 286 and 386SX motherboards can accept up to 16Mb, but many of them only have sockets for 4Mb to 8Mb. On some of them you might be able to use 4Mb chips, or you might have to use a plug-in memory board. This is not usually a problem with most 386DX and 486 system motherboards. Some of them have SIMM connectors that accept up to 128Mb of DRAM.

Bus systems

Memory on a plug-in board might slow your system down considerably. The 286 CPU can run at a frequency of 20 MHz, the 386SX at 25 MHz, the 386DX at 40 MHz, and the 486 at 50 MHz. But all of these ISA systems communicate with their plug-in boards and any other I/O devices over a 16-bit bus at about 8 MHz. One reason for this is so these systems are compatible with the early boards and software. The CPUs of the 386DX and 486 systems have a 32-bit bus that they use to communicate with memory. This means that they can access and process data at the CPU speed.

Dual in-line packages

The early DRAM chips had two rows of eight pins. They were bulky and used up a lot of motherboard space. The 16 pins also imposed limits on them. Later, 1Mb DIPs were developed that had 18 pins.

You won't find DIPs on motherboards very often now. They are used mostly for VGA cards and special uses.

Single in-line memory modules

Your computer motherboard probably has sockets for SIMMs. SIMMs are assemblies of 256K, 500K, 1Mb, or 4Mb miniature DRAM chips. There are usually nine chips on a small board that is plugged into a special connector. These chips require a very small amount of motherboard space. Figure 6-1 shows a baby 386 motherboard with 2Mb of SIMM RAM installed in the upper left corner. Figure 6-2 shows two different types of DIP socket and chip. Figure 6-3 shows two SIMMs. The one at the top is a 1Mb SIMM, the lower one is a 4Mb SIMM.

Single in-line packages

Some motherboards have SIP memory. These are similar to SIMMs except that they have pins. Figure 6-4 shows a 1Mb SIP module. At the present time, 4Mb DRAM chips are the largest generally available. Several companies, including IBM, are developing 16Mb and 64Mb DRAM chips.

The need for more memory

One of the upgrades you probably need is more memory. For some applications, you might need several megabytes more. In the old days, you could get by with just 64K of memory. But many of the new software programs, such as spreadsheets, databases, and accounting programs, require a lot of memory. Lotus 1-2-3 Release 3 requires about 2Mb of RAM in order to run, and OS/2 2.0 requires about 4Mb, but runs even better with 8Mb.

6-1 A baby 386 motherboard with 8Mb of SIMM memory installed in the upper left corner.

6-2 A portion of a memory board that has both 16-pin and 18-pin sockets. Note the difference in the 256K and the 1024K or 1Mb chip. Note also the -15 on the 256 indicating 150 ns and the -10 on the 1024 indicating 100 ns. This type of memory board and chip is practically obsolete.

6-3 SIMM chips. The top module is 1Mb, the bottom is 4Mb.

6-4 SIP chips. This is a 1Mb module.

Things to consider before you buy memory

There are several different factors to consider before buying memory, including type, size, and speed. If you plan to add extra memory, be sure you get the kind and type that are right for your machine. Make sure it is fast enough for your system. Check your documentation; it should tell you what speed and type of chips to buy.

Dynamic RAM

This is the most common type of memory used today. Each memory cell has a small etched transistor that is kept in its memory state, either on or off, by a very small capacitor. Capacitors are similar to small rechargeable batteries. Units are charged with a voltage to represent 1s and left uncharged to represent 0s. But those that are charged begin losing their charge immediately. They must be constantly "refreshed" with a new charge. A computer spends 7 percent or more of its time refreshing DRAM chips. Also, each time a cell is accessed, it must be refreshed before it can be accessed again. If it has a speed of 70 ns, it takes 70 ns plus the time it takes to recycle, which might be 105 ns or more before the cell can be accessed again.

Refreshment and wait states

The speed of the DRAM chips in your system should match your system CPU. You might be able to install slower chips, but your system will have to work with wait states. Wait states deprive your system of one of its greatest benefits—speed. If the DRAM is too slow, the CPU and the rest of the system have to sit and wait while the RAM is being accessed and refreshed. What a terrible waste of time. If the CPU is operating at a very high frequency, it might have to wait one cycle, or one wait state, for the refresh cycle. This wait state might be only a millionth of a second or less, and that might not seem like much time. But if the computer is doing several million operations per second, it can add up.

It takes a finite amount of time to charge the DRAM. Some DRAM chips can be charged much faster than others. For instance, the DRAM chips needed for an XT at 4.77 MHz might take 200 ns to be refreshed. A 486 running at 25 MHz needs chips that can be refreshed in 70 ns or less time. Of course, the faster chips cost more.

Interleaved memory

Most of the newer faster systems use interleaved memory to prevent wait states. The memory is always installed in multiples of two. You can install two banks of 512K, 2Mb, 4Mb, 8Mb, 16Mb, 32Mb, 64Mb, or 128Mb memory. Half of the memory is refreshed on one cycle, and the other half is refreshed on the next cycle. If the CPU needs to access an address that is in the half already refreshed, it is available immediately. This can reduce the amount of waiting by about half.

Static RAM

Static RAM is made up of actual transistors. They are turned on to represent 1s and left off to represent 0s, and they stay in that condition until they receive a change signal. They do not need to be refreshed, but they revert back to 0 when the computer is turned off or if the power is interrupted. They are very fast and can operate at speeds of 25 ns or less.

A DRAM memory cell needs only one transistor and a small capacitor. Each SRAM cell requires four to six transistors and other components. So besides being more expensive, SRAM chips are physically larger and require more space than

DRAM chips. Because of the physical and electronic differences, SRAM and DRAM chips are not interchangeable. The motherboard must be designed for SRAM.

Cache memory

The speed and static characteristics of SRAM make it an excellent tool for cache systems. The 486 chip has an on-board built-in 8K cache system. It is very fast, but 8K is fairly small. Many of the 486 motherboard designers have included sockets for up to 256K of SRAM cache.

When running an application program, the CPU loops in and out of certain memory areas and uses the same memory over and over. If this often-used memory is stored in the cache, it can be accessed by the CPU much more quickly.

You can't arbitrarily add cache to any system. The motherboard has to be designed for it. If you need a very fast system, you should look for a motherboard that has a cache on it. Most of the motherboards with cache systems are designed for the 386DX and 486; only a few 386SX cache motherboards are available.

Hit rate A well-designed cache system might have a *hit rate* of over 90 percent. This means that each time the CPU needs a block of data, it finds it in the nearby, fast cache. A good cache system can increase the speed and performance of your computer considerably.

486 cache The 486 has an 8K cache system built into the chip. This built-in cache gives the 486 about a 90 percent hit rate. The 486DX also has a math coprocessor in among its 1.2 million transistors.

It takes a large number of transistors for a cache, even one as small as 8K. Cyrix built a 1K cache into their 486 clone. They claim that this gives them an 80 percent hit rate. Cyrix also left the coprocessor off their 486 clone, but they package an external coprocessor with each CPU. By reducing the number of transistors on their CPU, they made the chip the same size as the 386 CPU. The Cyrix 486, along with the coprocessor, is currently selling for $119. That is about $500 less than the Intel 486DX.

Flash memory

Intel has developed flash memory that is similar to erasable programmable read-only-memory (EPROM). It is on small plug-in cards that are about the size of a credit card. It is available on some small palm-size computers, such as the PSIONs. It is still rather expensive, but several companies have begun development along the same lines. A JEIDA standard has been proposed that would make the cards interchangeable among the various laptops.

CMOS

The complementary metal-oxide semiconductor (CMOS) uses very little power to keep itself alive. They are actually SRAM transistors that store your system setup. Several of the configurable computer features, such as the time, date, type of disk drives, and other features are stored in CMOS. A lithium or rechargeable battery keeps the data alive when the computer is turned off. If your computer is not used for a long period of time, you might have to reset the time. If you have to reset the time quite often, you might need a new battery. The IBM ATs used batteries that only lasted a couple of years. Most motherboards today have lithium batteries that last about 10 years.

You should take a pad and write down all of the features stored in your CMOS setup. If you lose the data in your CMOS and you don't know what type of hard drive is in the setup, you will not be able to access the data on your hard drive.

Clock rate

Computers operate at very precise clock rates. The CPU is controlled by timing circuits and crystals. The original PCs and XTs operated at 4.77 MHz. The CPUs of some of the 286s operate at as high as 20 MHz. Many 386s operate at 40 MHz, and some 486s operate at as high as 66 MHz.

Many systems are just too fast for some of their other components. Some computers are designed with built-in wait states so they can use slower memory. Some of the newer BIOS chips allow you to insert wait states. Wait states can cause a computer to operate 25 to 50 percent slower than one without wait states. For ordinary applications, this is probably only a few billionths of a second. But for some applications, it can add up and seems like an eternity.

Table 6-1 contains information that will give you a rough idea about what speed chips you should buy for your system. Again these are only rough figures. Your system might be designed to operate a bit differently. Check your system specifications and documentation, or check with your vendor.

Table 6-1. Memory speed

CPU speed (MHz)	Wait state	DRAM speed (ns)
4.77	0	200
6–8	1	120–150
6–8	0	100–120
8–10	1	100–120
8–10	0	80–100
10–12	1	100
12–20	1	80
16–20	0	70
25–33	0	60
40–50	0	40–53

Buying chips

Buying chips that are faster than what your system can use only costs you extra money. It doesn't hurt to use faster chips, or even to intermix faster ones with slower ones. Just make sure you buy the type that fits in your system. For instance, 64K and 256K DIP chips have 16 pins, while 1Mb chips have 18 pins (see Fig. 6-2). The 1Mb chip is also larger than the 256K chip. You cannot use a SIMM module unless your motherboard is designed for it.

Size or chip capacity

The most common chip sizes today are 1Mb and 4Mb. Older systems use 64K and 256K chips. The size and speed of the chip is usually printed on the top of the chip. For instance, a 256K, 150-ns chip might have the manufacturer's logo or name and some other data. But somewhere among all this is "25615." The 15 indicates 150 ns (the zero is always left off). A 1Mb, 100-ns chip might have "102410" (see Fig. 6-2).

It takes eight chips of each size listed to make the stated size. For instance, it takes eight chips to make 64K, eight to make 256K, eight to make 1Mb, and eight to make 4Mb. Almost all computers use an extra ninth chip for parity checking. This chip checks and verifies the integrity of the memory. It is usually the same type of chip as the eight used to make up the bank. The chips are usually arranged in banks or rows of nine.

The XT and early 286 motherboards had their RAM located in the front left corner of the motherboard. They all used DIP-type chips. To make 640K, most boards filled the first two banks—banks 0 and 1—with 256K chips, equaling 512K. The next two banks—banks 2 and 3—were then filled with 64K chips to make 128K, for a maximum 640K.

Many of the early 286 and 386 systems filled all four banks with 256K DIP chips for a total of 1Mb. Although the 286 is capable of addressing 16Mb with special software, for most ordinary uses it is limited to 640K. Boards that have the extra 384K can use it for a RAM cache, print spooling, or for other extended memory needs with the proper software. Even the 386 and 486 are limited to 640K without special software that takes advantage of extended memory.

Prices

Table 6-2 lists some current advertised SIMM prices from a discount house. Memory prices are very volatile and fluctuate considerably. Also note that the price list is from a discount house. The prices at the average store might be higher.

Table 6-2. Current memory prices

256K × 9	80 ns	$ 11.95
256K × 9	70 ns	$ 13.00
1Mb × 9	80 ns	$ 34.88
1Mb × 9	70 ns	$ 36.00
1Mb × 9	60 ns	$ 42.00
1Mb × 9	53 ns	$ 65.00
1Mb × 9	40 ns	$ 89.00
4Mb × 9	80 ns	$125.00
4Mb × 9	70 ns	$132.00
4Mb × 9	60 ns	$146.00

Remember, it takes nine chips to make a bank, so it takes four banks of 256K × 9 SIMMs to make 1Mb. At $13 each for the 70-ns type, it costs $52 for 1Mb. It only takes one SIMM to make 1Mb using a 1Mb × 9 module. This 1Mb costs $36. It only takes one SIMM to make 4Mb using a 4Mb × 9 module. The cost of this 4Mb is $132, or about $33 per megabyte.

Installing the chips

One of the first things you should do is discharge any static electric charge you have. This is especially important if you are working in an area that is carpeted. Touch some metal object, such as a lamp that is plugged into an outlet, to discharge yourself. Static electricity is discussed in chapter 2.

You can mix chips of different speeds in the same bank, such as 100 ns and 120 ns, but you are then limited to the 120-ns speed. You should not use a chip slower than the speed of your CPU. You cannot mix chips of different capacities, such as 64K and 256K, in the same bank.

The chips have a small notch at one end or a round dot in one corner. The notch or dot indicates the end that has pin 1. The socket has a matching notch or outline on the board indicating how the chip should be plugged in. Ordinarily, all of the chips on a board are installed and oriented in the same direction.

To install a chip, set the leads in one side of the socket, then with a bit of pressure against that side, line up the leads on the other side and press the chip in. Be careful not to bend the leads. Make sure all the leads are inserted in the sockets. It is very easy to have one slip out. If this happens you will have memory errors when you try to run the system.

If you are installing memory on a PC or XT, you have to reset the dipswitch on the motherboard to reflect the amount of memory. Some of the older ATs have a jumper that has to be set.

To install SIMMs or SIPs, look for markings on the modules. Pin 1 should be marked and there is usually a mark on the motherboard sockets for pin 1. The motherboard also has markings for the individual banks, such as bank 0, bank 1, bank 2, etc. The SIMM sockets usually have a small plastic catch on each end to lock and hold the modules in place. To remove a SIMM, simply push the plastic catch away from the end of the module and lift the module out.

The PC, XT, and AT bus

The PCs and XTs use an eight-bit bus. The AT systems, which include the 286, 386, and 486, use a 16-bit and 32-bit bus. The eight-bit 8088 communicates with its RAM over a 20-line bus. With these 20 lines, it is possible to address any individual byte in 1Mb; that is, 2^{20} = 1,048,576 bytes of RAM. The 16-bit 286 communicates with its RAM over a 24-line bus. These 24 lines can address 16Mb, or 2^{24} = 16,777,216 bytes. The 32-bit 386 and 486 CPUs communicate with their RAM over a 32-line bus. They can address 4Gb, or 2^{32} = 4,294,967,296 bytes.

Although the 386 and 486 can address 4Gb of RAM, without special software, DOS does not let you access more than 640K. Several software programs are available that let you break this 640K barrier.

In its virtual memory mode, the 386 can address 64 terabytes (Tb), or 64 trillion bytes. This is the amount of data that can be stored on 3.2 million 20Mb hard disks. *Virtual memory* is a method that uses part of a hard drive as RAM. Many large programs won't run unless the entire program resides in RAM. So the program is partially loaded in the available RAM and the rest of it is loaded in a virtual RAM section of the hard drive. Of course, having to access the disk for data slows down the processing considerably. The virtual disk system must be implemented by the operating system.

Types of memory

There are three types of memory—conventional, expanded, and extended. Figure 6-5 shows how memory is arranged in the computer system.

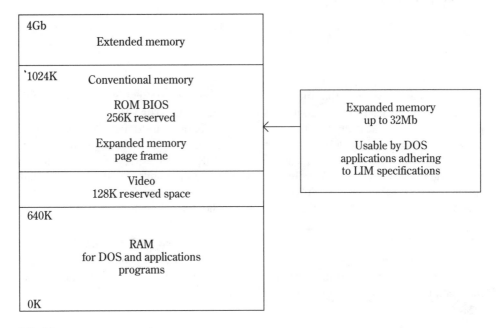

6-5 Memory arrangement.

Conventional memory

This is the memory that includes the 640K of RAM. The 384K of memory above 640K is reserved for video, ROM BIOS, and other functions.

Extended memory

Extended memory is memory that can be installed above 1Mb. If it weren't for the 640K limitation of DOS, it would be a seamless continuation of memory. Windows 3.1 and several other software applications let 286s and larger computers use this memory.

Expanded memory

Some large spreadsheets require an enormous amount of memory. A few years ago in a rare instance of cooperation, Lotus, Intel, Microsoft, and some other large corporations got together and devised a system and standard specification called LIM EMS 4.0. It allows a computer, even a PC or XT, to address up to 32Mb of expanded memory.

The memory is divided into pages of 16K each. Expanded memory finds a 64K window that is not being used above the 640K conventional memory. Pages of 16K expanded memory are then switched in and out of this window. LIM EMS also includes functions that allow multitasking so that several programs can be run simultaneously. The system can treat extra memory on the 286, 386, and 486 as extended memory with the proper software and drivers. Expanded memory is seldom used today.

Memory modes

There are two different memory modes—the real mode and the standard or protected mode.

Real mode

The real mode is the mode that most of us have been using until now. When any application is being processed, the program is loaded into RAM. The CPU uses the RAM to process any data that is input. Computations and changes are done in memory, then are sent back to the disk, screen, printer, or other device. For most single-user applications, this processing is done in the standard 640K or less of RAM. Operating in the real mode doesn't cause many problems if you are running fairly small programs that can fit in the available RAM. But if you are trying to update a spreadsheet that has 2Mb in it, you are in trouble. It is like trying to put a gallon of Jello in a quart bowl.

Protected mode

In the protected mode, the AT-type machines can run several programs at the same time if they have extended memory. Each program runs in a 640K area of memory. In effect, this memory has a wall around it so it won't interfere with any other memory area.

OS/2 2.0

Operating system/2 (OS/2) was originally designed for high-end advanced applications. The development was a joint effort by Microsoft and IBM. After several missed deadlines by Microsoft, IBM took over all responsibility for OS/2. In April 1992, IBM released OS/2 2.0. This system allows you to break the 640K barrier, do multitasking, and use the protected mode and virtual memory, provides networking facilities, and can run all DOS software. The Presentation Manager portion of OS/2 is much like Windows, so OS/2 provides high-level DOS functions plus Windows functions. OS/2 2.0 is a 32-bit operating system, so it will not run on an XT or 286 system. It can run on anything from a 386SX on up.

Windows 3.1

Windows runs on top of DOS. Windows 3.1 also lets you go beyond the 640K barrier. It lets you do multitasking and lets you take advantage of the 486's virtual and protected modes. It works with a mouse and performs even better than a Macintosh. Windows is also very inexpensive. Every system should have Windows 3.1. If you have an older copy of Windows, you can upgrade to Windows 3.1. You can get more details by calling (800) 426-9400. Windows 3.1 is still a 16-bit system, but Microsoft is developing Windows New Technology (Windows NT), a 32-bit system that should compete head to head with OS/2 2.0.

DESQview

DESQview is an excellent program that lets you take advantage of the 386 and 486 virtual and protected modes. It lets you run multiple DOS programs simultaneously, switch between them, run programs in the background, and transfer data between them. DESQview is very inexpensive and no 486 system should be without a copy. For more details call (213) 392-9701.

How much memory do you need?

This depends primarily on what you intend to do with your computer. For word processing or small applications, you can get by with 640K. You should have at least 4Mb if you expect to use Windows, large databases, or spreadsheets. Having lots of memory is like having a car with a large engine. You might not need that extra power very often, but it sure feels great being able to call on it when you do need it.

7
Upgrading your ROM BIOS

WHEN A COMPUTER IS SOLD IT HAS A BIOS THAT IS DESIGNED TO HANDLE ANY software or hardware that is presently available, but thousands of new products are introduced every day. If you have an older computer, there is a lot of software and hardware that you might not be able to use. You might not be able to use a 1.44Mb or 2.88Mb floppy drive or an IDE hard drive. You might not be able to run Windows, or some of the Novell and Netware software. You might also be missing out on a lot of essential utilities such as disk diagnostics, disk surface analysis, and other major component tests and diagnostics. You might also be wasting a lot of time while your BIOS tries to do its job.

The BIOS chip developers constantly introduce new versions of their chips trying to keep current. Chances are they have a BIOS that can give new life to your old computer. Replacing your ROM BIOS is rather inexpensive, and so it's easy, anyone can do it. It is one of the better upgrades you can do for your computer.

ROMs and EPROMs

The ROM BIOS is a program that is burned onto EPROM chips which are made up of special light-sensitive transistor circuits. Some of the BIOS system resides in the CMOS. These are very low-power transistor circuits that are kept alive with an onboard battery when the computer is off. EPROM chips are made up of special transistors and are available in 64K, 128K, 256K, and 512K sizes (see Fig. 7-1).

A clear glass window is placed over the transistor circuits on the chip. These circuits are sensitive to ultraviolet (UV) light. The transistor circuits are electronically programmed in an EPROM programmer or burner. The program can be read from a floppy or a hard disk and is fed to the burner. The individual transistors on the chip are set to on or off to reflect the 1s and 0s of the software program. Thus, the program is copied to the chip just as if it were being copied to another floppy or to a hard

7-1 EPROM chips. From left to right: 512K, 256K, 128K, and 64K.

disk. Once the chip is programmed, the glass window of the chip is covered with opaque tape. If something goes wrong, if the program is not exactly right, or if it needs to be updated, it can be erased and reprogrammed. To erase the program, the tape is removed from the glass window and the chip is exposed to UV light.

Some of the functions of ROM BIOS
POST
The function of the BIOS is quite similar to a boss in a small factory. It gets there early, checks all the equipment to make sure it is in working order, then opens the doors for business. It first does a power on self-test (POST). It checks the RAM chips for any defects. The BIOS then checks the keyboard, the floppy and hard drives, the printer, and other peripherals. If it finds something wrong, it reports an error and displays a code number. See chapter 18 for a listing of POST codes.

Hard drive types
When IBM introduced the AT in 1984, their BIOS recognized only 15 types of hard drives. If your drive wasn't on the list, you were in trouble. IBM also had a diagnostic or setup disk that was used to tell the computer such things as the type of floppy and hard drives and the type of monitor that was installed. A floppy disk was needed to set the time and date.

The compatible BIOS developers soon came out with BIOS chips that allowed these functions to be set from the keyboard. You don't need the floppy disk. Also, the list of hard drives was upgraded from 15 to 46 different types. A forty-seventh type is included that lets the user input any characteristics or types not included in the 46 types listed. Many of the clone ROM BIOSs also include other goodies, such as letting you switch from standard speed to turbo from the keyboard. They all now include the ability to recognize 1.44Mb floppy drives. The newer releases also recognize 2.88Mb floppy drives. Incidentally, most hard disk controllers, monitor adapters, and several other peripheral devices have their own BIOS chips.

BIOS utilities
Many of the developers have added utilities to their BIOSs. Some have comprehensive diagnostics. These diagnostics can be used to do a low-level format on a hard disk, can test and determine the optimum interleave factor, and can do a surface

analysis of the disk and mark the bad sectors. They can check the performance of the hard and floppy drives, measure their access speed, measure the data transfer rate, and measure the rotational speed of the drives. They can run tests on the keyboard, the monitor and adapter, the serial and parallel ports, and several other very useful diagnostic tests.

The AMI BIOS has the best diagnostic utilities. It is one of the few that can support COM3 and COM4. At this time, most other BIOS chip developers only support COM1 and COM2. If you want to use COM3 and COM4, you must use special software such as PROCOMM.

Boot program

If everything is okay, a signal is sent to drive A to run the boot program. If there is no disk in drive A, the computer then tries to find a boot program on the hard drive. This boot program initializes the peripheral equipment, runs the config.sys and autoexec.bat programs and allows you to start doing business.

Interrupt control

The BIOS receives several interruptions or requests for services. Depending on the type of request, the BIOS might shut down everything and work to satisfy that one request. A minor request might have to wait until the present task is finished.

Depending on the software and the type of computer, the BIOS might have the facilities to accomplish several tasks at the same time, or do multitasking. With the proper hardware and software, the BIOS might even be able to do multiusing functions, allowing several computers to access it and utilize its software and hardware. The BIOS must be able to work with many different types of requests and orders. There are thousands of different software programs and hardware. The BIOS must be able to take the orders and route them to the proper hardware device, such as the screen, keyboard, disks, printer, or modem.

Sometimes the BIOS is asked to do something it doesn't have the equipment or the ability to do. Because the BIOS is very conscientious, it will keep trying to accomplish the impossible task. If you leave your computer on and come back a week later, it might still be trying to satisfy the request, and it might ignore any requests from the keyboard to stop. Depending on the type of problem, you might have to do a *warm boot*—Ctrl-Alt-Del—to restart the computer. You might even have to turn the power off and do a *cold boot* to completely clear the computer.

Compatibility

Many of the chips used to make a computer, such as the CPU and the RAM chips, might be made by many different companies. IBM designed and developed their own ROM BIOS for their PCs using EPROM chips. Because IBM was the biggest, the industry leader, and the standard setter, a lot of software was written for the IBM PC and its BIOS system.

Just as it is possible to copy software from one disk to another, it is also possible to copy the contents of one EPROM chip to another with an EPROM burner. Of course, it is illegal to make and distribute copies of software that are copyrighted, but that hasn't stopped a lot of people from doing it. The same is true for illegal copying of ROM chips. In order to be compatible with IBM, several of the early clone makers copied the IBM BIOS. Naturally IBM was not too happy about this and threatened to sue.

Phoenix Technologies and Award are two of the several companies that began developing a compatible BIOS for the clone makers. Because they cannot copy the IBM BIOS, their BIOSs can never be 100 percent compatible. But they do almost everything that IBM does, and in some cases, they do things better than IBM, such as reducing time required for checking RAM.

It wasn't long before there were more compatible clones in existence than IBM PCs. It didn't take long for the software developers to take note of this fact. They soon began writing programs that could run on any machine, not just IBM. Today there are very few, if any, programs that have BIOS compatibility problems.

BIOS size

The early BIOS programs were relatively simple. PCs and XTs used a single 64K chip for the BIOS. The ATs used two 128K chips. But the ever-changing technological advances have forced changes. Most of the 286, 386, and 486 machines use two 256K chips for a total of 512K of memory.

Shadow ROM

Some manufacturers have installed the entire ROM BIOS on a single 512K chip. This slows the BIOS down considerably because the ROM is addressed in an eight-bit format. If the BIOS is installed on two chips, a high and a low, or an odd and an even, each can be addressed eight bits at a time. This is, then, essentially a 16-bit system. Even 16 bits is very slow, so some of the high-end 386 and 486 systems offer an option of loading the ROM BIOS into 32-bit system RAM. This shadow ROM can then be addressed 32 bits at a time.

BIOS differences

I have several computers in my office. One of them has a clone 286 motherboard that was designed and built in late 1984. The vendor I bought it from tried both the Phoenix and the Award BIOS in it. They both worked and I ended up with the Award BIOS. A while back I tried to install a 1.44Mb floppy drive. Of course, my 1984 BIOS had never heard of such a thing. I also wanted to install a new hard drive that didn't fit any of the 15 types listed. I also had a few other minor problems, so I decided it was time to upgrade my BIOS.

I went to a nearby dealer who used the Phoenix BIOS in his systems. He cautioned me that it might not work in my system, but he sold me a set. I figured that if it worked with Phoenix in the beginning, it should work now; but it didn't. It would not boot at all. I went to another dealer who used the Phoenix BIOS, and he had another version. It worked perfectly.

In the early days, things were a lot simpler. There were not nearly as many options and choices available, so there were fewer compatibility problems. Now each motherboard manufacturer designs motherboards that are a bit different than the others. They buy a BIOS license from a developer and many of them customize the software for their motherboards. A BIOS that has been customized for one mother-board might not work on another. Most vendors will give you a money back guarantee in case a replacement doesn't work.

IBM XT and AT

You usually won't have too much trouble upgrading an XT BIOS. Most of the new ones are very compatible. It is very worthwhile, especially if you are installing high-density disk drives. Most of the new XT BIOSs recognize the 1.2Mb and 1.44Mb drives.

If you have an older IBM PC or XT, you might have some trouble getting a new IBM BIOS. You might be better off installing a clone BIOS. It will cost you a lot less money, and it will provide more utility and capability for your computer than you had before. Putting a clone BIOS in an IBM won't cause it to lose any of its perceived value as long as you keep that IBM logo on the front panel.

You shouldn't have any trouble replacing your old 286 AT BIOS with a 286 BIOS from any of the major vendors. However, you might have some trouble replacing a PS/2 BIOS. Although the PS/2 models 25 through 40 are ISA machines, IBM installed a BIOS that is not compatible with other ISA machines. If you have an older PS/2, you will probably have to go to IBM for an upgrade.

How to install a BIOS

I mentioned in chapter 6 that you should have a copy of your CMOS setup. If you have not done that, you should do it before you remove your BIOS. If you don't have a listing of your setup, especially your hard drive type, you might not be able to access it. Once you install a new BIOS, you must enter all the information for a complete setup.

The companies that make the BIOSs for computers use different methods of accessing the setup. They might ask you to press Ctrl-Alt-Esc, or just Del, or Alt-Esc, or any of several other combinations. Check your documentation. If you don't have the documentation, you can usually force the setup to appear by holding down one of the keyboard keys. The BIOS detects that it has a stuck key and gives you the option of going to the setup or bypassing the problem.

Step 1—remove the cover and locate the BIOS   Remove the cover and look for the BIOS chips. They can be almost anywhere. They are similar to the chips shown in Fig. 7-2. The XT motherboard has a single 28-pin chip near the center, usually with a white label on it. The 286, 386, and 486 usually have two 28-pin chips.

You might have to remove one or more plug-in boards to get to the BIOS. Before you remove any boards or cables, make a diagram of how they are connected and installed. Be especially careful to note where the BIOS chips are located and how they are oriented. Note the small notch or other markings on the chips indicating which end has pin 1. One of the chips will be marked either HI or ODD, or simply H or O. The other will be marked LO or EVEN, or L or E. Most motherboards are stamped with a chip number. The IC numbers usually begin with a U. Look for the U number of each of the BIOS chips and write it down on your diagram.

7-2 ROM BIOS chipsets from Quadtel, Award, Phoenix, and DTK.

Step 2—remove the old BIOS After you make your diagram, remove the chips. A small screwdriver can be used to lift the chips from each end. There are metal covers on the back panel used to cover the openings for unused slots. One of these covers makes a great tool for lifting out chips. Be careful that you do not get your screwdriver or lifter under the socket itself. There is space under some sockets, and if you pry up on it, you could damage the board or socket. Make sure that your lifter is under the chip only, then lift one end, then the other.

Step 3—plug in the new BIOS Carefully plug in the new BIOS chips. Make sure that you replace the HI or ODD chip and the LO or EVEN chip in its proper socket. CAUTION! Make sure the chips are oriented properly so that pin 1 goes into pin 1 on the board. If you plug them in backwards, they will be destroyed! If necessary, use a flashlight to check that all of the pins are inserted into the sockets. If one of the pins gets bent, remove the chip and use long-nose pliers to straighten it out.

Step 4—replace the cover Replace any boards and cables that were removed. Plug in the power cable and turn on the system. It will probably tell you there are errors in the setup. You have to reenter all of the setup information. You have to set the date, the time, the type of drives, and the type of monitor you are using. If it boots properly after changing the setup, then replace the cover and give yourself a pat on the back for doing a good job.

The future

Intel and Phoenix are developing a BIOS that uses Intel's flash memory. Flash memory is somewhat similar to EPROMs, except that it can be erased and reprogrammed with software. It is currently being used in several laptops, and might eventually replace the hard drive in some applications.

A BIOS in flash memory can be immediately upgraded from data on a floppy disk. New operating environments, utilities, peripherals, and other enhancements can be easily installed in flash memory BIOS.

Sources

Most BIOS developers do not supply chips to end users. They usually draw up a license agreement with a motherboard manufacturer and supply them with the BIOS software on a disk. The manufacturer then uses the supplied software to burn as many BIOS chips as needed for their motherboards. The BIOS companies might also license some distributors such as these:

- Advanced Software ((800) 798-2467). They can provide a BIOS for almost any computer. They also have a low-cost diagnostic POST card and several other computer components.
- DTK Computer Company. They design motherboards. Unlike some of the other manufacturers, they also design their own BIOSs. If you have one of their older systems and you need to upgrade, contact your vendor or their main office at (818) 810-8880.
- Micro Firmware ((800) 767-5465). They stock more than 50 different ROM BIOS sets.
- Unicore Software ((800) 800-2467). They are a BIOS distributor for both Award and Quadtel.
- Upgrades Etc. ((800) 955-3527). They carry AMI, Phoenix, and Award products. They can provide BIOS upgrades for almost any kind of computer. They also carry several other computer components.
- USA Electronics ((800) 332-8434). Among their many advertised components is the AMI BIOS. A spokesman at the company says the AMI BIOS will work in 95 percent of other computer systems.

8
Floppy drives and disks

MY FIRST COMPUTER HAD TWO SINGLE-SIDED 140K DRIVES. IT WAS SLOW AND required a lot of disk swapping. Floppy systems have come a long way since those early days. The 140K systems were soon replaced with 320K double-side systems, then 360K, then 1.2Mb, 1.44Mb, 2.88Mb, and now even 21Mb on a floppy disk.

Floppy disks and floppy drives are a very important part of your computer. The majority of all software comes to us on floppy disks. Floppy disks are also needed to archive programs and backup your hard disk.

How floppy drives operate

A floppy drive spins a disk much like a record player. The floppy disk is made from a type of plastic material called polyethylene terephthalate. This is coated with a magnetic material made of iron oxide. Basically, it is similar to the tape used in cassette tapes. The drive has a head that records (writes) and plays back (reads) the disk much like the record/playback head in a cassette recorder.

When the head on a disk drive writes or records on the iron oxide surface, a pulse of electricity causes the head to magnetize that portion of the track beneath the head. A spot on the track that is magnetized represents a 1, and a spot that is not magnetized represents a 0. When the tracks are read, the head detects this magnetism and creates a small voltage signal representing a 1 (or a 0 if it is not magnetized).

Several large companies manufacture floppy drives, including Sony, Toshiba, Fuji, TEAC, and others. Most of the drives are fairly close in quality, but there are minor differences. For instance, I have two 1.2Mb drives made by Toshiba, one slightly newer than the other. The older one is much quieter and operates much more smoothly than the newer one. On my older Toshiba drive, a fairly large stepping motor is used to position the heads. It is very quiet and works smoothly as it moves the heads to the desired track. The newer drive uses a small cylindrical stepping motor

85

with a worm gear. It groans and is very noisy as it moves the heads from track to track. Otherwise, both have worked perfectly. Figure 8-1 shows the two drives. The one on the right has a large stepper motor, but the drive on the left has a very small motor.

8-1   Two Toshiba 1.2Mb floppy drives. The drive on the right has a large actuator motor at the top right corner. The one on the left has a small cylindrical motor with a worm gear.

360K drives

About 40 million 360K drives are still in use, and many software programs are still distributed on 360K disks. But many of the programs have grown so large that they are being distributed on 1.2Mb or 1.44Mb disks in a compressed form. If you need 360K disks, most vendors will furnish them. The old 360K format has served us well, but it is now obsolete.

If you have an older computer, then you probably have a 5¼-inch, 360K floppy drive, or maybe two. If they are very old, they are probably full height, or about 3½ inches high. If they are original IBM drives, then they have a rubber O-ring for a drive belt from the motor to the disk spindle. This rubber O-ring deteriorates and stretches with time. When the O-ring stretches, the drive speed slows down, and sometimes the spindle won't turn at all.

I replaced an IBM 5¼-inch, 360K floppy drive in 1985 because it kept giving me errors when reading floppies. A new IBM drive cost $425. I didn't realize it at the time, but I could have replaced the O-ring.

High-density drives

From the outside, 360K and 1.2Mb drives look very much alike. The main difference is that 1.2Mb drives use a higher head current to record to the higher-density format. The 5¼-inch, 1.2Mb drives will read and write to the 360K format as well as to the high-density format. The head current is reduced when recording or writing on a 360K disk.

The 3½-inch, 1.44Mb and 720K drives also look very much alike. The main difference is that the 1.44Mb drive has a microswitch that checks for the square hole in the right rear corner of 1.44Mb disks. The 1.44Mb drives will read and write to the 720K format as well as to the high-density format. The 720K drives are obsolete. Although both the 360K and 720K drives are obsolete, many vendors are still advertising and selling them for about the same price as high-density drives. Figure 8-2 shows a 1.2Mb and a 1.44Mb floppy drive.

8-2 A 1.2Mb and a 1.44Mb floppy drive.

Advantages of high-density drives

Installing high-density floppy drives is a useful upgrade that is relatively inexpensive and easy to do. Even if you have fairly new half-height 360K drives, it is well worth the cost and effort to replace them with high-density drives.

I have about 500 floppy disks full of programs. They take up quite a lot of space, and I sometimes have a difficult time finding what I need. Someday I am going to transfer all of them to high-density disks. If I use 1.2Mb floppies, I will need 150 disks to store all the data on my 360K disks, or 125 disks if I use 1.44Mb floppies.

I also have several hard disks that must be backed up constantly. It takes over one hundred 360K floppies to back up 40Mb. It only takes 34 of the 1.2Mb disks or 26 of the 1.44Mb floppies to back up 40Mb. And it takes even fewer disks if you use one of the newer backup softwares. Most of today's backup software compresses the data. I discuss backups in chapter 10.

The all-media floppy drives

Many computers provide only three or four bays to mount drives. You might not have space to mount two floppy drives, two hard drives, a tape backup, and a CD-ROM. The CMS Enhancements ((714) 222-6316) noted this problem and created an all-media floppy drive that combines a 1.2Mb and a 1.44Mb floppy drive in a single unit. This allows both drives to be installed in a single drive bay. The two drives are never used at the same time, so there is no problem. They can even share most of the drive electronics. The CMS drive costs about $150. Several other manufacturers such as TEAC and Canon have now designed similar drives (see Fig. 8-3).

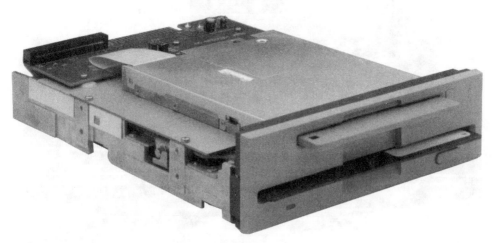

8-3   A TEAC combination 3½-inch and 5¼-inch floppy drive.

Extended-density drives

Several companies are now offering 3½-inch extended-density (ED) 2.8Mb floppy drives. The 2.8Mb disks have a barium ferrite media and use perpendicular recording to achieve the extended density. In standard recording, the particles are magnetized so that they lay horizontally in the media. In perpendicular recording, the particles are stood vertically for greater density.

The ED drives are downward compatible and can read and write to 720K and 1.44Mb disks. At the present time, ED drives are still rather expensive, at about $350 for the drive and about $10 each for the disks.

IBM has installed 2.88Mb drives in some of their new PS/2 models, but I wouldn't buy one, especially at today's prices. For just a little more money, you can buy a 20Mb floppy drive.

Very high-density drives

Floppy technology continues to advance, and several new higher-capacity drives and disks are now available. Brier Technology ((408) 435-8463) and Insite ((408) 946-8080) have developed very high-density (VHD) 3½-inch drives that can store over 20 Mb on a disk. There is no standard among the competing systems, and they use different methods to achieve the very high density.

One of the problems that had to be overcome in VHD drives was tracking. The drives have little trouble reading and writing to the 135 tracks per inch (tpi) of the standard 3½-inch disk, but 20Mb requires many more tracks that are much closer. Brier Technology's Flextra uses special disks that have magnetic servo tracks embedded beneath the data tracks. The Insite disks have optical servo tracks that are etched into the surface with a laser beam. The heads lock onto the servo tracks for accurate reading and writing to the data tracks. The Insite drive has a head with two different gaps. This allows it to read and write to the 20Mb format as well as the 720K and 1.44Mb formats.

The Brier drive is being distributed by Q'COR ((800)-548-3420). Several companies, including Iomega, are now distributing the Insite Floptical.

The VHD drives cost about $450 and special disks for these systems cost about $20 each.

Floppy controllers

A floppy drive must have a controller. In the early days they were a separate board full of chips. Now they are built into a single VLSI chip that is integrated with a hard disk controller or IDE interface. They might also be integrated with a multifunction board or be built in on the motherboard.

The ED drives require a controller that operates at 1 MHz. The other floppy controllers operate at 500 kHz. Eventually this controller will be integrated with the other floppy controllers.

Bernoulli drives

Iomega has a high-capacity Bernoulli floppy disk system. This system allows the recording of up to 90 Mb on special floppy disks. Using Stacker compression software, these 90Mb floppies will hold 180Mb. With a Bernoulli drive, you need never run out of hard disk space. The Bernoulli can be used instead of a hard disk or in conjunction with a hard disk. Figure 8-4 shows an externally mounted 5¼-inch drive. This shows the SCSI plug-in interface, the cable, and a 90Mb floppy disk. Several 5¼-inch 90Mb internal drives that fit in any standard bay are also available. Because

8-4 An external Iomega 90Mb Bernoulli floppy drive, floppy disk, cable, and SCSI interface card.

the floppies can be removed and locked up, they are excellent in a security environment. Bernoulli drives list for about $800 and each floppy costs about $100.

Bernoulli disks spin much faster than a standard floppy forcing the flexible disk to bend around the heads without actually touching them. This is in accordance with the principle discovered by the Swiss scientist, Jakob Bernoulli (1654–1705). The average seek time for a Bernoulli system is 32 ms. The better hard drives have seek times of about 15 ms.

Data compression

Data compression can double your disk capacity. Programs such as Stacker from Stac Electronics ((800)-522-7822) or SuperStor from AddStor ((800)-732-3133) can double the size of a disk. DR DOS 6.0 comes with SuperStor as one of its utilities. MS_DOS 6.0 also comes with data compression.

At one time, data compression wasn't completely trusted. But bulletin boards have been using it for years with very few problems. Compression has matured, and it is now trustworthy and reliable. Compression programs are now fast and transparent to the user. Many backup programs use compression so that fewer disks are needed.

Stacker and AddStor can double the size of any disk. Stacker works great on

VHD floppies and on Bernoulli disks. I have used Stacker for over two years with no problems. AddStor puts a small file on floppy disks that makes them readable by a system that does not have the compression program.

Differences between floppy disks

The 5¼-inch, 360K and 3½-inch, 720K disks are called *double-sided double-density* (DS/DD). The 5¼-inch, 1.2Mb and 3½-inch 1.44Mb disks are called high-density (HD). The 3½-inch double-density disks are marked DD; the high-density disks are marked HD. But the 5¼-inch, 360K and 1.2Mb disks usually have no markings. They look exactly alike, except the 360K disks usually have a reinforcing ring or collar around the large center hole. The high-density 1.2Mb disks do not have the ring (see Fig. 8-5). The 360K disk shown in the photo has a white collar or ring, most of the new disks have a black ring.

8-5   A 360K disk (left) and a 1.2Mb disk (right). The only difference is the reinforcing ring around the center hole of the 360K disk. It is shown white here, but most are now black.

One of the major differences between 720K and 1.44Mb disks is that the high-density 1.44Mb disks have two small square holes at the rear of the plastic shell, while the 720K disks have only one. The 3½-inch drive has a microswitch on the right side that protrudes upwards. If it finds a hole on the right side of the disk, it knows that it is a 1.44Mb disk. If there is no hole, it is treated as a 720K disk. Figure 8-6 shows the front and back of two 1.44Mb disks on the left and two 720K disks on the right. There might be times when you want to use a 1.44Mb disk as a 720K disk. You can cover the hole with any kind of tape and the disk will format at 720K.

The square hole on the left of the shell has a small black slide that can be moved to cover the hole. A microswitch on the drive checks the hole when the disk is inserted. If the hole is covered, the switch is pressed downward, allowing the disk to be written on. If the hole is open, the switch protects the disk so that it cannot be written on or erased. The 3½-inch write-protect system is just the opposite of the system used by the 5¼-inch disks. The 5¼-inch disks have a square hole that must be covered

8-6 The front and back of
3½-inch floppy disks.
The two on the left are
1.44Mb, the two on the
right are 720K. Note
that the 1.44Mb disks
have two square holes
at the rear corners, the
720K only one. The
hole on the right rear
corner of the two lower
disks has a black slide
that covers the hole to
write-protect the disks.

with opaque tape to prevent writing or unintentional erasing of the disk. You must
use opaque tape. The 5¼-inch system uses a light that shines through the square hole.
If the detector in the system sees light through the hole, then it can write on the disk.
Some people have used clear plastic tape to cover the hole, with disastrous results.

360K and 1.2Mb disks

The 360K and 1.2Mb disks look exactly alike except for the hub ring on the 360K
disks. However, there is a large difference in their magnetic materials that determines
the oersted (Oe) of each. Oersted is a measure of the resistance of a material to being magnetized. The lower the Oersted, the easier the material is to magnetize. The
360K disks have an Oersted of 300; the 1.2Mb disks have an Oersted of 600. The 360K
disks are fairly easy to write to, and require a fairly low head current. The 1.2Mb disks
are more difficult to magnetize, so a much higher head current is required. The current is switched to match whatever type of disk you tell the system you are using.

It is possible to format a 360K disk as a 1.2Mb disk, but several bad sectors will
be found, especially near the center where the sectors are shorter. These sectors will
be marked and locked out. The system might report that you have over 1Mb of space
on a 360K disk. I do not recommend you use such a disk for any data that is important. The data will eventually deteriorate and become unusable.

720K and 1.44Mb disks

The 720K disks can store twice as much data as the 360Ks, and the 1.44Mb disks can
store four times as much in a smaller space. They have a hard plastic protective shell,
so they are not easily damaged. They also have a spring-loaded shutter that automatically covers and protects the disk opening when it is not in use.

It is possible to insert a 5¼-inch floppy upside down, backwards, or sideways. The 3½-inch disks were designed so they can only be inserted one way. They have arrows at the top left of the disk indicating how they should be inserted into the drive. They also have notches on the back that prevent them from being completely inserted upside down.

Disk format structure

Tracks

A disk must be formatted before it can be used. This consists of laying out individual concentric tracks on each side of the disk. If it is a 360K disk, each side is marked or configured with 40 tracks, numbered 0 to 39. If it is a 1.2Mb, 720K, or 1.44Mb, each side is configured with 80 tracks, numbered 0 to 79. The tracks have the same number on the top and bottom of the disk. The top is side 0 and the bottom is side 1. When the head is over track 1 on the top, it is also over track 1 on the bottom. The heads move as a single unit to the various tracks using a head positioner. When data is written to a track, as much as possible is written on the top track, then the head is electronically switched, and data is written to the same track on the bottom side. It is much faster and easier to electronically switch between the heads than to move them to another track.

Cylinders

If you could strip away all of the other tracks on each side of track 1 on side 0 and track 1 on side 1, it would be very flat, but it would look like a cylinder. If a disk has 40 tracks, such as a 360Kdisk, it has 40 cylinders; the 1.2Mb and 1.44Mb disks have 80 cylinders.

Sectors

Each of the tracks are divided into sectors. Each track of a 360K disk and 720K disk is divided into nine sectors; each track of a 1.2Mb disk is divided into 15 sectors. Each track of a 1.44Mb disk is divided into 18 sectors, and each track of a 2.88Mb disk is divided into 36 sectors. Each sector contains 512 bytes. Multiplying the number of sectors times the number of bytes per sector times the number of tracks times two sides gives the amount of data that can be stored on the disk. For instance, a 1.2Mb disk has 15 sectors times 512 bytes times 80 tracks times 2 sides—$15 \times 512 \times 80 \times 2$—equals 1,228,800 bytes. The system uses 14,898 bytes to mark the tracks and sectors during formatting, so there is actually 1,213,952 bytes available on a 1.2Mb floppy (see Table 8-1).

Table 8-1. Capacities of various disk types

Disk type	Tracks per side	Sectors per track	Unformatted capacity	System use	Available to user	Maximum directories
360K	40	9	368,640	6,144	362,496	112
1.2Mb	80	15	1,228,800	14,898	1,213,952	224
720K	80	9	737,280	12,800	724,480	224
1.44Mb	80	18	1,474,560	16,896	1,457,664	224
2.88Mb	80	36	2,949,120	33,792	2,915,328	224

Clusters or allocation units

DOS allocates one or more sectors on a disk and calls it a cluster or allocation unit. On the 360K and 720K disks, a cluster or allocation unit is two sectors. On the 1.2Mb and 1.44Mb disks, each allocation unit is one sector. Only single files or parts of single files can be written into an allocation unit. If two different files are written into a single allocation unit, the data becomes mixed and corrupted.

File allocation table (FAT)

During formatting, a file allocation table (FAT) is created on the first track of the disk. This FAT acts like a table of contents for a book. Whenever a file is recorded on a disk, the file is broken up into allocation units. The head looks in the FAT to find empty units, then records parts of the file in any empty units it finds. Part of the file might be recorded in sector 5 of track 10, part in sector 8 of track 15, and anyplace else there are empty sectors. The location of all the various parts of the file is recorded in the FAT. With this method, parts of a file can be erased, changed, or added to without changing the entire disk.

Tracks per inch

The 40 tracks of a 360K disk are laid down at a rate of 48 tracks per inch (tpi), so each of the 40 tracks is $\frac{1}{48}$ inch wide. The 80 tracks of a high-density 1.2Mb disk are laid down at a rate of 96 tpi, so each track is $\frac{1}{96}$ inch. The 80 tracks of the 3½-inch disks are laid down at a density of 135 tpi or $\frac{1}{135}$ inch per track.

Read accuracy

The 5¼-inch disks have a 1⅛-inch center hole. The drives have a conical spindle that comes up through the hole when the drive latch is closed. This centers the disk so that the heads are able to find each track. The plastic material that the disk is made from is subject to environmental changes and wear and tear, and the conical spindle might not center each disk exactly, so head-to-track accuracy is difficult with more than 80 tracks. If you have trouble reading a disk, it might be off center. Sometimes it helps if you remove the disk and reinsert it. Most 360K disks use a reinforcing hub ring, but it probably doesn't help much. The 1.2Mb floppies do not use a hub ring. Except for the hub ring, the 360K and 1.2Mb disks look exactly the same. The tracks of the 3½-inch floppies are narrower and greater in density per inch than those on 5¼-inch disks. But because of the metal hub, their head tracking accuracy is much better.

Some differences between floppies and hard disks

Hard disks have very accurate and precise head tracking systems. Some hard disks have densities up to 3000 tpi. Hard disks rotate at 3600 to 6400 rpm. The heads and disk surface would be severely damaged if they came in contact at this speed. The heads of a hard disk "fly" over the surface of the disk at a few millionths of an inch above it.

Floppy disks have a very smooth lubricated surface. They rotate at a fairly slow 300 rpm. Magnetic lines of force deteriorate very fast with distance, so the closer the heads are to the disk surface, the better they can read and write. The heads directly contact floppy disks.

Formatting

Assuming that the 1.2Mb drive is the A drive, to format a 360K disk with a 1.2Mb drive, type FORMAT A /4. To format to 1.2Mb, you need high-density disks. If the system is configured and the controller allows it, you only have to type FORMAT A:. If you insert a 360K disk, it will format to 1.2Mb, and several bad sectors will be found.

To format a 720K disk on a 1.44Mb drive, type FORMAT B: /T:80 /N:9. To format a 1.44Mb disk, just type FORMAT B:, or you might have to type FORMAT B: /T:80 /N:18.

Formatting. bat files

Here are some batch files that save me a lot of time when formatting disks. Here is how I made my batch files:

```
COPY CON FM36.BAT
C: FORMAT A: /4
^Z

COPY CON FM12.BAT
C: FORMAT A: /T:80 /N:15
^Z

COPY CON FM72.BAT
C: FORMAT B: /T:80 /N:9
^Z

COPY CON FM14.BAT
C: FORMAT B: /T:80 /N:18
^Z
```

The ^Z indicates the end of the file. It is made by pressing F6, or the ^ over the numeral 6 and Z. With these batch files I only have to type fm36 for a 360K disk, fm12 for a 1.2Mb disk, fm72 for a 720K disk, or fm14 for a 1.44Mb disk.

The above statements and .bat files apply to DR DOS 6.0 and versions of MS-DOS through version 4.01. MS-DOS version 5.0 tries to format a 360K disk as a 1.2Mb disk in a high-density drive unless you tell it differently. A switch has been added that can be invoked with the FORMAT command. It eliminates the need to type in parameters for the various formats. To format a 360K disk, type FORMAT A:/f:360; for a 1.2Mb disk type FORMAT A:/f:1.2; for a 720K disk, type FORMAT B:/f:720; and for a 1.44Mb disk, type FORMAT B:/f:1.44. All of these commands can be considerably shortened if they are made into .bat files similar to those above.

If you try to reformat a disk with MS-DOS 5.0 that has been previously formatted, it tries to format it the same way. For instance, if you made a mistake and formatted a 360K disk as a 1.2Mb disk, MS-DOS 5.0 insists on formatting it as a 1.2Mb disk if you don't use the /f:360 switch.

Disk costs

All floppy disks are now quite reasonable. The 360K DS/DD disks sell for as little as 19 cents each, and the 720Ks are going for as little as 33 cents each. The 1.2Mb HD disks are selling at discount houses for as little as 33 cents each. The 1.44Mb HD disks are selling for as little as 55 cents each. These are real bargains. You can buy 10 of the 1.44Mb disks or 14.4Mb of storage for $5.50. This is about 38 cents per megabyte. You can buy 10 of the 1.2Mb HD disks for only $3.30. You can store 12Mb of data on them at a cost of less than 28 cents per megabyte. If you use a good compression software such as Norton or Fastback Plus, you could store more than 28Mb on ten 1.44Mb disks or about 24Mb on ten 1.2Mb disks.

Discount disk sources

Here are just a few companies that sell disks at a discount. There are several others. Check the computer magazines for ads.

Americal Group	(800) 288-8025
The Disk Barn	(800) 727-3475
MEI/Micro Center	(800) 634-3478
MidWest Micro	(800) 423-8215

What to buy

I recommend the 1.2Mb and 1.44Mb drives. Or if you can afford it, buy the Insite Floptical 20Mb drive. It is about the best 3½-inch drive you can buy. If you live near a large city, there should be lots of stores nearby, as well as computer shows and swap meets. If you don't live near a good source, the next best thing is mail order. Look in the computer magazines for ads.

How to install a floppy drive

To install your drive, you need a Phillips and a flat-blade screwdriver. It helps if they are magnetized. But be careful with magnetized tools around your floppy disks. Magnetism can partially erase or damage your disks. You might also find it helpful to have long-nose pliers.

Step 1—set any switches or jumpers   You should receive some sort of documentation with your drive. The drive might have jumpers that must be set to configure it to the type of system you have. Check the documentation and set the jumpers before you install the drive. I once overlooked the setting of a jumper on a drive I installed in one of my 386 machines. It seemed to work fine, but if I typed DIR, the computer would display the directory of whatever disk was in the drive. If I removed the disk, inserted another, and typed another DIR, the computer would display the directory from the first disk. The other drive on my system worked fine, so I knew something was wrong with the new drive. When I got out the documentation and checked the jumper settings, I found I had not set one of the jumpers properly.

The documentation that comes with most drives and other components is often very poorly written and organized, and you might have trouble understanding it. Your dealer might not be able to help you, especially if you buy from a mail-order house. This is a good reason why you should belong to a user group. Such a group can be a tremendous help if you have problems.

The 3½-inch drives are much smaller than the standard 5¼-inch drives, and usually come with an installation kit that includes an expansion bracket so the drive can be mounted in any standard 5¼-inch drive bay (see Fig. 8-7). Four screws mount the drive to the bracket. If the drive is to be used in an XT, the bracket assembly has threaded holes for mounting in the XT drive slots. If the drive is to be used in a 286 or 386 chassis, you might have to install plastic or metal slide rails on each side of the bracket assembly. Some of the newer cases have small bays that accept 3½-inch drives without an expansion bracket.

8-7 A 5¼-inch, 1.2Mb floppy drive (left), a 3½-inch, 1.44Mb drive (center), and a controller (right).

Step 2—remove the cover The first thing to do, of course, is unplug the power. If you have one of the older standard cases, remove the cover by removing each of the screws in the four corners and the one screw in the top of the back panel. Slip the cover off.

Once the cover is off, make a rough diagram of the cables and how and where they are connected. Pay close attention to the position of the colored wire on each ribbon cable. Now you can remove your old drives. If you are going to use the same controller, leave the cable plugged into it.

Step 3—mount the drive   Mount the drive in the chassis. If the drive is not mounted with slide rails, line the holes up on the sides of the drive and in the bay, and the insert screws.

Step 4—reconnect cables   The flat ribbon cable to the drive should have three connectors as shown in Fig. 8-8. The connector on one end has a split and twist in

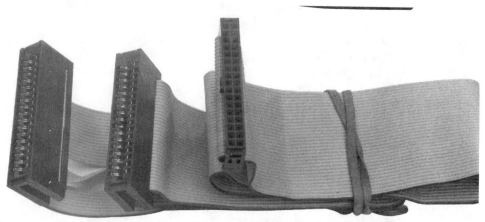

8-8   A 34-wire ribbon cable with three connectors for floppy drives. The end connector on the left has some twisted wires. It goes to drive A. The middle connector is for drive B, if you have one. The end connector on the right goes to the floppy controller card.

8-9   Installing the cable to drive A. This connector can be plugged in backwards. Note that the slot on the edge connector of the drive is between contacts 2 and 3. The colored wire on the cable goes to pin 1 of the connector.

some of the wires. This connector goes to drive A. (see Fig. 8-9). This is your boot drive. In most cases, this should be your 1.2Mb or 5¼-inch drive. The middle connector goes to the drive B, and the end connector plugs into the controller (see Fig. 8-10). CAUTION! The connectors can be plugged in backwards. Note that the edge connector on the drive has a narrow slit between contacts 2 and 3. That end of the board has contact number 1, and the colored wire on the ribbon cable goes to pin 1 of the connector. You might also see a number etched on the board. All of the even numbered contacts are on the front of the board, and the odd numbers are on the back. You might see a small number 2 near the narrow slit and a 34 on the other end.

8-10 Connecting the ribbon cable to the controller. Note that this connector can be plugged in backwards. Look for the pin 1 indication on the board and orient the cable so that the colored wire side goes to pin 1.

The power to the drives is a four-wire cable from the power supply (see Fig. 8-11 on the next page). This cable can be plugged in only one way. After you install your drive, try it out before you replace the cover. Try formatting a blank disk, then write a file to it, and read it back. Congratulations! Pat yourself on the back for a job well done.

8-11 Connecting the power plug to the drive. It can only be plugged in one way.

9
Choosing and installing a hard drive

IF YOU ARE COMPLETELY NEW TO COMPUTING, A HARD DRIVE IS AN ASSEMBLY OF platters or rigid disks with a magnetic plating. Depending on the capacity, there might be several disks on a common spindle. There is a read/write head on the top and bottom of each disk. The head "flies" just a few millionths of an inch from the disk on a cushion of purified air. Figure 9-1 shows a hard drive with the cover removed.

A hard disk is a very precise piece of machinery. The tracks might be only a few millionths of an inch apart, and the head actuator must move the heads quickly and accurately to the specified track. In the early 1980s, a 20Mb hard drive cost over

9-1 A hard drive with the cover removed.

$2500. You can buy a 20Mb hard drive today for about $100, or a 200Mb drive for about $500. For such a precise piece of machinery, that is absolutely amazing.

The need for a hard drive

It is possible to run a computer with only floppy drives, but it is slow and time consuming. It involves an endless amount of disk swapping. Many of today's programs are very large. OS/2 2.0 comes on twenty-one 1.44Mb disks in a compressed form. It is almost impossible to run programs such as this with just a floppy system. With today's low prices, I can't imagine why anyone would run a PC without a good hard drive. To do any kind of productive computing, you need a hard drive.

Types of drives

The two most popular types of drives are the integrated disk electronics (IDE) and small computer system interface (SCSI) types. The enhanced small device interface (ESDI) type is a good high-end drive, but it is usually more expensive than an equivalent IDE or SCSI drive. The older modified frequency modulation (MFM) and run length limited (RLL) drives are rugged and reliable, but they are slow and limited in capacity. Like the 360K and 720K drives, they are practically obsolete.

SCSI

SCSI (pronounced scuzzy) drives have most of the disk controlling functions integrated onto the drive. This makes a lot of sense because the control electronics can be optimally matched to the drive. The electronics still require an interface card to transmit the data in eight-bit parallel back and forth to the disk, much like a parallel printer port. Because SCSI drives can handle eight bits of data at a time, they can have very fast transfer rates. The MFM, RLL, and ESDI drives are serial systems, transferring data one bit at a time over the lines. SCSI systems allow recording of up to 54 sectors per track, compared to 17 sectors for MFM systems, so more than twice as much data can be stored on a disk. They can also be more than twice as fast as MFM systems.

Many companies are making smaller-capacity low-end SCSI drives. Seagate has several such models. The low-end models format each track to 26 sectors, the same as the RLL drives. I recently bought a low-end SCSI system, a Seagate ST138N, 30Mb, 28-ms drive. (Seagate uses an N after the model number to denote SCSI.) It is a stepper motor system, which makes it a bit slow, but it is reliable and rugged.

SCSI systems need a host adapter, or interface card, to drive them. A Seagate ST02 host adapter with a built-in floppy controller costs about $40. The ST02 interface has a very brief installation guide. Several jumpers on the board configure it to your system's interrupts, BIOS address, and the type of floppy drives you have.

SCSI drivers Most hard drives require that you enter the drive type in the CMOS setup. The setup lists several drive types that describe the hard disk characteristics. The setup allows only two drives, and they must be the same type. The SCSI interface has its own drivers so it is not entered in your setup, and you can add up to eight SCSI drives along with the other drives. More about the CMOS setup later.

The main reason I bought a SCSI drive was for backup. This type of backup is very fast, and for my purposes, it is much better than using floppy disks. I can copy files from my main IDE drives to the SCSI drive very quickly and easily. I don't have to worry about swapping floppy disks in and out; I don't have to worry about labeling and storing floppy disks; and I can quickly find any file that I want and copy it back to the original disk.

There are many different types of SCSI controllers with many different functions. The prices range from $40 for a simple adapter to over $1000 for a high-end EISA interface. Some of the high-end adapters can handle eight or more devices in a chain.

IDE or AT-type drives

Several companies have developed drives with integrated drive electronics. They are sometimes called AT drives because they were first developed for use on the 286 AT. The drives are similar to SCSI drives in that all of their controller electronics are integrated on the drive. Figure 9-2 shows a 5¼-inch, 40Mb, MFM drive on the left and two IDE hard drives. The 3½-inch IDE drive in the center is 80Mb and is about two years old. The IDE drive on the right is a fairly new Quantum 240Mb drive. The 80Mb drive is 1½ inches high. The 240Mb drive is newer and is only 1 inch high; exactly the same dimensions as a 3½-inch floppy drive.

9-2 A 40Mb MFM drive (left), an 80Mb IDE drive (center), and a 240Mb IDE drive (right).

IDE drives need only a very inexpensive interface to connect with the bus. Figure 9-3 shows a multifunction card that is an interface for IDE drives, is a floppy drive controller, and has two parallel printer ports and two serial ports. This interface can be plugged into any of the eight motherboard slots. Because the interface is so simple, some vendors have designed motherboards with the interface built-in by providing a set of pins on the motherboard. A single cable is plugged into these pins to control two IDE drives. This saves the cost of a controller and also saves one of your slots.

Many motherboards also have a built-in controller for floppy drives. A set of pins similar to the hard drive connector pins are provided. When plugging the connector into the pins for the floppy and hard drives, be very careful that you locate pin 1 on

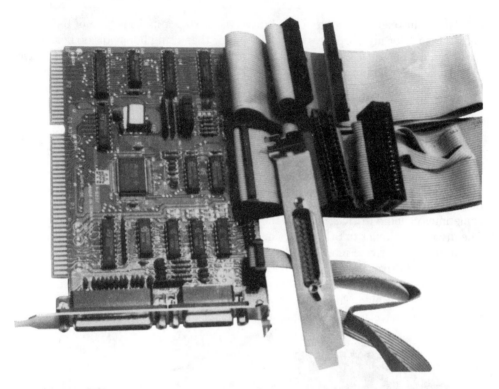

9-3   A multifunction board that has an IDE interface. It can control two floppy drives and two
IDE hard drives, and has a parallel printer port and two serial ports.

the board and plug the cable in so that the colored wire goes to the pin 1 side. The
cable has a different colored wire on the side that goes to pin 1.

The IDE drives cost about the same as the SCSI types. A recent *Computer
Shopper* had several ads that listed 200Mb IDE and SCSI drives for less than $500.
One major difference is that the IDE interface might cost nothing if it is built-in, or
about $10 if you have to buy a plug-in board.

ESDI

The ESDI (pronounced ezdy) system is another modification of the MFM system. Most
of the ESDI drives are large capacity, usually over 100Mb. ESDI drives can be formatted to 34 sectors or more per track, so they can store more than twice as much data as
the 17 sectors of standard MFM systems. They have a very fast access speed, usually
15 ms to 18 ms, and a data transfer rate of 10 to 15 megabits or more per second.

The ESDI systems don't offer as many options as the SCSI systems, but they are
often more expensive. They are good drives, but they are being phased out, and if
you buy one, you might be left with an orphan. Orphan products are those that are
no longer being manufactured or have no technical support.

MFM

MFM was an early standard method for disk recording. In the early 1980s, Seagate Technology developed the ST506/412 interface for MFM, and it became the standard. This method formats several concentric tracks on a disk like those laid down on a floppy disk. The MFM systems divide the tracks into 17 sectors per track, with 512 bytes in each sector. They usually have a transfer rate of 5 megabits per second. The MFM method can be used with drives from 5Mb up to several hundred megabytes. The MFM drives are physically large, limited in capacity, clunky, and slow. Most manufacturers have stopped making them.

RLL

The RLL system is a modification of the MFM system. RLL drives, when used with an RLL controller, format the disk to 26 sectors per track. This allows the storage of 50 percent more data than the 17 sectors per track on an MFM drive. For instance, a 20Mb drive can store 30Mb; a 40Mb drive can store 60Mb. They have a transfer rate of 7.5 megabits; 50 percent faster than MFM systems. Not all drives are capable of running RLL. Seagate uses an R after the model number to denote their RLL drives. Except for being just a bit faster and being able to store 50 percent more data, the RLL drives cost about the same as the MFM types. They are more limited than the IDE and SCSI drives, and these drives are also being phased out.

Capacity

When you consider capacity, buy the biggest you can afford. You might have heard of Mr. C. Northcote Parkinson. After observing business organizations for some time, he formulated several laws. One law says, "Work expands to fill up available employee time." A parallel law that paraphrases Mr. Parkinson's immutable law might say, "Data expands to fill up available hard disk space."

Don't even think of buying anything less than 100Mb; 200Mb is even better. New software has become more and more friendly and offers more and more options. Most of the basic application programs, such as spreadsheets, databases, CAD programs, word processors, and many others, require 2Mb to 3Mb of disk space. OS/2 2.0 requires over 25Mb of disk space.

Speed or access time

Speed or access time is the time it takes a hard drive to locate and retrieve a sector of data. This includes the time it takes to move the head to the track, settle the head in place, and read the data. For a high-end, very fast drive, this might be as little as 9 ms. Some of the older drives and systems required as much as 100 ms. An 85-ms hard drive might be fine for a slow XT, but a 28-ms drive might not be fast enough for a 386. For disk-intensive uses, a 15-ms IDE, SCSI, or ESDI system is advisable. Of course, the faster the hard drive, the more expensive it will be.

Type of actuator—stepper or voice coil

The head actuator is the method used to move the head to the desired track. Most of the less-expensive hard drives use a stepper motor that moves the heads in discrete increments across the disk until they are over the track to be read or written. You can hear a definite click as they move from track to track.

The voice coil actuators are quieter, a bit faster, more reliable, and more expensive. Voice coil drives can be recognized from their spec sheets. They show an odd number of heads. Actually they have an even number of heads, one on the top and bottom of each disk, but one head and disk surface is used as a servo control for the heads. By using calibrated voltages and the servo tracks, a voice coil system can smoothly, quietly, and quickly move the heads to the desired track. The high-end SCSI, IDE, and ESDI drives use voice coil technology.

Cost per megabyte

If two drives from different manufacturers have the same specifications, you might consider the cost per megabyte. For instance, a 210Mb drive might cost about $500 or 500/210 = $2.38 per megabyte. A 340Mb drive might cost about $900 or 900/340 = $2.65 per megabyte. A 668Mb drive might cost about $1250 or 1250/668 = $1.87 per megabyte. Just a couple of years ago, the least expensive hard drive cost about $4.50 per megabyte. Within a couple of years you should be able to buy a 600Mb drive for about $1 per megabyte.

Physical size

The original full-height drives were about 3½ inches high and almost 6 inches wide. The disk platters were 5¼ inches in diameter. It wasn't long before the technology advanced to where you could get the same capacity in a half-height 5¼-inch form. But 5¼-inch platters have to be fairly thick in order to be rigid enough. As the technology advanced still further, you could get the same capacity in a half-height 3½-inch form. These smaller disk platters were made thinner, so more platters could be placed in the same amount of space. The smaller-diameter platters have less mass and need less wattage to spin them. Because they are smaller, it takes less time for the actuators to move the heads to a particular track. The access time is therefore much less.

I worked for Ampex Corporation during the early 1970s. They developed one of the first hard drives for military use. It was 16¼ inches in diameter and was ¼-inch thick. It could store 1.5Mb on each side for a total of 3Mb. Figure 9-4 shows the large hard disk on the left. In the top center is a 5¼-inch disk that can store over 100Mb. The upper right disk is a 3½-inch platter that can also store about 100Mb. The two bright disks in the lower portion of the photo are CD-ROM disks. The larger one can store over 600Mb, the smaller one about 250Mb.

Several companies are now manufacturing 2½-inch and 1.8-inch drives. Hewlett-Packard has announced that they will manufacture a 1.3-inch drive that can store 20Mb (see Fig. 9-5). These new and smaller hard disks will be used in many areas,

9-4 An early Ampex 3Mb hard disk (left) and several modern hard disk platters.

9-5 The Hewlett-Packard 1.3-inch, 20Mb hard drive. Hewlett-Packard Company.

such as laptops and cameras. One of the biggest uses is expected to be in automobiles. A great number of automobile functions, such as fuel use, automatic transmission, brakes, air conditioning, headlights, and others, will be controlled by a computer and hard disk. To give you a perspective, Figure 9-6 shows outline drawings that give you a idea of the size of a 1.3-inch, 1.8-inch, and a 2-inch hard disk platter.

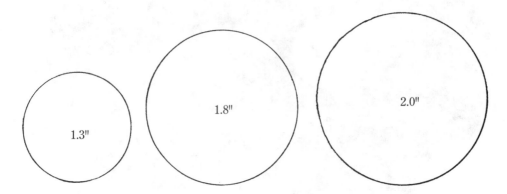

9-6 Full-size drawings representing the sizes of a 1.3-, 1.8-, and a 2.0-inch hard disk platter.

Interfaces and controllers

If you buy an IDE drive, it might have the interface built-in or you may have to buy an inexpensive plug-in interface board. If you buy a SCSI drive, you need to buy a plug-in interface board. If you buy an MFM, RLL, or ESDI hard drive you need a controller card that plugs into one of the slots in your computer.

In the past, very few hard drive companies made controllers for their hard drives. But many are now making controllers for their high-end ESDI drives and interfaces for their SCSI drives. The controllers and drives are then tested and tuned for optimum operation and sold as a pair.

Most hard drive controllers have floppy drive controllers integrated onto the same board. This saves space and is very convenient. These HDC/FDC boards will control 360K, 1.2Mb, 720K, and 1.44Mb drives, as well as two hard drives. There should be HDC/FDC controllers available soon that include 2.88Mb floppy drives. Note that the advertised price of most disk drives does not include the controller or the necessary cables. An HDC/FDC controller costs as little as $40. The cables may cost from $5 to $10.

Mean time before failure

Disk drives are mechanical devices. If used long enough, every disk drive will fail. Manufacturers test their drives and assign them an average lifetime that ranges from 40,000 to 150,000 hours. Of course, the larger the figure, the longer the drive should last (and the more it will cost). These are average figures, much like the figures quoted for a human lifespan. Some hard drives die very young, while some become obsolete before they wear out.

I have difficulty accepting some of the manufacturer's mean time before failure (MTBF) figures. For instance, to put 150,000 hours on a drive, it would have to be used 8 hours a day, every day, for over 51 years. If it were operated 24 hours a day, 365 days a year, it would take over 17 years to put 150,000 hours on it. Because hard drives have only been around about 10 years, I am pretty sure that no one has ever done a 150,000-hour test on a drive.

Hard cards

Several companies have developed hard drives on plug-in cards. These cards have the drive on one end of the card and the controller on the other. They are less than 1 inch thick and plug into any slot on your motherboard. They make it very easy to add a second hard drive to your system. Figure 9-7 shows a Plus Development Company hard card.

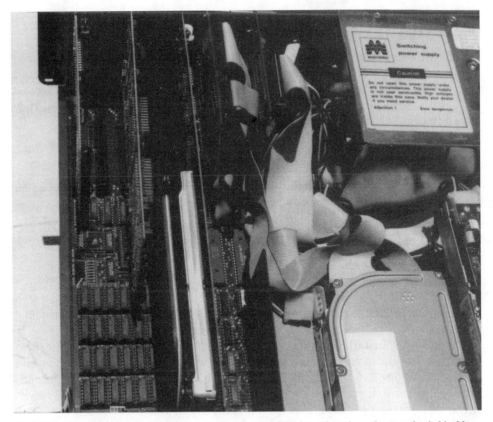

9-7 The Plus Development Hardcard 40 (the slim bright colored card near the left). Note that it only takes up one slot space. Similar hard drives on a card are available with 200Mb or more.

Bernoulli drives

I discussed the 90Mb Iomega Bernoulli drives in chapter 8 because they are floppies. But they can be used instead of or with a hard drive system. You can have two hard drives and up to eight Bernoulli drives because they work off either a SCSI adapter or a proprietary adapter system.

SyQuest's SyDOS drives

Syquest ((800) 437-9367) has several models of removable hard disk cartridges. They are similar to Bernoulli drives in cost and capacity—Bernoulli has 90Mb, SyQuest has 88Mb. Like Bernoulli, they are available in external and internal drives that operate off a SCSI adapter. Read the ads carefully. Some vendors advertise the drives at a very low price, then in very small letters at the end of the ad it says, "controller card optional." SyQuest also has a parallel port model that can be used with laptops, PS/2s, or any computer with a parallel port. These drives are great for backup, for removal and security, and for data transport.

Parallel port hard drives

I discussed these systems in chapter 5. These drives can be plugged into the parallel port of a laptop, a PS/2, or any desktop computer. They come in several capacities from 20Mb to more than 300Mb. They are great for backup or for adding a second hard drive. Because these drives plug into the computer's only parallel port, they usually include a parallel port connector for the printer.

Data compression

I discussed data compression in chapter 8. It can give you all of the benefits of a second hard drive with much less trouble and expense.

Installing a hard drive

Step 1—remove the cover   First, remove the cover. Refer to the procedure outlined in chapter 2.

Step 2—set the switches and jumpers   Check the instructions that came with the drive and set any switches or jumpers that are required. Unless you are installing a second hard drive, you might not have to set any.

Step 3—XT installation   If you are installing the drive in an XT, place the drive in an open bay and mount it on the brackets with screws. If it is a half-height size and you only have one floppy drive, you might want to install it in the lower bay beneath your floppy drive. If you have two floppy drives, or you are installing a full-height drive, then you should install it in the left-hand bay. If you are installing a 3½-inch drive, it is not absolutely necessary, but you might want to mount it in an expansion frame so that it fits in the bay just like a 5¼-inch drive. The threaded holes in the side of the drive should line up with the holes in the bracket. Start all the screws, then tighten them. Be careful because it is easy to strip the threads. There are also screw holes on the bottom of the drive. The bottom of the case has openings for access to these holes. If you have a magnetized screwdriver for this operation, it helps. Unless I will be moving the computer around a lot, I seldom install the screws in the bottom.

All of the access holes in the bottom of the case, and all other holes, should be covered with tape before the computer is used. The fan in the power supply should draw air only through the vents in the front of the computer. It passes this air over the components to cool them. If there are additional openings in the case, it cuts down on the efficiency of the cooling system.

Step 3a—AT, 286, or 386 installation You might have to install slide rails on the drive. There are several holes in the side of the drive. The easiest way to determine which ones to use is to try them. The tapered end of the rail should go toward the rear. Insert the drive in the bay, and check for the proper fit. If you are lucky and have started the screws in the right holes, install the rest of the screws in the rails.

Step 4—installing controller and cables Now that you have the drive installed, you need to check the instructions that came with your controller. Set any switches and jumpers on the controller board as necessary. Plug the board into an empty slot, preferably one near the drive so the cables don't have to be draped over other boards.

Attach the cables to the drive. There are two flat ribbon cables, one with 20 wires, the other with 34 wires. One edge of the cables has a different colored wire indicating pin 1. It is possible to plug the connector in backwards. The drive edge connectors have a slit in the board between pins 2 and 3, and the colored wire goes to this side of the connection (see Fig. 9-8).

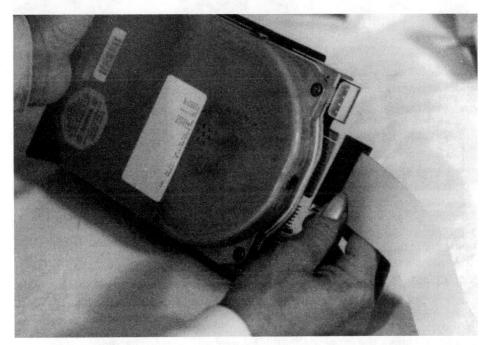

9-8 Connecting the 34-wire cable to the hard drive. Note the slit is between contacts 2 and 3 on the edge connector of the drive. Pin 1 is near that end. The colored wire of the cable indicates pin 1.

If your controller can handle both floppies and a hard drive, you will have one 34-wire ribbon cable from the floppies and one from the hard drive. The controller will have two sets of pins for the attachment of the 34-wire cable connectors. Your controller instructions should tell you which cable goes to which row of pins. Ordinarily, the row of pins in the center is for the hard drive, and the one toward the rear is for the floppies. The connectors can be plugged in backwards, so be sure to check the board for a small number 1 or some indication as to which pin is pin 1. Plug in the connector so that the colored wire is at that end. If the pins are in a horizontal row, pin 1 will usually be oriented toward the front (see Fig. 9-9). If the pins are vertical, then pin 1 is usually toward the top of the board. If you determine the orientation of one connection, all of the others should be the same.

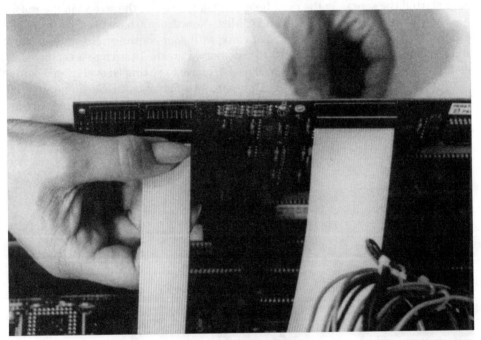

9-9 Connecting the 34-wire and 20-wire ribbon cables to the controller board. Make sure that the colored side of the cable goes to pin 1 on the board.

There are also two sets of 20-wire pins. The row closest to the hard drive 34-wire connector is for hard drive number 1. If you install a second hard drive, the 20-wire cable plugs into the second set of pins—those toward the bottom if oriented horizontally, or toward the front if oriented vertically.

If you are installing an IDE or SCSI drive, you will have a single 50-wire cable. In most drives, the cable can only be plugged in one way. If the IDE interface is built-in on the motherboard, you might have only a set of pins. You have to determine which is pin 1 and orient the cable so that the colored wire goes to that side.

Step 5—install drive power cables The power cable for the drive is a four-wire cable from the power supply. It can only be plugged in one way (see Fig. 9-10).

Step 6—installing a second hard drive You never know when your hard drive might fail, and you should always have it backed up. A hard drive can be backed up to another hard drive in just seconds. The probability that both drives will fail at the same time is quite small.

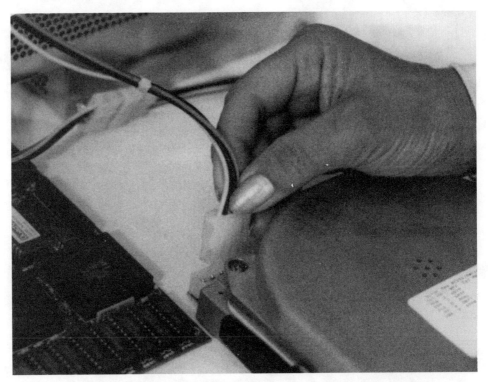

9-10 Connecting the power cable to the hard drive. It can be plugged in only one way.

I mentioned the fact that the need for storage is seldom satisfied. Even if you have a disk with 1Gb of storage, you will soon be trying to store 2Gb of data on it. A second hard drive can help solve this problem. Most controllers can control two hard drives, so it is easy to add a second hard drive. Some controllers allow you to use different types and sizes of drives. Others only control a second drive if it is the same type and size as the first one.

If you can afford it, you should buy two drives of the same type. If you can't afford it at this time, buy a well-known brand. Several drive manufacturers have gone out of business, and if you buy an off-brand drive, you might not be able to get a second one later to match your first one. If you decide to add a second hard drive later, you should get some sort of documentation with your drive that tells you what switches or jumpers to set on the drive. Follow any instructions that come with the drive.

The second drive should have a terminating resistor pack that should be removed. Only drive C should have a terminating resistor pack. Figure 9-11 shows a couple of hard drives with a terminating resistor pack and the configuration pins. There should also be a row of pins with a jumper so that it can be configured as drive number 2. If you have a ribbon cable with no twisted wires at the end connector, this should go to drive number 1, which should have its pins jumpered for disk 1. (NOTE: Some systems call the first drive 0 and the second drive 1.)

9-11   Your drives might be different than these, but most of them have resistor packs and shorting bars that are used to configure the drives. Check the documentation for your disks.

The 34-wire ribbon cable has a connector on each end and one near the center. The cable might have some twisted wires at the end connector and look very much like the cable used for the floppy drives. If the cable has a twist, the number 1 drive and the number 2 drive will both be jumpered as drive 2. Again, you should follow the instructions you receive with your drive.

Formatting hard disks

Formatting organizes the disk so data can be stored and accessed easily and quickly. If data recording was not organized, it would be very difficult to find an item on a large hard disk. I have about 3000 files on my two hard disks. Those files are on tracks and sectors that are numbered. A FAT is set up on the disk to record the location of each file on the disk. The FAT is similar to a table of contents in a book. When a request is sent to the heads to read or write to a file, it goes to the FAT, looks for the location of the file, and goes directly to it. The heads can find any file, or any part of any file, quickly and easily. Incidentally, I often forget what is in each of the 3000 files on my hard disks or where I have stored something. I use Magellan from Lotus to instantly tell me where any of my data is stored. It is great.

Formatting is not something that is done every day, and it can be rather difficult in some cases. Very little literature on the subject is available. Unless you are fairly knowledgeable, try to have your vendor format your hard disk for you. One reason disks do not come from the manufacturer preformatted is that there are so many options and different controller cards. The controller cards are designed so they will operate with several different types of hard drives, and most have dip-switches that must be set to configure your hard drive. Usually some documentation comes with the hard drive controller, but like most manuals and documentation, the instructions are sometimes difficult to understand, especially if you are a beginner.

Low-level format

A floppy disk is formatted in a single procedure, but a hard disk requires two levels of format—a low level and a high level. You should receive some sort of documentation with your hard disk and controller. Most hard disks have their low-level format performed at the factory, especially the SCSI and IDE drives.

The low-level data recorded on a hard disk by a low-level format can deteriorate with time. Several programs are available that can check MFM and RLL drives and reformat them if necessary. Two of these are SpinRite ((714) 362-8800) and Disk Technician ((619) 274-5000). These programs do not work with SCSI, IDE, and some other nonstandard drives.

You should never try to low-level format IDE and SCSI drives unless you have specially designed software for that purpose. One company that provides diagnostic software for IDE drives is Micro2000 ((818) 547-0125). Their Micro-Scope diagnostic software can low-level format IDE drives. It can also perform several other diagnostic tests on hard drives and all floppy drives. It can read, write, and edit data on any track of a floppy or hard disk, as well as check the IRQ assignment of devices in the event of a conflict.

If the hard disk has been low-level formatted, you can type FDISK, to partition your disk. If it does not allow you to FDISK, or if you are using a controller other than an MFM type, then you must do a low-level format. If it has not been formatted, use whatever software or instructions you received with the disk.

Using the debug command

CAUTION! Do not try to low-level format SCSI or IDE drives without special software. Some vendors provide special software with their drives.

With many MFM and RLL controllers, you can use the DEBUG command to invoke a low-level format. Type DEBUG, and when the hyphen (-) comes up, type G=C800:5. It will look like this:

```
A>DEBUG
-G=C800:5
```

This message will be displayed: This is a FORMAT routine. It will DESTROY any existing data on your disk! Press <RET> if you wish to continue or <ESC> to abort.

Bad sector data

If you press Return, you will be asked several questions. One question is if you want to input any bad sector data. It is almost impossible to manufacture a perfect hard disk, and the disks usually come with a list of bad sectors that the manufacturer discovered during testing. If they are very bad, your controller might detect them, but if they are marginal, it might not. When you input the list of bad sectors, DOS marks them so they will not used. More than 100K of space might be in bad sectors, but it will be a small percentage compared to the disk's capacity.

Utility programs for low-level formatting

Some controllers will not let you use the DEBUG command to do a low-level format. Several utility programs can do it for you.

Check-It	(800) 531-0450
Disk Technician	(619) 274-5000
DOSUTILS	(800) 752-1333
Micro 2000	(818) 547-0125
QAPlus	(408) 438-8247
SpinRite	(714) 362-8800

FDISK options

If the low-level format has been done, you can do the high-level format. Boot from your floppy drive with a copy of DOS and type DIR C:. If the message comes up, Invalid drive specification, put a copy of DOS that has the FDISK command on it in drive A.

When you type FDISK, using MS-DOS 5.0, the message MS-DOS Version 5.00 appears.

```
Fixed Disk Setup Program
Copyright Microsoft Corp. 1983, 1991
FDISK Options
Current Fixed Disk Drive: 1
Choose one of the following:
1. Create DOS partition or logical DOS drive
2. Set active partition
3. Delete partition or logical DOS drive
4. Display partition information
5. Change current fixed disk drive
```

Enter choice: [1]
Press ESC to exit FDISK

If you choose 1, and the disk has not been prepared, a screen like this comes up:

Create DOS Partition or Logical DOS Drive
Current Fixed Drive: 1
Choose one of the following:
1. Create primary DOS partition
2. Create extended DOS partition
3. Create logical DOS drive(s) in the extended DOS partition
Enter choice: [1]
Press ESC to return to FDISK Options

If you want to boot from your hard drive (and I can't think of any reason why you would not want to), then you must create a primary DOS partition and make it active.

Partition size

DOS 3.3 and earlier versions could only handle hard disks up to 32Mb. If you bought a 40Mb hard disk, you could only use 32Mb of it unless you used special software such as DiskManager. DOS 4.0 and later versions allow very large partitions, up to 2Gb. I recommend you make your partitions no more than 50Mb. If there are several partitions on a disk and one of them fails, you might be able to recover the data in the other partitions. If your disk is one large partition and it fails, you might not be able to recover any of the data, especially if the FAT is destroyed. Central Point's PC Tools and DOS 5.0 can be set up to make a copy of the FAT. If the primary FAT is destroyed, you can still use the copy.

DOS uses all of the alphabet letters for disk drives. It reserves A and B for floppy drives and C for the boot drive. If you have a very large disk, you can make 23 other logical partitions, or drives D through Z.

High-level format

After the FDISK options are completed, return to drive A and high-level format drive C. Because you want to boot off this drive, you must also transfer the system and hidden files to the disk as it is being formatted so you must use a /S to transfer the files. Type FORMAT C: /S. DOS will display a message that says:

WARNING! ALL DATA ON NON-REMOVABLE DISK DRIVE C: WILL BE LOST!
Proceed with Format (Y/N)

If you press Y the disk light should come on, and you might hear the drive stepping through each track. After a few minutes, it will display:

Format complete
System transferred
Volume label (11 characters, ENTER for none)?

You can give each partition a unique name, or volume label if you wish.

You can test your drive by doing a warm boot—pressing Ctrl-Alt-Del. The computer should reboot. Now that drive C is completed, if you have other partitions or a second disk, format each of them.

Some hard drive basics

A hard drive uses many of the same methods of recording and reading that are used with floppy disks. Here are some basics explaining how a hard drive operates.

Tracks and sectors

A hard disk is similar to the floppy in that it is a spinning disk that has a coating that can be magnetized. Hard disks also have tracks that are similar to floppy disk tracks. A 360K floppy disk has only 40 tpi, while a hard disk might have from 300 tpi to 3000 tpi. Each of the 40 tracks of a 360K floppy are divided into nine sectors per track. Older hard disks have 17 sectors per track, and some newer ones have up to 54 sectors per track.

Speed of rotation and density

Another major difference between floppy and hard disks is the speed of rotation. A floppy disk spins at about 300 rpm. The early hard disks had a rotation speed of 3600 rpm. Some of the newer systems spin at up to 6400 rpm.

As the disk spins beneath the head, a pulse of voltage through the head causes the area of track beneath the head to become magnetized. A hard disk spins much faster than a floppy, so the duration of the magnetizing pulses can be much shorter and at a higher frequency. The recording density depends to a great extent on the changes in magnetic flux. The faster the disk spins, the greater the number of changes. This allows much more data to be recorded in the same amount of space.

Timing

Everything that a computer does depends on precise timing. Crystals and oscillators are set up so certain circuits perform a task at a specific time. These oscillating circuits are usually called clock circuits. The clock frequency for the standard MFM method of reading and writing to a hard disk is 10 MHz. The head sits over a track that is moving at a constant speed. Blocks of data are written or read during the precise timing of the system clock. Because the voltage must be plus or zero, that is two states, in order to write 1s and 0s, the maximum data transfer rate is only 5 megabits per second for MFM, just half of the clock frequency. The RLL systems transfer data at a rate of 7.5 megabits per second, and the SCSI and ESDI systems have transfer rates of 10 to 15 megabits or more.

You have probably seen representations of magnetic lines of force around a magnet. The magnetized spot on a disk track has similar lines of force. To read the data on the disk, the head is positioned over the track and the lines of force from each magnetized area cause a pulse of voltage to be induced in the head. During a precise block of time, an induced pulse of voltage represents a 1, and the absence of an induced pulse represents a 0.

Head spacing

The amount of magnetism placed on a disk when it is recorded is very small. It must be small so that it does not affect other recorded bits or tracks near it. Magnetic lines of force decrease as you move away from a magnet by the square of the distance. Thus, it is desirable that the heads be as close to the disk as possible.

In a floppy drive, the heads actually come in contact with the disk. This causes some wear, but not very much, because the rotation is fairly slow and the plastic disks are coated with a special lubricant. However, the heads of a hard disk system never touch the disk. The fragile heads and the disk would be severely damaged if they made contact at speeds of 3600 to 6000 rpm. The heads fly over the spinning disk, just microinches above it. The air inside the hard drive must be pure because the smallest speck of dust or dirt could cause the head to crash. Most hard drives are sealed at the factory. You should never open one.

Disk platters

The surface of the hard disk platters must be very smooth. Because the heads are only a few millionths of an inch above the surface, any unevenness could cause a head crash. The hard disk platters are usually made from aluminum, which is nonmagnetic, and lapped to a mirror finish. They are then coated or plated with a magnetic material. Some companies are now using tempered glass as a substrate for the platters.

The platters must be very rigid so that the close distance between the head and the platter surface is maintained. If the platter is made smaller, it can be thinner and still have the necessary rigidity. Smaller disks also need less power and smaller motors.

You should avoid any sudden movement of your computer or any jarring while the disk is spinning, because it could cause the head to crash onto the disk and damage it. Most newer hard drive systems automatically move the heads away from the read/write surface to a parking area when the power is turned off.

Clusters

A sector is only 512 bytes, but most files are much longer than that. Many systems lump two or more sectors together and call it a cluster. If an empty cluster is on track 5, the system will record as much of the file as it can there, then move to the next empty cluster, which might be on track 20. The location of each part of the file is recorded in the FAT so the computer will have no trouble finding it.

Fragmentation

If a disk has just been formatted, all parts of a file are recorded contiguously; that is, in sectors near each other. After you use your hard disk for a while, the parts of these files are likely to be located all over the disk or fragmented. This is caused by erasing and modifying files. The computer can find all of the parts of a file, but it might have to do a lot of searching. This can slow the overall speed of the disk.

You could do a complete backup of your hard disk, then high-level reformat it, and then restore all of your files. But that could take a lot of time and trouble. Most utility programs can defragment a hard disk without having to reformat it. A utility program that can be used for defragmentation is Disk Organizer. It is a low-cost shareware program. It is available from most bulletin boards or from the author at (707) 961-1632. For a donation of $30, you receive a manual and future updates.

Another excellent utility program that everyone should have is PC Tools. If you can't find it, call (503) 690-8088 for the nearest distributor. Of course, no one should be without Norton Utilities. This program can be used for defragmentation and has dozens of other essential tools.

Multiple platters

Most hard drives have from 2 to 10 or more disks or platters. All the disks are stacked on a single shaft with just enough spacing between them for the heads. Each disk has a head for the top surface and one for the bottom. If the system has four disks, then it has eight heads. All the heads are controlled by the same positioner, and they all move together. If head number 1 is over track 1, sector 1, then all the other heads are over track 1, sector 1 on each disk surface.

Cylinders

If you could strip away all of the tracks except track number 1, top and bottom, on all of the platters, it would look somewhat like a cylinder. Cylinder refers to each of those tracks with the same number on a stack of platters or on a double-sided disk. A hard drive might have 4 platters with 1024 tracks on each of the 8 sides—8 × 1024 = 8192 tracks—but it still has only 1024 cylinders.

Head actuators or positioners

There are several different types of head positioners or actuators. Some use stepper motors to move the heads in discrete steps to a certain track. Some use a worm gear or screw-type shaft that moves the heads in and out. Others use voice coil technology.

The voice coil of a loudspeaker is made up of a coil of wire, wound on a hollow tube, and attached to the material of the speaker cone. Permanent magnets are then placed inside the coil and around the outside. Whenever a voltage is passed through the coil of wire, it causes magnetic lines of force to be built up around the coil. Depending on the polarity of the input voltage, these lines of magnetic flux are either the same or opposite to the lines of force from the permanent magnets. If the polarity of the voltage, for instance, a plus voltage, causes the lines of force to be the same as the permanent magnet, then they repel each other and the voice coil moves forward. If they are opposite, they attract each other, and the coil moves backwards.

Some of the better and faster hard drives use voice coil technology with a closed loop servo control. The voice coil moves the heads quickly and smoothly to the track area. Feedback information from the closed loop positions the head to the exact track very accurately. These drives use one surface of one of the disks to store data and track locations. Most specification sheets give the number of heads on a drive. If you see one that has an odd number of heads such as 5, 7, or 9, it probably uses the other head for servo information.

Setup routine

When you install a hard drive, your BIOS must be told what kind it is. The BIOS also must know the number and type of floppies you have, the time, the date, and other information. The setup routine asks several questions, then configures the BIOS for that configuration. This part of the BIOS configuration is in low-power CMOS and is on all the time, even when the computer is turned off.

One of the questions that the routine asks is what type of hard drive you have. There were only 15 different types when the AT was introduced in 1984. There are now hundreds. Most new BIOS ROMs list 46 types. If yours is not among the 46 listed, the BIOS allows you to input the parameters of any that are not listed. You should receive some information from your vendor that tells you the number of heads, cylinders, and other specifications of your hard drive.

Booting from a floppy

CAUTION! Never boot with a floppy disk version that is different from the version used to format the hard disk. A short boot record is contained on the hard disk, and if a different version is used to boot up, you might lose all of the data on your disk.

Sources

Local computer stores and computer swap meets are a good place to find hard drives. You can at least look them over and get some idea of the prices and what you want. Mail order is a very good way to buy a hard drive. The many computer magazines contain hundreds of ads. Check the list of magazines in chapter 17.

10
Backup

IF YOU BUY A SOFTWARE PROGRAM THE VERY FIRST THING YOU SHOULD DO IS write-protect the floppies. It is very easy to become distracted and write over an expensive program disk in error and ruin the program. The vendor might give you a new copy, but it will probably entail weeks of waiting and much paperwork.

If you are using 5¼-inch floppies, you should cover the square write-protect hole with a piece of opaque tape. Don't use clear tape. The drive focuses a light through the square hole. If the light detector senses a light, it allows the disk to be written on, read, or erased. If the hole is covered with opaque tape, the disk can be read, but it cannot be written on or erased. Some vendors distribute their programs on disks without the square hole.

If you are using 3½-inch disks, you should move the small slide on the left rear so that the square hole is open. The 3½-inch write-protect system is the opposite of the 5¼-inch system. The 3½-inch system uses a microswitch. If the square hole is open, the switch allows the disk to be read, but not written on or erased. If the slide covers the hole, the disk can be written on, read, or erased. It takes less than a minute to write-protect a disk, and it will save you lots of frustration and weeks of valuable time.

After you make sure the disks are write-protected, the second thing you should do is to use DISKCOPY to make exact copies of your original disks. The originals should then be stored away. Only the copies should be used. If you damage the copy, you can always make another copy from the original. A simple, easy way to protect your original program disks from dirt and dust is to seal them in plastic sandwich bags.

Unerase software

Anyone who works with computers for any length of time is bound to make a few errors. One of the best protections against errors is to have a backup. The second best protection is to have a good utility program such as Norton Utilities or PC Tools.

These programs can unerase a file or even unformat a disk. When a file is erased, DOS goes to the FAT and deletes the first letter of each file name. All of the data remains on the disk unless a new file is written over it. If you erase a file in error, or format a disk in error, do not do anything to it until you have tried using a recover utility. Don't use the DOS Recover utility except as a last resort. Use Norton Utilities ((213) 319-2000), Mace Utilities ((504) 291-7221), PC Tools ((503) 690-8090), DOS-UTILS ((612) 937-1107), or any of several other recovery utilities. These utilities let you restore your files by replacing the missing first letter of the file name.

The early versions of DOS made it very easy to format your hard disk in error. If you were on your hard disk and typed FORMAT, it would immediately begin to format your hard disk and wipe out everything. Later versions do not format unless you specify a drive letter. These versions also allow you to include a volume label, or name, on the drive when you format by including /v. Or you can add a label name later by using the LABEL command. If the drive has a volume label, it cannot be formatted unless the drive letter and correct volume name are specified. You can display, delete, assign,or change the name of a volume by typing LABEL. The label name is also displayed when CHKDSK is run.

Many people have erased files in error, and they will probably do it again. Some of them will not have backups and unerase software. In a fraction of a second, you can wipe out data that might be worth thousands of dollars, or might have taken hundreds of hours to accumulate, or might be impossible to duplicate. Yet many people do not back up their precious data. Most of these people are those who have not had a major catastrophe. Just as sure as there are earthquakes in California, if you use a computer long enough, you can look forward to at least one disaster. There are thousands of ways to make mistakes, and there is no way to prevent them. But if your data is backed up, it doesn't have to be a disaster. It is a lot better to be backed up than sorry.

Jumbled FAT

The FAT keeps a record of the location of all the files on a disk. Parts of a file can be located in several sectors, but the FAT knows exactly where they are. If for some reason track 0,— where the FAT is located,— is damaged, erased, or becomes defective, you will be unable to read or write to any of the files on the disk.

Because the FAT is so important, programs such as PC Tools and Mace Utilities make a copy of the FAT and store it in another location on the disk. Every time you add a file or edit one, the FAT changes, and these programs make a new copy each time the FAT is altered. If the original FAT is damaged, you can still get your data by using the alternate FAT.

Head crash

The heads of a hard disk "fly" over the disk just a few microinches from the surface. They have to be close in order to detect the small magnetic changes in the tracks. The disk spins at 3600 to 6400 rpms, and if the heads contact the surface, they can scratch it and ruin the disk. A sudden jar or bump to the computer while the hard disk is spinning can cause the heads to crash. You should never move or bump your computer while the hard disk is running. Mechanical failures and other factors can also cause a crash. You should never move or bump your computer while the hard disk is running.

Most of the newer disks have a built-in park utility. When the power is removed, the head is automatically moved to the center of the disk where there are no tracks. Many older disks do not have this utility. It is also possible for the heads to crash if the power is suddenly removed, such as in a power failure. The technology of hard disk systems has improved tremendously over the last couple of years. They are still mechanical devices, however, and as such, you can be sure that eventually they will wear out, fail, or crash.

Mean time before failure

Most hard disks are now relatively bug-free. Manufacturers quote MTBF figures of 40,000 to 150,000 hours. These figures are only an average. There is no guarantee that a disk won't fail in the next few minutes. A hard disk is made up of mechanical parts, and if it is used long enough, it will wear out or fail. Despite the MTBF claims, hard disks do fail, and there are many businesses that do nothing but repair hard disks that have crashed or failed.

Crash recovery

A failure can be frustrating and time-consuming, and make you feel utterly helpless. In the unhappy event of a crash, depending on its severity, it is possible that some of your data can be recovered, one way or another. There are companies that specialize in recovering data and rebuilding hard disks. Many of them have sophisticated tools and software that can recover some data if the disk is not completely ruined. If it is possible to recover any of the data, Ontrack Computer Systems ((612) 937-1107), among others, can probably do it. Look in the computer magazines for ads. A couple of companies that I have used to recover data include California Disk Drive Repair ((408) 727-2475) and Rotating Memory Service ((916) 939-7500). The cost for recovery services can be rather expensive, but if you have data that is critical, it is well worth it. However, it is a lot cheaper to have a backup.

Small logical drives are better

Early versions of DOS would not recognize a hard disk larger than 32Mb. DOS now allows you to have a drive C or D of 512Mb or more. Don't do it. If this large hard disk crashes, you might not be able to recover any of its data. If the same disk is divided into several smaller logical drives, and one of the logical sections fails, it might be possible to recover data in the unaffected logical drives.

Some reasons why people don't back up

Don't have the time This is not a good excuse. If your data is worth anything at all, it is worth backing up. It takes only a few minutes to back up a large hard disk with some of the newer software.

Too much trouble   It is a bit of trouble unless you have an expensive auto-mated tape backup system. Backup can require a bit of disk swapping, labeling, and storing. But with a little organizing, it can be done easily. If you keep all of the disks together, you don't have to label each one. Just stack them in order, put a rubber band around them and label the first one of the lot. Yes, it is a bit of trouble to make backups, but if you don't have a backup, consider the trouble it would be to redo all your files. The trouble that it takes to make a backup is infinitesimal.

Don't have the necessary disks, software, or tools   Depending on the amount of data to be backed up and the software used, you might need quite a few disks. Of course, it requires a lot fewer disks if high-density disks are used. Again, it takes only a few minutes and a few disks to make a backup of only the data that has been changed. In most cases, the same disks can be reused to back up your files each day. Several discount mail-order houses sell 360K disks for as little as 19 cents each, 39 cents each for 1.2Mb and 720K disks, and 59 cents each for 1.44Mb disks. Look through the computer magazines for ads.

Failures and disasters only happen to other people   People who believe this are those people who have never experienced a disaster. There is nothing anyone can say to convince them. They just have to learn the hard way.

A few other reasons why you should back up

General failure   Outside of ordinary care, there is little you can do to prevent a general failure. A failure can be caused by a component on the hard drive elec-tronics or in the controller system, or any one of a thousand other things. Even things such as a power failure during a read/write operation can cause data corrup-tion.

Theft and burglary   Computers are easy to sell so they are a favorite target for burglars. It is bad enough to lose a computer, but many computers have hard disks filled with data that is even more valuable than the computer. It is a good idea to put your name and address on several of the files on your hard disk. It is also a good idea to scratch identifying marks on the back and bottom of your computer's case. You should also write down the serial numbers of your monitor and drives. Another good idea is to store your backup files in an area away from your computer. This way, there is less chance of losing both your computer and your backups in a burglary or fire. You can always buy another computer, but if you have a large database of cus-tomer orders, files, and history, how can you replace that?

Archival   Another reason to back up is for archival purposes. No matter how large the hard disk is, it will eventually fill up with data. Quite often, there are files that are no longer used or used only once in a great while. I keep copies of all the let-ters I write on disk. I have hundreds of them. Rather than erase them, I put them on a disk and store them away.

Fragmentation   After a hard disk is used for a while, files begin to fragment. Data is recorded on concentric tracks in separate sectors. If part of a file is erased or changed, some of the data might be in a sector on track 20 and another part on track

40. There might be open sectors on several tracks because portions of data have been erased. Hunting all over the disk slows the disk down. If the disk is backed up completely and then erased, the files can be restored so that they are again recorded in contiguous sectors. The utility programs mentioned earlier can unfragment a hard disk by copying portions of the disk to memory and rearranging the data in contiguous files.

Data transfer Often it is necessary to transfer a large amount of data from one hard disk to another. It is quite easy and fast to use a good backup program to accomplish this. It is easy to make several copies that can be distributed to others. This method can be used to distribute data, company policies and procedures, sales figures, and other information to several people in a large office or company. The data can also be shipped or mailed to branch offices, customers, or to others almost anywhere.

Methods of backup
Software

There are two main types of backup—the image backup and file oriented backup. An *image backup* is an exact bit-for-bit copy of the hard disk copied as a continuous stream of data. This type of backup is rather inflexible and does not allow for a separate file backup or restoration. The *file oriented* backup identifies and indexes each file separately, thus separate files or directories can be backed up and restored. It can be very time consuming to have to back up an entire 40Mb or more each day. With a file oriented system, once a full back up is made, you only have to make incremental backups of those files that are changed or altered.

DOS stores an archive attribute in each file directory entry. When a file is created, DOS turns the archive attribute flag on. If the file is backed up using DOS BACKUP or any of the commercial backup programs, the archive attribute flag is turned off. If this file is later altered or changed, DOS turns the attribute flag back on. At the next backup, you have the program search the files and look for the attribute flag. You then back up only those files that have been altered or changed since the last backup. You can view or modify a file's archive attribute by using the ATTRIBUTE command.

Once the first backup is made, all subsequent backups need only be made of any data that has been changed or updated. Most backup programs recognize whether a file has been changed since the last backup. Most of them can also look at the date stamped on each file and back up only those within a specified date range.

DOS backup.com

One of the least expensive methods of backup is to use the backup.com and restore.com that comes with MS-DOS. There is a price to pay in that it is slow, time-consuming, and rather difficult to use, but it will do the job if nothing else is available.

DR DOS is an operating system from Digital Research, which is now part of Novell. DR DOS 6.0 is a direct replacement for MS-DOS. The backup.com included with DR DOS 6.0 and MS-DOS 6.0 use data compression and are better than many of the commercial backup programs, and they're free with DOS software.

Commercial backup software

Here are just a few commercial backup programs. There are many others.

Norton Backup   Norton Backup ((213) 319-2000) is one of the newest and fastest backup programs on the market. It is also one of the easiest to use. It compresses data so that fewer disks are needed.

Norton Desktop for Windows   This software package has several very useful utilities including emergency unerase, manual or automatic backup, and utilities for creating batch files and managing directories and files under Windows.

Fastback   Fastback ((504) 291-7221) was the first backup software program that was fast. They are now past version 3.0. It is easy to learn and use, and compresses data so that fewer floppy disks are needed.

Back-It 4   Back-It is from Gazelle Systems ((800) 233-0383). Back-It has recently been revised to version 4.0. This new version uses very high-density data compression, as much as 3 to 1. It is also very fast and uses a sophisticated error correction routine. Unlike some of the other systems, Back-It 4 allows you to use different format floppies at the same time.

PC Tools   PC Tools comes bundled with a very good backup program. The backup program is now sold separately to anyone who doesn't want to buy the whole bundle.

XTree   XTree is an excellent shell program for disk and file management. It has several functions that make computing much easier. You can use it to copy files from one directory or disk to another. I often use it to make backups when I only have a few files to back up.

Q-DOS III   Q-DOS III, from Gazelle Systems ((801) 377-1288), is another excellent shell program that is similar to XTree. It can be used to select and copy files to another hard disk or to floppies.

DOS XCOPY   The XCOPY command is a part of MS-DOS versions higher than 3.2. Several switches can be used with XCOPY (a switch is a /). For instance, XCOPY C:*.* A:/A copies only those files that have their archive attribute set to on. It does not reset the attribute flag. XCOPY C:*.* A:/M copies the files, then resets the flag. Whenever a disk on drive A is full, you merely have to insert a new floppy, and hit F3 to repeat the last command. It will continue to copy all files that have not been backed up. XCOPY C:*.* A:/D:03-15-92 copies only those files created after 15 March 1992. Several other very useful switches can be used with XCOPY. There are many very good backup software packages available. Check through the computer magazines for ads and reviews.

Tape

Several tape backup systems are on the market. Tape backup is one of the easiest ways to make sure your data is safe. The cost of tape drives has come way down, and they are now relatively inexpensive, starting at about $200. The tape cartridges cost from $5 to $15.

Most tape drives require the use of a controller similar to a disk controller, so they will use one of your precious slots. On the positive side, some companies have developed tape drives that can operate off the floppy controller. They call them floppy tapes. The tape drives also require one of your disk mounting bays, unless it is an external model.

One of the big problems with software backup is that you have to sit there and put in a new disk whenever one gets full. One big plus for tape is that it can be set up so it is done automatically. You don't have to worry about forgetting to backup or wasting time doing it.

Tape drives are very easy to install. You should get some documentation with any unit you purchase. Set any switches or jumpers for configuration, then follow the instructions in chapter 8 for installing a floppy drive.

Parallel port tape systems A few companies are manufacturing tape backup systems that are plugged in the parallel port of your computer. The same drive can be used on several computers. One such drive is Backpack from MicroSolutions ((815) 756-3411). Sigen ((408) 737-3910) also has parallel port tape drives. Figure 10-1 shows a parallel port tape backup system from ADPI ((513) 339-2241). ADPI calls it the "One For All" because it can be used on any ISA, EISA, or PS/2 system. Check the ads in the computer magazines for other vendors.

Digital audio tape Several companies offer digital audio tape (DAT) systems for backing up large hard disk systems. DAT systems offer storage capacities as high as 1.3Gb on a very small cartridge. DAT systems use a helical scan recording that is similar to that used for video recording. DAT tapes are 4 mm wide (0.156 inches). DAT cartridges are much smaller than quarter-inch tape cartridges, yet they can store about twice as much data.

Very high-density drives

Several companies are now making high-density 2.8Mb floppies and very high-density 20Mb floppies. Insite Peripherals and Brier Technology have developed 3½-inch floppies that can store 20Mb. A Bernoulli drive can put 90Mb on a 5¼-inch floppy disk.

Even though they cost a bit more, a high-density floppy drive is better than a tape. Tape drives are only used for backup, but a high-density floppy has much more utility, possibly even obviating the need for a hard disk.

Data compression

I discussed data compression in chapter 7. It can be used with any floppy or hard disk to double the storage capacity. For more details on drives and data compression please refer to chapter 7.

Second hard drive

The easiest and fastest of all methods of backup is to have a second hard drive. It is very easy to install a second hard drive. It doesn't have to be a large one; a 30Mb or 40Mb will do fine. With a second hard drive as a backup, you don't need backup software. A good backup software might cost $200 or more. You can buy a 40Mb MFM hard drive for about $100.

The average hard drive has an access speed of about 28 ms. Floppy disks operate at about 300 ms, which can seem like an eternity when compared to the speed of even the slowest hard drive. Depending on the number of files, how fragmented the data is, and the access speed, a second hard drive can back up 20Mb in a matter of seconds. To back up 20Mb using even the fastest software requires 15 to 20 minutes

10-1   A parallel port tape backup system. Analog and Digital Peripherals, Inc.

and a lot of disk swapping. Depending on the type of disks you use for backup, and the type of software, you might need 15 to 20 disks to back up 20Mb. Some backup software makes extensive use of data compression, so fewer disks are needed.

Another problem with using backup software is that it is often difficult to find a particular file. Most backup software stores the data in a system that is not the same as DOS files. Usually there is no directory like that provided by DOS. Even the DOS BACKUP files show only a control number when you check the directory.

External plug-in hard drives

Several companies are now manufacturing small 20Mb to 80Mb hard drives that operate off the parallel or serial connector. Many of them are battery-powered so they can be used with laptops. They can also be used to back up data from a large desktop system or to transfer data from one system to another. Pacific Rim Systems ((415) 782-1013) has a 20Mb and 40MB system. MicroSolutions ((815) 756-3411) and Micro Sense ((800)-544-4252) also have parallel port hard drives.

Hard cards

You can buy a hard drive on a card for $300 to $600, depending on the capacity and the manufacturer. It might be worthwhile to install a card in an empty slot and dedicate it to backup. If you have no empty slots, you might consider plugging in the card once a week or so to make a backup, then remove the card until it is needed again. This entails removing the cover from the machine each time, but I remove the cover from my computer so often I only use one screw on it to provide grounding. I can remove and replace my cover in a very short time.

Backup, backup, backup

No matter what type of system or method is used, if your data is worth anything at all, you should be using something to back it up. You might be one of the lucky ones and never need it, but it is much better to be backed up than to be sorry.

11
Monitors

ONE OF THE BEST UPGRADES YOU CAN MAKE TO YOUR COMPUTER IS A GOOD monitor. The monitor is your primary link with your computer. The time you spend at your computer is spent staring at the monitor. It is a critical part of your system, and it represents a large percentage of the cost of a system.

Color and cost

I like color. Even if I do nothing but word processing, I like to have a good color monitor. But color costs. Several improvements have been made in the electronics that go into a monitor, such as new chip sets and VLSI. These improvements have helped to reduce the cost of manufacturing somewhat. But not much has been done to reduce the cost of the major monitor component, the cathode-ray tube (CRT). Manufacturing a CRT requires a lot of tedious and labor-intensive effort. We are very fortunate in that there are many manufacturers who make many different types, sizes, and kinds of monitors.

Available options

Because there are so many types of monitors and so many options, you will have some difficult decisions to make when choosing a new monitor. You have a very wide choice as to price, resolution, color, size, and shape. You can buy a 12-inch monochrome monitor for as little as $65. A CGA monitor costs $75 to $100, while an EGA monitor costs $100 to $150. The VGA and Super VGA monitors cost from $200 to $5000, depending on such things as size, resolution, scan rate, bandwidth, brand, and adapter. You shouldn't even consider a monochrome or obsolete CGA or EGA monitor unless you absolutely can't afford anything else.

Monitor basics

If you know a bit about monitor basics, you can make a more-informed decision as to which monitor to buy. In IBM language, a monitor is a display device, which is probably a better term, because the word *monitor* is from the Latin meaning "to warn." But despite IBM, most people still call it a monitor.

Basically a monitor is similar to a television set. The face of a TV set or monitor is the end of a CRT. These are vacuum tubes, and they have many of the same elements of the old vacuum tubes that were used before the advent of the semiconductor age.

Electron beams

The CRT has a filament that is heated, causing it to boil off a stream of electrons. These electrons have a potential of about 25,000 volts. They are "shot" from an electron gun toward the front of the CRT where they slam into the phosphor on the back of the screen. As the electrons hit the small dots of phosphor, they cause the dots to light up.

The thin electron beam moves rapidly across the screen, from top left to right, lighting up the dots of phosphor. The phosphor continues to glow for awhile, and we see the traces that are created. When the beam gets to the right edge of the screen, it drops down one line, turns off, moves quickly back to the left side, turns on again, and begins to write another line across the screen.

Persistence of vision   When you watch a movie, you are seeing a series of still photos, flashed one after the other onto a screen. Due to your persistence of vision, it appears to be continuous motion. It is this same persistence of vision that allows you to see motion and images on your television and video screens.

Controlling the beam   In a magnetic field, a beam of electrons reacts very much like iron. Like iron, a beam of electrons can be attracted or repelled by the polarity of a magnet. Electromagnets are made by winding a coil of wire around a piece of iron. When voltage is passed through the coil of wire, it creates a magnetic field. The polarity of the magnetic field depends on the polarity of the voltage. The strength of the field depends on several factors, such as the number of windings, the type of iron core, and the force and intensity of the voltage.

In a CRT, the beam of electrons must pass between a system of electromagnets before it reaches the screen of the CRT. In a basic system there is an electromagnet on the left, one on the right, one at the top, and one at the bottom. Voltage through these electromagnets is varied, causing the magnetic force to increase or decrease. The beam of electrons can be repulsed by one side and attracted by the other, or pulled to the top or forced to the bottom. With this electromagnetic system, a beam of electrons can be bent and directed to any spot on the screen. It is much like holding a hose and directing a high-pressure stream of water to an area.

Scan rates

When you look at the screen of a TV set or monitor, you see a full screen only because of your persistence of vision and the type of phosphor used on the back of the screen. Actually, the beam of electrons starts at the top left corner of the screen, and under the influence of the electromagnets, it is pulled across to the top right corner.

It lights up the pixels as it sweeps across. It is then returned to the left side, dropped down one line, and swept across again.

Fields and frames   A TV is set up so that 262.5 lines are written from the top to the bottom of the screen in $\frac{1}{60}$ of a second. This is one field. The beam is returned to the top left and a second field of 262.5 lines is written across the screen and interlaced with the first field. The two interlaced fields make one frame, or the equivalent of a still photo. Thus, 525 lines are written on the screen in about $\frac{1}{30}$ of a second, so 30 frames are written to the screen in 1 second.

Vertical scan rate   The time it takes to fill a screen with lines from top to bottom is the vertical scan rate. It is $\frac{1}{30}$ of a second for a TV set, but some of the newer multiscan or multifrequency monitors have variable vertical scan rates from $\frac{1}{40}$ to $\frac{1}{100}$ of a second. Of course, the higher the vertical scan rate, the more fields are written, and the greater the resolution.

Horizontal scan rate   The horizontal scan rate is the speed of the beam from side to side. The horizontal scan rate of a standard TV set is 15.75 kHz. (Note that 15,750 divided by 525 lines = 30.) This is also the frequency used by CGA systems. If you look closely at a TV screen or an old CGA monitor, you will see a lot of space between the lines. The EGA systems have horizontal scan rates of about 22 kHz, while VGA systems have rates of 31.5 kHz or more. The multiscan monitors vary from 15.5 kHz to 100 kHz. Higher resolutions require higher frequencies.

Pixels

Resolution is also determined by the number of picture elements (pixels) that can be displayed. The following figures relate primarily to text, but graphics resolution is similar to text. A standard CGA monitor can display 640×200 pixels. It can display 80 characters in one line with 25 lines from top to bottom. If you divide 640 by 80 you find that one character is 8 pixels wide. There can be 25 lines of characters, so $200/25 = 8$ pixels high. The entire screen can have $640 \times 20 = 128{,}000$ pixels.

Most monitor adapters have text character generators built onto the board. When you send an A to the screen, the adapter goes to its library and sends the signal for the performed A to the screen. Each character occupies a cell made up of the number of pixels depending on the resolution of the screen and the adapter. In the case of a CGA monitor, if all the dots within a cell were lit up, there would be a solid block of dots eight pixels wide and eight pixels high. When the A is placed in a cell, only the dots necessary to form an outline of the A are lit. It is very similar to the dots formed by a dot matrix printer when it prints a character.

A graphics adapter, along with the proper software, allows you to place lines, images, photos, normal and various text fonts, and almost anything you can imagine on the screen. An EGA monitor can display 640×350 pixels, or $640/80 = 8$ pixels wide and $350/25 = 14$ pixels high. The screen can display $640 \times 350 = 224{,}000$ total pixels. Enhanced EGA and VGA monitors can display $640 \times 480 = 307{,}200$ total pixels, with a character being 8 pixels wide and 19 pixels high.

The Video Electronics Standards Association (VESA) has chosen 800×600 as the Super VGA standard, which is $800/80 = 10$ pixels wide and $600/25 = 24$ pixels high. IBM suggested that 1024×768 be the XGA standard.

Many newer systems are now capable of 1024×768, 1280×1024, 1664×1200, and more. With a resolution of 1664×1200, you have 1,996,800 pixels that can be lit up. We have come a long way from the 128,000 pixels possible with CGA.

Monochrome versus color

A monochrome monitor has a single electron gun and a single color phosphor. It writes directly on the phosphor and can provide very high resolution for text and graphics. It is even possible to get monochrome analog VGA, which can display in as many as 64 different shades. Large monochrome monitors are ideal for some desktop publishing (DTP) systems and even some CAD systems. However, these large monochrome monitors are almost as expensive as the equivalent size color monitor.

Color TVs and monitors are much more complicated than monochrome systems. During the manufacture of a color monitor, three different phosphors—red, green, and blue—are deposited on the back of the screen. Usually a very small dot of each color is placed in a triangular shape. There are three electron guns, one for each color. By lighting up the three different colored phosphors selectively, all the colors of the rainbow can be generated.

The guns are called red, green, and blue (RGB), but the electrons they emit are all the same. They are called RGB because each gun is aimed so that it hits a red, a green, or blue dot on the back of the monitor screen. These guns are very accurately aimed so that they converge or impinge only on their assigned color.

Dot pitch The distance between a dot of one color to the next dot of the same color is called the dot pitch. The dots per inch determine the resolution. A high-resolution monitor might have a dot pitch of 0.31 mm. (1 mm = 0.0394 inches, 0.31 mm = 0.0122 inches or about the thickness of an average business card). A typical medium-resolution monitor has a dot pitch of 0.31 mm. One with very high resolution has a dot pitch of 0.26 mm or less. The smaller the dot pitch, the more precise the monitor is and the more difficult they are to manufacture. Some of the Sony monitors use stripes instead of dots. Their specifications indicate stripe pitch, which is about the same as the better dot pitch specs, or 0.25 mm to 0.31 mm. Some low-cost monitors have a dot pitch of 0.42 mm to 0.52 mm. The 0.52-mm monitors might be suitable for playing some games, but it would be difficult to do any productive computing on such a system.

Interlaced versus noninterlaced

Higher resolutions demand higher horizontal frequencies and more precise and higher-quality electronics, which, of course, require a higher cost to manufacture. As pointed out earlier, a TV set writes 262.5 lines from top to bottom, then moves back to the top and interlaces another 262.5 lines between the first lines. This interlacing works fairly well for TV sets and is relatively inexpensive.

IBM decided that interlacing might help them avoid the higher costs of high horizontal frequencies, so they designed some of their VGA systems with an interlaced horizontal system similar to a TV system. Instead of increasing the horizontal frequency, these systems paint every other line across the screen from top to bottom, then return to the top and paint the lines that were skipped.

Theoretically, it sounds like a great idea, but practically, it doesn't work too well because it causes a very annoying flicker. This flicker can be very irritating for some people who have to work with this type of monitor for very long. The flicker is not readily apparent, but some people have complained of eyestrain, headaches, and fatigue after prolonged use of an interlaced monitor. If the monitor is used for short periods of time, by different people, then the interlaced type is probably okay.

Some companies make monitors that use interlacing in some modes and noninterlacing in other modes. Most companies don't advertise the fact that their monitors use interlacing. The interlaced models are usually a bit lower in price than the noninterlaced types. If you get a chance, compare the interlaced and noninterlaced types. You might not be able to tell the difference.

Multiscan

Some software programs call for a wide range of vertical and horizontal frequencies. Most multiscan monitors can satisfy these requirements. This makes multiscan monitors quite versatile and flexible. Most of the early multiscan monitors could accept both digital and analog signals. If you had an older EGA or even a CGA card, multiscan monitors could work with them. Many of the new monitors accept only VGA analog signals.

The VGA introduced by IBM on their PS/2 systems in 1987 was not a multiscan monitor. It operated at a fixed frequency. A multiscan design costs more to build, and many low-cost VGAs are designed to operate at a single, fixed frequency. They are not as versatile or flexible as multiscan.

Many companies are manufacturing monitors with multifixed frequencies. These monitors have two or more fixed frequencies. Again, they are not as flexible as the true multiscan monitors, but they do cost less. I am using a 19-inch Sampo TriSync, which has three different frequencies. I paid $1000 for it, and for my purposes, it does everything I need. Multiscan monitors sell for as little as $300 to as much as $4000 for some of the large 19- to 30-inch sizes.

Landscape versus portrait

Most monitors are wider than they are tall. These are called landscape styles. Others are taller than they are wide. These are called portrait styles. Portrait monitors are used for desktop publishing and other special applications.

Screen size

The stated screen size is very misleading and almost fraudulent. The size is supposed to be a diagonal measurement. There is a border on all four sides of the screen. The usable viewing area on a 14-inch monitor is about 9.75 inches wide and about 7.75 inches high. One reason is because the screen is markedly curved near the edges on all sides. This curve causes distortion, so the areas are masked off and not used.

Adapter basics

Just as a hard disk must have a controller, a monitor must have an adapter that plugs into the motherboard. The PS/1 and PS/2 systems and many of the ISA systems have a monitor adapter built-in on the motherboard. The adapter that you buy should match your monitor. Use an interlaced adapter with an interlaced monitor. An adapter that can send only interlaced signals probably will not work with a noninterlaced monitor. Some high-end adapters are able to adjust and operate both interlaced and noninterlaced monitors.

It won't do you much good to buy a high-resolution monitor unless you buy a good adapter to drive it. Like the hard disk manufacturers, many of the monitor manufacturers do not make adapter boards. Just as a hard disk can operate with several different types of controllers, most monitors can operate with several different types of adapters.

The original IBM PC came with a green monochrome monitor and a monochrome display adapter (MDA) that could display text only. The Hercules Company saw the folly of this limitation and developed the Hercules monographic adapter (HMGA), setting a new standard. It wasn't long before IBM and a lot of other companies were selling similar MGA cards that could display both graphics and text. These adapters provide a high resolution of 720×350 on monochrome monitors.

IBM then introduced their color monitor and color graphics adapter (CGA). It provides only 640×200 resolution. The CGA system is a digital system that allows a mix of red, green, and blue. The cables have four lines, one each for red, green, and blue, and one for intensity. This allows two different intensities for each color, on for bright and off for dim. So there are four objects, each of which can be in either of two states, or two to the fourth power (2^4); therefore CGA has a limit of 16 colors. The CGA monitors have very large spaces between the pixels, and their resolution and color are terrible.

An enhanced graphics adapter (EGA) can drive a high-resolution monitor to display 640×350 resolution. The EGA system has six lines and allows each of the primary colors to be mixed together in any of four different intensities, so there are 2^6 or 64 different colors that they can display.

Analog versus digital

Up until the introduction of the PS/2 with VGA, most displays used the digital system. But digital systems have severe limitations. Digital signals are of two states, either fully on or fully off. The signals for color and intensity require separate lines in the cables. It takes six lines for an EGA monitor to display 16 colors out of a palette of 64. Digital systems are obsolete.

The analog signals that drive the color guns are voltages that are continuously variable. It takes only a few lines for the three primary colors. The intensity voltage for each color can then be varied almost infinitely to create as many as 256 colors out of a possible 262,144. To display more than 256 colors requires a true-color adapter.

Very high-resolution graphics adapters

Most of the adapters sold today are 16-bit boards. A few eight-bit boards can still be found for a very reasonable price, but they are a bit slow, especially if you are doing any kind of graphics or if you are using a GUI program such as Windows. If you have more time than money, they might be all you need. Another problem is finding an eight-bit VGA board. They are practically obsolete, so not many vendors carry them. Even the 16-bit VGA and Super VGA boards are slow when running GUIs. Several companies have developed video accelerator boards. Another solution is to use a motherboard with a local bus option and special local bus adapters. These items are discussed later in this chapter.

Many of the high-resolution adapters have up to 1Mb or more of video RAM (VRAM) on board. VRAM chips are slightly different than DRAM chips. They have two ports and can be accessed by one port while being written to on the other. VRAM chips look very much like older DIP DRAM chips, but they are not interchangeable with DRAM. VRAM chips are rather inexpensive and are easy to install. Check your adapter board and add more memory if necessary. Figure 11-1 shows a VGA card with 1Mb of memory and empty sockets for another 1Mb.

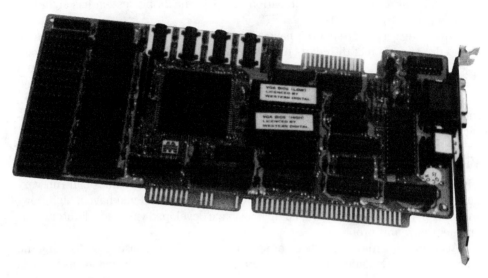

11-1   A 16-bit VGA card.

A single complex graphic might require 1Mb or more of memory. By having the memory on the adapter board, it saves having to go through the bus to the conventional RAM. Some adapter boards even have a separate plug-in daughterboard. Many of them have their own coprocessor on board, such as the Texas Instruments 34010 or the Hitachi HD63483.

True color

Most of the standard low-cost VGA cards are capable of only 16 colors. True color or pure color require video boards with lots of fast memory, a coprocessor, and complex electronics. *True color* means that the video board can drive a monitor to display a large number of shades in separate, distinct hues or pure colors (see Table 11-1). True color also means that the board is expensive. A good adapter for true color might cost more than the monitor. Here is a brief table:

Table 11-1. Pure color

Bits	Shades	Depth
4	16	
8	256	
15	32,768	5:5:5
16	65,536	5:6:5: or 6:6:4
24	16.7 million	8:8:8

Depth   True color usually refers to displays with 15-, 16-, or 24-bit depths. *Depth* means that each of the individual red, green, or blue (RGB) color pixels has a large amount of information about each color. The 15-bit system has five bits of information for each of the three colors. The 16-bit system has six for red, six for green, and four for blue, or a combination of 5:6:5. The 24-bit system has eight bits for each color (see Table 11-1).

Dithering   If a board doesn't have enough power to display true distinct colors, it uses dithering to mix the colors to give an approximation. Dithering takes advantage of the eye's tendency to blur colors and view them as an average. A printed black-and-white photo uses all black dots. But several shades of gray can be printed depending on the number of black dots per inch. A mixture of red dots with white ones can create a pink image. Gradual color transitions can be accomplished by using dithering to intersperse pixels of various colors.

Video accelerator adapters

Windows and other GUI programs that depend on intensive graphics can run very slowly. You might have to sit and twiddle your thumbs even if you have a high-powered 386 or 486 machine. Several companies have developed video accelerator cards that help solve this problem.

Accelerator cards add a processor specifically for the purpose of performing the type of graphic calculations that GUI programs require. The performance increase is somewhat comparable to that achieved by adding a math coprocessor to your system. Accelerator cards can be used in any AT-type system.

Here is a list of a few companies that manufacture accelerator cards. Call them for their product specs and prices.

Actix Systems	(800) 927-5557
ATI Technologies	(416) 756-0718
CSS Laboratories	(800) 966-2771
Dell Computer	(800) 624-9897
Diamond Computer	(408) 736-2000
Matrox Electronics	(800) 361-4903
Number Nine Computer	(800) 438-6463
Orchid Technologies	(800) 767-2443
STB Graphics	(800) 234-4334
Truevision Inc.	(800) 344-8783
Weitek Corp.	(800) 800-0811
Western Digital Paradise	(800) 832-4778

Some software companies have developed software that can speed up GUIs considerably. The software usually costs much less than an accelerator card.

Local bus adapters

The bus between the CPU and system RAM usually operates at the CPU frequency, but the I/O bus speed is only 8 MHz to 10 MHz. This is so for the lowly 286 as well as the fastest 486. The 32-bit 386 and 486 CPUs communicate with their RAM over a special 32-bit bus. But for I/O communications, all AT-type ISA systems have a bus that is only 16 bits wide.

When a video signal has to travel over the eight-bit bus of an XT for some high-end graphics and CAD programs, it can be painfully slow. Even with a 16-bit bus, it can be very slow for some applications. Because of this, some companies developed a 32-bit system called a local bus. They created the local bus by adding an extra connector in front of one of the 16-bit connectors on the motherboard. The contacts of the extra connector are similar to the MCA connector. The local bus provides a 32-bit bus for the monitor adapter. This 32-bit bus can also operate at the CPU frequency, which can speed up Windows and GUI processing by several magnitudes.

The Opti Company developed the first chip set that was used on local bus motherboards. Several companies have developed special high-resolution adapters for the local bus system. If you do a lot of graphics work with your computer, you might want to check out these systems.

Most companies sell the local bus and adapter as a unit. The 486 local bus motherboard and adapter sells for $900 to $1200. The price variation depends on the frequency of the CPU, the brand name, and the built-in functions.

VGA-to-video adapters

Several companies have developed special VGA cards that can transform VGA output to a television signal. This National Television Standards Committee (NTSC) signal can then be recorded on a VCR or displayed on a TV screen. These adapters can be used to create presentations or computerized special effects.

US Video ((203) 964-9000) has several adapters. Their TVGA card can drive a monitor up to 1024 × 768 and also output NTSC signals. They also have several other cards for special effects. Other companies that have similar products include Jovian Logic Corp. ((415) 651-4823) and Willow Peripherals ((212) 402-0010).

What to look for

If possible, go to several stores and compare various models. Turn the brightness up and check the center of the screen and the outer edges. Is the intensity the same in the center and the outer edges? Check the focus, brightness, and contrast with text and graphics. There can be vast differences even in the same model from the same manufacturer. I have seen monitors that displayed demo graphics beautifully, but were not worth a damn when displaying text in various colors. If possible, try it out with both text and graphics.

Ask the vendor for a copy of the specs. Check the dot pitch. For good high resolution, the dot pitch should be no greater than 0.31 mm, even better would be 0.28 mm or 0.25 mm. Check the horizontal and vertical scan rate specs. For a multiscan monitor, the wider the range, the better. A good system should have a horizontal range from 30 kHz to 40 kHz or better. The vertical range should be from 45 Hz to 70 Hz or better.

Bandwidth

The *bandwidth* of a monitor is the range of frequencies its circuits can handle. A multiscan monitor accepts horizontal frequencies from 15.75 kHz to about 40 kHz, and vertical frequencies from 40 Hz to about 90 Hz. To get a rough estimate of the bandwidth required, multiply the resolution pixels times the vertical scan or frame rate. For instance, a Super VGA, or VESA standard, monitor should have 800 × 600 × 60 Hz = 28.8 MHz. But the system requires a certain amount of overhead for retrace,—the time needed to move back to the left side of the screen, drop down one line, and start a new line,—so the bandwidth should be at least 30 MHz. If the vertical scan rate is 90 Hz, then the bandwidth is 800 × 600 × 90 = 43.2 MHz or at least 45 MHz. A very high-resolution monitor requires a bandwidth of 1600 × 1200 × 90 = 172.8 MHz or about 180 MHz counting the overhead. Many of the very high-resolution units are specified at 200-MHz video bandwidth. Of course, the higher the bandwidth, the more costly and difficult the monitor is to manufacture.

Controls

You might also check for controls to adjust the brightness, contrast, and vertical and horizontal lines. Some manufacturers place them on the back or in other areas that are difficult to get to. It is much better if the controls are accessible from the front so you can see what the effect is as you adjust them.

Glare

If a monitor reflects too much light, it can be like a mirror and be very distracting. Some manufacturers coat their screens with a silicon formulation to cut down on reflectance. Some etch the screen for the same purpose. Some screens are tinted to cut down on glare. If possible, try the monitor under various lighting conditions. If you have a glare problem, several companies and mail-order houses offer glare shields that cost from $20 to $100.

Cleaning the screens   Because there is about 25,000 volts of electricity hitting the back of the monitor face, it creates a static attraction for dust. This can distort the screen and make it difficult to read. Most manufacturers provide an instruction book with their monitors that suggests how the screen should be cleaned. If you have a screen that is coated with silicon to reduce glare, you should not use any harsh cleansers on it. In most cases, plain water and a soft paper towel will work fine.

Tilt and swivel base

Most people place their monitor on top of their computer. If you are short or tall, have a low or high chair, or have a nonstandard desk, the monitor might not be at eye level. A tilt and swivel base allows you to position the monitor to best suit you. Many monitors now come with this base. If yours does not have one, many specialty stores and mail-order houses sell them for $15 to $40.

Several supply and mail-order houses offer an adjustable arm that clamps to the desk. The arm has a small platform that the monitor sits on, and the arm can swing up and down and from side to side. These are handy and can free up a lot of desk space. They cost from $50 to $150.

Cables

Some monitors come without cables. Vendors sell them separately for $25 to $75 extra. Even those monitors that have cables might not have cables with the type of connectors that fit your adapter. There is little or no standardization for cable and adapter connectors. Make sure that you get the proper cables to match your adapter and monitor.

Monitor and adapter sources

I subscribe to *PC Magazine*, *PC Week*, *Byte*, *Personal Computing*, *InfoWorld*, *PC World*, *Computer Shopper*, *Computer Buyer's Guide*, and about 50 other computer magazines. Most of these magazines have test labs that do extensive tests of products for their reviews. Because I can't personally test all of these products, I rely heavily on these reviews. I can't possibly list all of the monitor and adapter vendors, so I suggest you subscribe to the magazines listed above and in chapter 17.

List price versus street price

Note that the prices quoted from manufacturers in most magazine reviews are list prices. Often the "street price" of the product will be as little as one-half the list price. I don't know why vendors insist on using a list price. Very few people pay list price for computer products.

What to buy if you can afford it

Buy the biggest and best multisync, color, Super VGA or XGA monitor you can afford. If money is no object, buy a 486 local bus motherboard and adapter and a 19-inch analog monitor with super high resolution. If you spend a lot of time staring at your screen, you will never be sorry for buying the best available.

Realistically, the determining factors for choosing a monitor should be what you are going to use it for and the amount of money you have to spend. If you expect to do any kind of graphics or CAD/CAM design work, you definitely need a good large-screen color monitor with very high resolution. A large screen is almost essential for some types of design work so that as much of the drawing as possible can be viewed on the screen. It takes a lot of time for the computer to redraw an image on the screen. You also need a high-resolution monitor for close-tolerance designs. For instance, if you draw two lines to meet on a low-resolution monitor, they might look as though they are lined up. But when the drawing is magnified or printed out, the lines might not be anywhere close to one another.

Most desktop publishing is done in black and white. A high-resolution monochrome monitor might be all you need for these applications. These monitors usually display several shades of gray. Many of these monitors are the portrait type; that is, they are higher than they are wide. Many of them have a display area of 8½ inches by 11 inches. Instead of 25 lines, they have 66 lines, which is the standard for an 11-inch sheet of paper. Many have a phosphor that lets you have black text on a white background. Some of the newer color monitors have a mode that lets you switch to pure white with black type. Some of the 19-inch and larger landscape-type monitors, which are wider than they are high, can display two pages of text side by side. These monitors are ideal for databases, spreadsheets, accounting, or desktop publishing.

Monitor testing software

If you are planning to buy an expensive high-resolution monitor, you might want to buy a software program called DisplayMate (see Fig. 11-2). It is a collection of utilities that performs several checks on your monitor. It measures the resolution for fine lines, the clarity of the image, and distortion, has gray and color scales, and has a full range of intensities and colors. It also checks the ability of the adapter to drive the monitor during these tests. It comes with a large 370-page manual that is very comprehensive. It tells you just about everything you need to know about monitors. The program lists for $149, but if you plan to spend $1500 or more for a monitor, it can be well worth it to test the monitor first. The program is available from Sonera Technologies ((908) 747-6886).

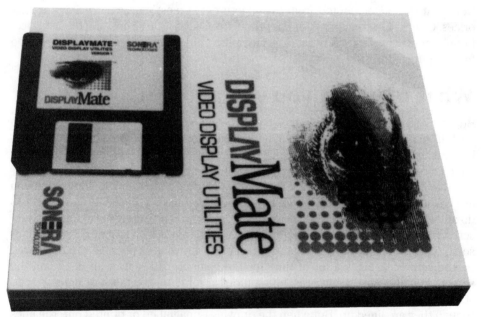

11-2   DisplayMate, a software program that can make a thorough check of your monitor.

12
Input devices

BEFORE YOU CAN DO ANYTHING WITH YOUR COMPUTER YOU MUST INPUT DATA TO it. There are several ways to input data including from a disk, modem, mouse, scanner, bar-code reader, voice data input, fax, or online from a mainframe or network. But by far, the most common way to get data into a computer is by way of a keyboard. For most common applications, it is impossible to operate a computer without a keyboard.

The keyboard is a most personal connection with your computer. If you do a lot of typing, it is very important to get a keyboard that suits you. Not all keyboards are the same. Some have a light mushy touch, some heavy. Some have noisy keys, others are silent with very little feedback.

Keyboards

Typewriter keyboards are fairly standard. There are only 26 letters in the alphabet and a few symbols, so most QWERTY typewriters have about 50 keys. I have had several computers over the last few years and each one of them has had a different keyboard. The main typewriter characters aren't changed or moved very often, but some of the control keys such as the Esc, Ctrl, PrtSc, and \, the function keys, and several others are moved all over the keyboard.

The original IBM keyboard had the Esc key just to the left of the 1 key in the numeric row. The 84-key keyboard moved the Esc key to the top row of the keypad. The tilde (~) and grave (^) key was moved to the original Esc position to the left side of the 1. The IBM 101-key keyboard moved the Esc key back to its original position.

For some unknown reason, IBM also decided to move the function keys to the top of the keyboard above the numeric keys. This is quite frustrating for WordStar users because the Ctrl key and the function keys are used quite often. The original position made them very easy to access.

Figure 12-1 shows four keyboards. Each of them has a different key arrangement. The keyboard on the bottom is a Focus FK5001. It is the one I use most often.

12-1 Four different keyboards.

It has the function keys to the left of the keyboard. It also has a duplicate set of function keys along the top. It has a built-in calculator to the right. When the calculator is turned off, the keypad works just like all other keyboards. This keyboard also has a slot at the top of the keyboard for holding program templates. It comes with several templates, such as WordStar, WordPerfect, Microsoft Word, Lotus 1-2-3, and dBASE IV. These templates show all the basic commands and are very helpful.

The two keyboards in the center in Fig. 12-1 are only slightly different. The shapes and sizes of the backspace and enter keys on the two keyboards are quite different. The keyboard at the top has a built-in trackball. It also has several keys that are positioned differently than on the other keyboards.

How a keyboard works

A keyboard is actually a computer containing a small microprocessor with its own ROM. The computerized electronics of the keyboard eliminate the bounce of the keys, can determine when you hold a key down for repeat, can store up to 20 or more keystrokes, and can determine which key was pressed first if you press two at a time.

In addition to the standard BIOS chips on your motherboard, there is a special keyboard BIOS chip. Each time a key is pressed a unique signal is sent to the BIOS. This signal is a dc voltage that is turned on and off a certain number of times within a definite time frame to represent 0s and 1s. In the ASCII code, if the letter A is pressed, the code for 65 is generated: 1 0 0 0 0 0 1.

Reprogramming key functions

The keys can be changed by various software programs to represent almost anything you want them to. One thing that makes learning computers so difficult is that every software program uses the function and other special keys in different ways. You might learn all the special keys that WordStar uses, but if you use a word processor such as WordPerfect or Microsoft Word, you have to learn the special commands and keys they use.

The major word processors, spreadsheets, and some other software let you set up macro programs. A macro program lets you record a series of keystrokes, such as your name and address, the time and date, or any other frequently used item so you can type it by pressing just one or two keys.

Keyboard sources

Keyboard preference is strictly a matter of individual taste. KeyTronic ((509) 928-8000) makes some excellent keyboards. They are the IBM of the keyboard world. Their keyboards have set the standard. KeyTronic keyboards have been copied by the clone makers, even to the extent of using the same model numbers. KeyTronic offers several models. They even let you change the little springs under the keys for different tensions. The standard is 2 ounces, but you can configure the key tension to whatever you like—1 to 3 ounces—for an extra $15. You can even exchange the positions of the CapsLock and Ctrl keys. These keyboards have several other functions that are clearly described in their large manual. Hundreds of clone makers offer keyboards that are very good for $35 to $90. Look through the computer magazines for ads.

Specialized keyboards

Quite often I have the need to do minor calculations. The computer is great for calculations, and several programs such as SideKick, Windows, and WordStar have built-in calculators. But most of these programs require that the computer be on and a file be open. Keyboards available from Shamrock ((800) 722-2898) and Jameco ((415) 592-8097) have built-in solar-powered calculators. The calculator can be used whether the computer is on or not.

Focus Electronics ((818) 820-0416) has a series of specialized keyboards. They have keyboards with built-in calculators, function keys in two locations, extra * and \ keys, and several other goodies. Their FK5001 keyboard has eight cursor arrow keys (see Fig. 12-1). With these keys the cursor can be moved right or left, up or down, and diagonally from any of the four corners of the screen. The speed of the cursor can be varied by using the 12 function keys. These eight cursor keys can do just about everything a mouse can do.

Besides their standard keyboards, KeyTronic has developed a large number of specialized ones. Instead of a keypad, one has a touch pad. This pad operates in several different modes. One mode lets it act like a cursor pad. By using your finger or a stylus, the cursor is moved much the same as with a mouse. This keyboard comes with templates for several popular programs such as WordStar, WordPerfect, DOS, and Lotus 1-2-3. Another KeyTronic model has a bar-code reader attached to it. This can be extremely handy if you have a small business that uses bar codes.

Keyboard covers

Special plastic covers are available that can protect keyboards against spills, dust, and other harsh environmental factors. There are some areas, such as the floor of a manufacturing area, where a cover is absolutely essential. Most covers are made from soft plastic that is molded to fit over the keys. They are pliable, but they will slow down any serious typist.

Several companies manufacture custom covers including CompuCover ((800) 874-6391) and Tech-Cessories ((800) 637-0909). Over 400 different keyboards are used in the United States. If you count the foreign keyboards, there are probably over 4000 different types worldwide. These companies claim they can provide a cover for most of them. The average cover costs about $25. This is a bit expensive, but one reason they are so expensive is that there are so many different keyboards. Quality Computer Products ((800) 752-1745) says their QCP 101 keyboard is spill-proof. But if you have a need to protect your keyboard from a harsh environment, and you don't have a special cover, plastic wrap makes a fairly good cover. It is flexible, it clings to the keyboard, and it is certainly inexpensive.

Mouse systems

One of the biggest reasons for the success of the Macintosh is it is easy to use. With a mouse and icons, all you have to do is point and click. You don't have to learn a lot of commands and rules. A person who knows nothing about computers can become productive in a very short time. The people in the DOS world finally took note of this and began developing programs and applications such as Windows for the IBM and compatibles. Dozens of companies now manufacture mice. Many software programs can be used without a mouse, but they operate much faster and better with a mouse. To be productive, a mouse is essential for programs such as Windows 3.1, CAD programs, paint and graphics programs, and many others.

Types of mice

The ball-type mouse   The vast majority of mice today are the ball type. The mouse has a small round rubber ball on the underside that contacts the desktop. As the mouse is moved, the ball turns. Inside the mouse, two flywheels—one for horizontal and one for vertical movements—contact the ball. You don't need a grid for ball-type mice, but you do need about 1 square foot of clear desk space to move the mouse about. The ball picks up dirt so it should be cleaned often.

The optical mouse   Some older mice use optics with an LED (light-emitting diode) that shines on a reflective grid. As the mouse moves across the grid, the reflected light is picked up by a detector and is sent to the computer to move the cursor. The spacings on the grid of an optical mouse might not provide sufficient resolution for designs that demand very close tolerances. In this case, you might be better off with a high-resolution mouse that utilizes a ball. Optical mice are practically obsolete, and if you have one, you might consider upgrading to the ball type.

Mouse interfaces

You can't just plug in a mouse and start using it. The software, whether Windows, WordStar, or a CAD program, must recognize and interface with the mouse. Mouse companies develop software drivers that allow their mice to operate with various programs. The drivers are usually supplied on a disk. The Microsoft Mouse is the de facto standard, and most other companies emulate the Microsoft driver.

Most mice require a voltage, usually 5 volts. Some come with a small plug-in transformer, and some have an adapter that you insert between the keyboard cable connector and the motherboard connector. Some mice require the use of one of your serial ports for their input to the computer. This can cause problems if you already have devices using COM1 and COM2. You might have to buy a board and use one of your plug-in slots to provide a serial interface for the COM ports.

Microsoft, Logitech, and several other mouse companies have developed a bus mouse. It interfaces directly with the bus and does not require the use of your COM ports. But the systems come with a board that requires the use of one of your slots.

The PS/2 systems have a built-in pointing device interface on their motherboard. The connector looks much like those used on ISA clone machines, but it is wired differently. Many of the clones also have built-in interfaces on their motherboards. Some of them use the IBM-type sockets. Depending on what type of system you have, if you buy a mouse, you might have to buy an adapter.

The mouse plugs into a serial port. The serial ports on some systems use a DB25-type socket connector. Others use a DB9 socket. Many mice now come with a DB9 connector and a DB25 adapter. Before you buy a mouse, you might check what type of serial port connector you have and order the proper type. You can buy an adapter for about $3.

Mouse cost

A good mouse costs from $50 to $100. One cost factor is what options of software packages and other goodies are included with the product. Another cost factor is resolution. Some mice are capable of only 100 dots per inch (dpi), the better ones have resolutions of 200 dpi to 350 dpi. Higher resolution is necessary for some CAD work and critical design work that requires close tolerances.

Mouse costs have come way down. I recently went to a local swap meet and bought a mouse for $10. I thought it was a bargain until I saw an ad from a discount house offering the mouse for $8.88. I felt like returning the one I bought and asking for my money back. Figure 12-2 shows the $10 mouse on the left, a $19 mouse in the center, and a $68 Logitech mouse on the right.

If you just need something to point and click, low-cost mice are perfectly all right. Of course, higher-resolution systems cost more. Many companies manufacture mouse systems. Check the ads in the computer magazines listed in chapter 17.

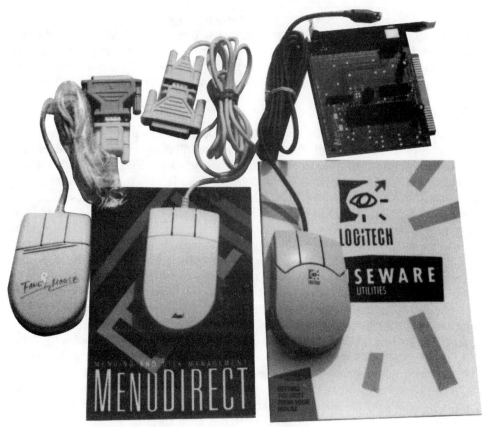

12-2 Three different mice. The one on the left cost $10, the one in the center $19, and the Logitech cost $68.

Trackballs

A trackball is a mouse turned upside down. Like the mouse, it must have a voltage from a transformer or other source. It also requires a serial port, or a slot if it is of the bus type.

Instead of moving the mouse to move the ball, the ball is moved by your fingers. The ball in a trackball is much larger than the ball in a mouse, so trackballs can have better resolution. Trackballs do not require as much desk space as an ordinary mouse. If your desk is as cluttered as mine, you definitely need a trackball. Several companies manufacture trackballs. Look through the computer magazines for ads.

Keyboard/trackball combination

Amtac ((718) 392-1703), Chicony ((714) 771-6151), and several other companies have keyboards with a built-in trackball. This gives you the benefits and capabilities of a mouse, without using up extra desk space. I bought a Chicony keyboard with a trackball for $68 (see Fig. 12-1). This was a real bargain when you consider that several other companies offer stand-alone trackballs that cost $75 or more. Check the computer magazines for ads.

Digitizers and graphics tablets

Graphics tablets and digitizers are similar to a drawing pad or drafting table. Most of them use some sort of pointing device that translates movement into digitized output. Some are rather small, but some are as large as a standard drafting table. They cost as little as $150 to over $1500. Most of them have a very high resolution, are very accurate, and are intended for precision drawing. Most of the tablets are serial devices, but some require their own interface board.

Some of the tablets have programmable overlays and function keys. Some work with a mouse-like device, a penlight, or a pencil-like stylus. The tablets can be used for designing circuits, for CAD programs, for graphics and freehand drawing, and even for text and data input. The most common use is with CAD-type software.

Scanners and optical character readers

Most large companies have mountains of memos, manuals, documents, and files that must be maintained, revised, and updated periodically. Several companies manufacture optical character readers (OCRs) that can scan a line of printed type, recognize each character, and input those characters into a computer just as if it were typed in from a keyboard. Once the data is in the computer, a word processor is used to revise or change the data, and print it out again. Or the data can be stored on floppies or a hard disk. If copies of the data are stored in a computer, the data can be searched very quickly for any item. Many times I have spent hours going through printed manuals looking for certain items. If the data had been in a computer, I could have found the information in just minutes.

Optical character readers have been around for several years. When they first came out they cost from $6000 to more than $15,000. They were very limited in the fonts they could recognize and were unable to handle graphics. But vast improvements have been made in the last few years. Many full-page scanners are now fairly inexpensive, starting at about $500. Some hand-held ones, which are rather limited, cost as little as $200. For $375, I bought a good hand-held scanner from Caere ((408) 395-7000).

Houston Instruments specializes in manufacturing plotters. They developed a scanning head for one of their plotters that can scan a large drawing, digitize the lines and symbols, and input them to a computer. The drawing can then be changed and replotted very easily. There are many manufacturers of input devices. Look in any of the computer magazines listed in chapter 17.

Bar codes

Bar codes are a system of black-and-white lines arranged in a system much like the dots and dashes of Morse code. By using combinations of wide and narrow bars and wide and narrow spaces, any numeral or letter of the alphabet can be represented. I discuss bar codes in greater detail in chapter 16.

Voice data input

Another way to input data into a computer is to talk to it with a microphone. This requires electronics that can take the signal created by the microphone, detect the spoken words, and turn them into digital information the computer can use.

The early voice data input systems were very expensive and limited. One reason was that voice technology requires lots of memory. But the cost of memory has dropped considerably in the last few years, and the technology has improved in many other ways. Voice technology involves "training" a computer to recognize a word spoken by a person. When you speak into a microphone, the sound waves cause a diaphragm, or some other device, to move back and forth in a magnetic field, creating a voltage that is analogous to the sound wave. If this voltage is recorded and played through a good audio system, the loudspeaker responds to the amplified voltages and reproduces a sound that is identical to the one input to the microphone.

A person speaks a word into a microphone creating a unique voltage for that word spoken by that particular person. The voltage is fed into an electronic circuit, and the pattern is digitized and stored in the computer. If several words are spoken, the circuit digitizes each of them and stores them. Each word has a distinct and unique pattern. Later when the computer hears a word, it searches through the patterns it has stored to see if the input word matches one of its stored words. Because every person's voice is different, the computer will not recognize the voice of anyone who has not trained it. Training the computer involves saying the same word several times so the computer can store several patterns of the person's voice. Once the computer is able to recognize words, it can perform some useful work. You can command it to load and run a program, or perform any of several other tasks.

Voice data input is very useful whenever you must use both hands to do a job but still need a computer to perform certain tasks. One area where voice data is used extensively is in military fighter planes. The pilot does not have time to manipulate computer keys because both hands are usually busy. The pilot can have the computer do hundreds of jobs by just telling it what he wants done.

Voice data is also useful on production lines where a person does not have time to enter data manually. It can also be used in laboratories where a scientist can't write down the findings or data. There might be times when the lighting must be kept too dim to input data to a computer manually. In other instances, a person might have to be several feet from the computer and still be able to input data. The person might even be miles away, yet can input data over a telephone line.

In most of the systems in use today, the computer must be trained to recognize a specific word, so the vocabulary is limited. But every word that can be spoken is derived from just 42 phonemes. Several companies are working on systems that take a sample of a person's voice containing these phonemes. Using the phonemes from this sample, the computer can recognize any word the person speaks.

Computerized voice output

Computer synthesized voice systems have been developed to do hundreds of tasks. Sensors can be set up so that when a beam is broken, it sends a signal to a computer to alert a person of danger. The Atlanta airport has an underground shuttle that moves people to the various airline gates. It has several sensors feeding into a computer. If a person stands in the doorway, it asks the person to move, and the train will not move until it is safe to do so.

Many automated banking systems allow you to dial into a computer. A computerized voice asks questions, lets you pay your bills, and moves money from one account to another, letting you do almost all of your banking by telephone. The telephone system has computerized voices for the time and for giving out numbers when you dial 411. Many more uses are being developed every day.

Computers and devices for the handicapped

Several computer devices have been developed to help the disabled person live a better life. Devices are available that allow the blind, the deaf, the quadriplegic, and other disabled people to communicate. There are special braille keyboards and keyboards with enlarged keys for the blind. The EyeTyper from Sentient Systems Technology has an embedded camera on the keyboard that can determine which key the user is looking at. It then enters that character into the computer. Words Plus has a sensitive visor that can understand input from a raised brow, head movement, or eye blinks. The Speaking Devices Corp. ((408) 727-5571) has a telephone that can be trained to recognize an individual's voice. It can store and dial 100 different numbers. The same company has a tiny earphone that also acts as a microphone. These devices are ideal for people who can speak, but cannot use their hands.

Devices for the disabled allow them to lead active, useful, and productive lives. They have become artists, programmers, writers, and scientists. These communication devices have allowed them a bit of freedom from the harsh prison of their disabilities. Several organizations can help in locating special equipment and lend support. If you know someone who might benefit from the latest technologies and devices for the handicapped, contact these organizations:

AbleData	(800) 344-5405
Accent on Information	(309) 378-2961
American Foundation for the Blind	(212) 620-2000
Apple Computer	(408) 996-1010
Closing the Gap, Inc.	(612) 248-3294
Direct Link for the Disabled	(805) 688-1603
Easter Seals Systems Office	(312) 667-8626
IBM National Support Center	(800) 426-2133
National ALS Association	(818) 340-7500
Trace Research and Development Center	(608) 262-6966

Get a tax deduction

Now that you have assembled your new computer, you might be retiring an older computer. You can advertise and sell it, but it's probably more trouble than it is worth. It might be worth more to you to give it away to a charitable organization. You can then deduct the reasonable value from your income tax. Charities are most happy to get anything you can give them, and it feels good making others happy.

13
Telecommunications

ADDING A MODEM TO YOUR COMPUTER CAN BE A VERY USEFUL UPGRADE. EVEN IF you already have a modem, maybe you should think about replacing it with a new high-speed model. Many modem boards are now integrated with fax boards. A modem board with a fax might cost no more than a modem alone. Communicating by fax is fast and efficient.

Reaching out

There are about 40 million computers installed in homes, offices, and businesses. About 20 million of these have a modem or some sort of communications capability. You can use a telephone to communicate with any of several million persons anywhere in the world. Likewise, a computer with telecommunications capabilities can communicate with several million other computers in the world. They can access over 10,000 bulletin boards in the United States, taking advantage of electronic mail, faxes, up-to-the-minute stock market quotations, and a large number of other online services such as home shopping, home banking, travel services, and many other services and databases.

Modems

A modem is an electronic device that allows a computer to use an ordinary telephone line to communicate with other computers equipped with modems. Modem is a contraction of the words *modulate* and *demodulate*. The telephone system transmits voice and data in analog voltage form. Analog voltages vary continuously up and down. Computer data is in a digital voltage form. Digital signals are a series of on and off voltages. The modem modulates the digital voltages from a computer and transforms them into analog voltages in order to transmit them over the telephone lines.

At the receiving end, another modem demodulates the analog voltages and transforms them back into digital voltages.

Transmission difficulties

Telephone systems were originally designed for voice and have a very narrow bandwidth. A person with perfect hearing can hear 20 cycles per second or hertz (Hz) up to 20,000 Hz. For normal speech, we hear 300 Hz to 2000 Hz.

Telephone analog voltages are subject to noise, static, and other electrical disturbances. The analog noise and static voltages are added and imposed on any data voltages being transmitted. The mixing of static and noise voltages with data voltages can corrupt and severely damage the data. The demodulator might be unable to determine which voltages represent data and which are noise.

Baud rate

These problems, and the state of technology at the time, limited the original modems to about 5 characters per second (cps), or a rate of 50 baud. The term baud comes from Emile Baudot (1845–1903), a French inventor. Originally, the baud rate was a measure of the dots and dashes in telegraphy. It is now defined as the actual rate of symbols transmitted per second. For the lower baud rates, it is essentially the same as bits per second. Remember, it takes eight bits to make a character. Just as we use periods and spaces to separate words, we must use one start bit and two stop bits to separate the on/off bits into characters. A transmission of 300 baud means that 300 on/off bits are sent in 1 second. Counting the start/stop bits, it takes 11 bits for each character. So 300 divided by 11 gives about 27 cps. Some of the newer technologies actually transmit symbols representing more than one bit. For baud rates of 1200 and higher, the characters per second and the baud rate can be considerably different.

There have been some fantastic advances in modem technologies. A couple of years ago, 2400-baud systems were the standard. Today they are practically obsolete. The industry has leaped over 4800- and 9600-baud systems to 14.4K systems. These units also incorporate the V.42 bis standard. This allows them to use 4:1 data compression and thus transmit at 57,600 bits per second (bps). When communicating with another modem, both the sending and receiving unit must operate at the same baud rate and use the same protocols. Most of the faster modems are downward compatible and can operate at slower speeds.

Ordinarily, the higher the baud rate, the less time it takes to download or transmit a file. This might not always be true, because at higher speeds, more transmission errors might occur. If errors occur, parts of the file, or the whole file, must be retransmitted. If the file is being sent over a long-distance line, the length of telephone connect time can be costly. If your modem is used frequently, your telephone bills can be very substantial, especially if you have a slow modem.

How to estimate connect time

You can figure the approximate length of time it will take to transmit a file. Divide the baud rate by 10. For instance, 1200 baud would be 120 cps, 2400 baud would be 240 cps. Look at the directory and determine the number of bytes in the file. Divide the number of bytes in the file by the characters per second. Then multiply that figure by 1.3 for the start/stop bits to get a final approximation. For instance, with a 1200-baud modem and a 40K file, divide 40K by 120 cps to get 333 seconds times 1.3 equals about 433 seconds, or 7.2 minutes.

If you transmit the same 40K file with a 2400-baud modem, it would be $40,000/240 = 167 \times 1.3 = 217$ seconds, or 3.6 minutes. With a 9600-baud modem, the same 40K file can be sent in about 55 seconds.

Besides the phone charges you have to pay, the major online service companies, such as CompuServe, Dataquest, and Dow Jones News/Retrieval, charge for connect time to their services. The connect time is much less with some of the high-speed modems. However, some companies charge more for high-speed modems.

Protocols

Protocols are procedures that have been established for exchanging data, as well as the instructions that coordinate the process. Most protocols can sense when data is corrupted or lost due to noise, static, or a bad connection. They will automatically resend the affected data until it is received correctly.

There are several protocols, but the most popular ones are Kermit (named for Kermit the frog), Xmodem, and Ymodem. These protocols transmit a block of data along with an error-checking code, then wait for the receiver to send back an acknowledgment. They then send another block and wait to see if it goes through okay If a block does not get through, it is resent immediately. Protocols such as Zmodem and HyperProtocol send a whole file in a continuous stream of data with error-checking codes inserted at certain intervals. They then wait for confirmation of a successful transmission. If the transmission is unsuccessful, the whole file must be resent.

Communications software

In order to use a modem, you must have the proper software. There are dozens of communication programs that can be used. Crosstalk ((404) 998-3998) was one of the earlier modem programs. They now have a Crosstalk for Windows version. It works with any Windows version, which makes it very easy to learn and use. ProComm ((314) 474-8461) is one of several low-cost shareware programs. In many areas it outperforms some of the high-cost commercial programs. The registration cost is $89. Qmodem ((319) 232-4516) is another excellent communications shareware program. Its registration cost is only $30. Shareware is available from bulletin boards or from any of the several companies that provide public domain software. Shareware is not free. You try it out and use it, and the developers ask that you register the program and send in a nominal sum. For a low cost, they usually provide a manual and some support.

Types of modems

There are two basic types of modems—the external desktop and the internal. Each type has its advantages and disadvantages. The external type requires some of your precious desk space and a voltage source. It also requires a COM port to drive it. Even if you use an external modem, if your motherboard doesn't have built-in COM ports, you will need an I/O board that will require the use of one of your slots. Most external modems have LEDs that light up and let you know what is happening during your call. Both the external and the internal models have speakers that let you hear the phone ringing or hear the busy signal. Some of the external models have a volume control.

The internal modem is built entirely on a board, usually a half or short board. They don't use up any of your desk space, but they do use one of your precious slots. And they don't have LEDs to let you know the progress of your call.

Hayes compatibility

One of the most popular early modems was made by Hayes Microcomputer Products. They are the IBM of the modem world and have established a de facto standard. There are hundreds of modem manufacturers, and except for some of the very inexpensive ones, almost all of them emulate the Hayes standard.

Installing a modem

If you are adding a modem on a board to a system that is already assembled, the first thing you do is remove the computer cover. Then find an empty slot, and plug it in. The board should have jumpers or switches that must be set to enable COM1 or COM2. If you have an I/O board in your system with external COM ports, or built-in COM ports on your motherboard, you must configure them for whichever port is used for the modem.

If you are installing an external modem, you must go through the same procedure to make sure the COM port is accessible and does not conflict. If you have a mouse, a serial printer, or some other serial device, you have to determine which port it is set to. You cannot have two serial devices set to the same COM port.

Plug in the modem board and hook it up to the telephone line. Unless you expect to do a lot of communicating, you don't need a separate dedicated line. If the modem has an automatic answer mode, this mode should be disabled unless you have a dedicated line. Check your documentation. There should be a switch or some means to disable it.

There should be two connectors at the back of the board. One labeled for the line in and the other labeled for the telephone. Unless you have a dedicated telephone line, you should unplug your telephone, plug in the extension to the modem and line, and then plug the telephone into the modem. If your computer is not near your telephone line, you might have to go to a hardware store and buy a long telephone extension line. After you have connected all of the lines, turn on your computer and try the modem before you put the cover back on.

A simple modem test   It is often difficult to determine which COM port is being used by a device. You can use the AT command to determine if your modem is working. At the DOS prompt C:> type ECHO AT DT12345>COM1:. If the modem is set properly, you will hear a dial tone, then the modem will dial 12345. If two devices are set for COM1 there will be a conflict. The computer will try for a while, then give an error message and the familiar "Abort, Retry, Ignore, Fail?" Diagnostic programs such as Check-It from TouchStone ((714) 969-7746) can also determine which ports are being used. They can also do several other very helpful diagnostic tests.

Fax/phone switch Having the modem and telephone on the same line should cause no problems unless someone tries to use the telephone while the modem is using it. Life can be a lot simpler if you have a switch that detects whether the incoming signal is for a fax, a modem, or voice. The switch routes the incoming call to the proper device. Several different models are available with different features. Companies that sell fax/phone switches include Computer Friends ((800)547-3303), Business Computer Systems ((800) 333-2955), and Command Communications ((303)750-6434).

External modem An external modem is connected to one of the COM ports with a cable. If you did not get a cable with your unit, you will have to buy one. If you have built-in COM ports the cable will cost about $5. If you have to use the bus to access the port, you will need a cable and an I/O board with serial ports.

Bulletin boards

If you have a modem, you have access to several thousand computer bulletin boards. There are over 100 in the San Francisco Bay area and about twice that many in the Los Angeles area. Many of them are free. You only have to pay the phone bill if they are out of your calling area. However, some of them charge a nominal fee to join, and some just ask for a tax deductible donation.

Some bulletin boards are run by private individuals and some by companies and vendors as a service to their customers. Some are run by user groups and other special interest organizations. There are over 100 boards nationwide that have been set up for doctors and lawyers.

Most bulletin boards are set up to help individuals. They usually have lots of public domain software and a space where you can leave messages for help, for advertising something for sale, or for just plain old chit-chat. If you are just getting started, you probably need some software. Public domain and shareware software are available that are equivalent to almost all of the major commercial programs. And the best part is, they are free.

Viruses

Some low-life individuals have hidden "viruses" in some public domain and even in some commercial software. This software appears to work as it should, but eventually it contaminates and destroys your files. Viruses often cause files to grow in size until they explode.

Most bulletin boards have public domain software to check for viruses. One of the better virus detectors is the McAfee Shareware Scan program. It is available for downloading from several bulletin boards or from the BBS at (408) 988-4004. If you download bulletin board software, check it with a virus software. It is best not to install unknown software on your hard disk. Run it from a floppy disk until you are sure that it is okay.

Illegal activities

Some bulletin boards have been used for illegal and criminal activities. Stolen credit card numbers and telephone charge numbers have been left on bulletin boards. Because of this, many bulletin board system operators (SYSOPS) are now carefully checking any software that is uploaded onto their systems. Many of them are now restricting access to their boards, and some of them have had to start charging a fee because of the extra time it takes to monitor the boards.

Where to find bulletin boards

There are several computer magazines that devote space to bulletin boards and user groups. In California, *MicroTimes* and *Computer Currents* have several pages of bulletin boards and user groups each month. *Computer Shopper* has the most comprehensive listing of bulletin boards and user groups of any national magazine. *Computer Shopper* alternates each month with a listing of user groups one month and a listing of bulletin boards the next. You can call Allen Bechtold of the BBS Press Service ((913) 478-3157). He can arrange to have a copy of the bulletin boards and user groups sent to you.

CCITT recommended standards

The communications industry is very complex, and there have not been many real standards. There are many different manufacturers and software developers, and each of them wants to differentiate their hardware or software by adding new features. But you might be unable to communicate with someone who is not using the same features.

A United Nations standards committee is helping to establish some standards. It is called the Comite Consulatif Internal de Telegraphique et Telephone (CCITT). This committee has representatives from over 80 countries and from several large private manufacturers. The committee makes recommendations only, and companies are free to use or ignore them. But more and more companies are now adopting the recommendations.

All CCITT recommendations for small computers have a V or X prefix. The V series is for use with switched telephone networks, which is almost all of them. The X series is for systems that do not use switched phone lines. Revisions or alternate recommendations have bis (second) or ter (third) added. Here are a few CCITT recommendations:

- V.22—a 1200-baud standard.
- V.22 bis—a 2400-baud standard.
- V.32—a 9600-baud standard.
- V.42—an error correcting protocol. It includes MNP-4 and LAP M error correction.
- V.42 bis—a standard for 4:1 data compression. Under ideal conditions, this standard permits data transmission speeds four times greater than the rated baud rate. With this much compression a 14.4K modem can transmit at 57,600 bps.
- X.25—a protocol for packet mode communications on data networks. It is used on systems such as Telenet and Tymnet.
- MNP—Microcom Networking Protocol. A series of 10 different protocols developed by the Microcom company. Several of their protocols are very similar to the CCITT V.42 series.
- LAP M and LAP B—other protocols that are supported by AT&T and Hayes. They are similar to the CCITT V.42 error correcting standard.

Sources

I will not list the names and manufacturers of modems because there are so many. Look in any computer magazine and you will see dozens of ads. A recent copy of *Computer Shopper* had ads for about 200 different types of modems from several different companies.

One company I do want to mention is USRobotics. They manufacture a large variety of modems, especially the high-end, high-speed types. They will send you a free 110-page booklet that explains all you need to know about modems. To get your free booklet, call (800) 342-5877.

Online services

One of the most popular of the large national online service companies is CompuServe ((800) 848-8199). They provide forums for help and discussions, mail boxes, and a large variety of information and reference services. A caller can search the databases and download information as easily as pulling the data off his own hard disk. The company charges a fee for connect time.

Prodigy is unlike the other online services. Prodigy does not charge for connect time. They charge only a very nominal monthly rate. They have phone service to most larger cities so you don't even pay a phone charge. They have an impressive list of services including home shopping, home banking, airline schedules and reservations, stock market quotations, and many others. One of its faults is that it is relatively slow, but because it is so inexpensive, I can live with it. You can contact Prodigy at (800) 776-3449. Other online service companies include

America Online	(800) 827-6364
GEnie	(800) 638-9636

E-mail

Many of the national bulletin boards offer electronic mail (E-mail) along with their other services. These services can be of great value to some individuals and businesses. E-mail subscribers are usually give a "post office box." This is usually a file on a large hard disk system. When a message is received, it is recorded in the file. The next time the subscriber logs on to this service he/she is alerted that there is "mail" in their box.

E-mail is becoming more popular and there are now several hundred thousand subscribers. The cost for an average message is about $1. The cost for overnight mail from the U.S. Post Office, Federal Express, and UPS is $11 to $13. Companies that provide E-mail include

AT&T Mail	(800) 624-5672
CompuServe	(800) 848-8990
DASnet	(408) 559-7434
MCI Mail	(800) 444-6245
Western Union	(800) 527-5184

LAN E-mail

Most of the larger local area network (LAN) programs provide an E-mail utility in their software. For those packages that do not provide this utility, there are programs available that work with installed LANs. The CCITT has recommended that X.400 be the standard for LAN E-mail. This standard provides the gateway to installed LANs. Another gateway system supported by Novell and Lotus is the Message Handling System (MHS). Companies that have LAN E-mail programs include

Action Technologies	(800) 624-2162
Inbox Plus	(415) 769-9669
Lotus Express	(800) 345-1043
MS-Mail	(206) 882-8080
PCC Systems	(415) 321-0430
Quickmail	(515) 224-1995

Banking by modem

Many banks offer systems that let you do all your banking with your computer and a modem from the comforts of your home. You never again have to drive downtown, hunt for a parking space, and stand in line for a half-hour to do your banking.

Telephone technology advances

There have been many advances in telephone technology. A box can be attached to your telephone that will display the number of the caller. If you know the number of someone you don't want to talk to, you can look at the number and decide whether to answer the phone or not. Certain numbers can be excluded so that your phone will not even ring. Because the caller's number is displayed by this box, it should help reduce computerized, unwanted, and obscene calls. It will also be an enormous help to police departments and fire departments and to pizza and fast-food deliver businesses.

Some people object to the caller ID system. A court in Pennsylvania declared it unconstitutional on the grounds that it is an invasion of privacy. It is difficult to understand the judge's ruling. How is it violating a person's rights if you want to know who is calling before you answer?

The Public Utilities Commission has imposed several restrictions on the use of caller ID in California. A person's ID will not be shown unless that person agrees. Most people and the telephone companies are unhappy with the restrictions. Because of the restrictions, it is doubtful caller ID will be instituted in California. Phonevision is another new technology that will soon be in many homes.

ISDN

ISDN is an acronym for integrated services digital network. Eventually the whole world will have telephone systems that use this concept. It is a system that can transmit voice, data, video, and graphics in digital form, rather than the present analog form. When this happens, you can scrap our modem. You will need only a simple interface to communicate. ISDN is already installed in several cities, but don't throw your modem away just yet. The new service will be rather expensive and will not be available in all locations for some time.

Facsimile boards and machines

Facsimile (fax) machines have been around for quite a while. Newspapers and businesses have used them for years. The early machines were similar to the early acoustic modems. Both used foam rubber cups that fit over the telephone receiver and mouthpiece for coupling. They were very slow and subject to noise and interference. Fax machines and modems have come a long way since those early days.

Modems and fax machines are quite similar, and related in many respects. A modem sends and receives bits of data. A fax machine sends and receives scanned letters, images, signatures, etc. A computer program can be sent over a modem, but not over a fax. A fax sends and receives the information as digitized data. A page of text or a photo is fed into a fax machine and scanned. As the scanning beam moves across the page, white and dark areas are digitized as 1s and 0s, which are transmitted over the telephone line. A modem converts the digital information that represents characters into analog voltages, sends it over the line, then converts it back to digital information.

Millions of fax machines are in use today. Very few businesses could not benefit from the use of a fax machine. It can be used to send documents, handwriting, signatures, seals, letterheads, graphs, blueprints, photos, and other types of data around the world, across the country, or across the room.

I mentioned earlier that it costs $11 to $13 to send an overnight letter, but that E-mail only costs about $1. A fax machine can deliver the same letter for about 40 cents and do it in less than 3 minutes. Depending on the type of business, and the amount of critical mail that is sent, a fax system can pay for itself in a very short time.

Stand-alone fax units

Several fax machines are stand-alone devices that attach to a telephone. They have been vastly improved in the last few years. Most of them are as easy to use as a copy machine. In fact, most of them can be used as copy machines.

Some companies are making stand-alone units that are fairly inexpensive, some for as little as $400. You might not be happy with a low-cost fax. You will probably be better off if you spend a bit more and get one with a paper cutter, high resolution, a voice/data switch, a document feeder, automatic dialing, automatic retry, delayed transmission, transmission confirmation, polling, built-in laser printing, and large memory. You might not need or be able to afford all of these features, but try to get a machine with as many as possible. Of course, the more features it has, the higher the cost.

Fax computer boards

Several companies have developed fax machines on plug-in boards. Many of the fax boards are integrated with a modem on the same board. The modem and fax combination costs only slightly more than either board separately.

Special software allows the computer to control the fax board. Using the computer's word processor, letters and memos can be written and sent over the phone lines. Letters or other information can be stored or retrieved from the computer's hard disk and transmitted. The computer can even be programmed to send the letters out at night when the rates are lower. But computer fax boards have one disadvantage. They cannot scan information unless there is a scanner attached to the computer. Without a scanner, the information that can be sent is limited to that which can be entered from a keyboard or disk. However, the computer can receive and store any fax that is sent to it. The digitized data and images can be stored on a hard disk and printed out on a printer. Hundreds of companies manufacture fax boards and products. Look for ads in the computer magazines.

Installing a fax board

Most fax boards are very easy to install and easy to operate. Use the same basic instructions that were outlined earlier for installing a modem board. Check your documentation and set any switches that are necessary, plug the board into an empty slot, replace the computer cover, and connect the telephone line. You should have received some software to control the fax. This should be installed on your hard disk. If you use a word processing program, such as WordStar, to create letters or text for fax transmission, the text must be changed into an ASCII file before it can be sent. Most word processors have this capability.

Scanners

Scanners were discussed briefly in chapter 12. They are not absolutely essential to the operation of a PC-based fax, but there might be times when it is necessary to transmit photographs, blueprints, documents, or handwritten signatures on contracts, and a host of other needs. So a scanner is needed to get the most utility from your fax.

Combination devices

Compex International ((800) 626-8112) has an all-in-one fax, scanner, printer, and copier. Speaking Devices Corp. ((408) 727-2132) has a unit with a fax, fax/phone switch, scanner, voice mail, and caller ID. Many more companies manufacture combination devices. Just look through the ads in the computer magazines.

Telecommuting

Every day millions of people risk their lives and fight the traffic. Many of these people have jobs they could perform at home, working on a computer, and sending the data to the office over a modem or fax. Even if you had to buy your own computer, modem, and fax, it still might be worth it. You could save the cost of gasoline, auto maintenance, and lower insurance. Being able to work at home is ideal for those who have young children, for the handicapped, or for anyone who hates traffic. Telecommuting can be a lifesaver.

14
Printers

FOR THE VAST MAJORITY OF APPLICATIONS, A COMPUTER SYSTEM IS NOT COMPLETE without a printer. If you have an older system, you probably have a dot matrix printer. Depending on what you use your system for, it might be all you need. But the printing from a dot matrix, especially the seven- and nine-pin machines, is terrible. If you write a lot of letters or anything that other people will see, you should think about an upgrade. Your correspondence, proposals, resumes, or writing of any kind are a reflection on you. You want to look your very best, and your printing should too.

More advances and new technologies in printing have developed over the last 10 years than in the first 550 years. There are hundreds of printer manufacturers, and the competition and new technologies have helped to bring down the cost of printers.

Printer types

There are several types of printers; some are more suitable for certain applications than others.

Dot matrix printers

Dot matrix printers come in a wide range of prices. The low-priced ones are not very fast and the print quality can be poor. They are also limited in fonts and graphics capability. Some of the higher-priced dot matrix printers can print near letter quality (NLQ) at a speed equivalent to some of the lasers. Many of them can also print different fonts and graphics. Some of them can even print fairly good color by using low-cost multicolor ribbons.

There are many applications where a dot matrix printer is all that is needed. For example, wide continuous sheets are necessary for some spreadsheet printouts. My LaserJet can't handle anything wider than 8½ inches. With the wide carriage on my Star dot matrix, wide sheets are no problem.

Number of pins Most dot matrix printers sold today have 24 pins. Some less-expensive printers have a vertical row of seven or nine pins. They are fairly reasonable in price and are sturdy and reliable. A 24-pin printer forms characters from two vertical rows of 12 pins. There are small electric solenoids around each of the wire pins in the head. An electric signal causes the solenoids to push the pins forward. The solenoids press one or more of the pins as the head moves across the paper so that any character can be formed. It is also possible to print some graphics, although this is usually very slow. Figure 14-1 is a representation of the pins in a seven-pin print head and how it forms the letter A.

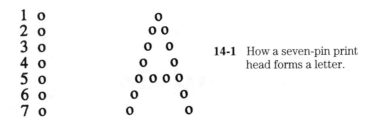

14-1 How a seven-pin print head forms a letter.

The numbers on the left represent the individual pins in the head before it starts moving across the paper. The first pin to be struck would be number 7, then number 6, then 5, 4, 3, 2 and 5, 1, 5, 2, 3, 4, 5, 6, 7.

A 24-pin head is similar to the 7-pin representation above, except that it has two vertical rows of 12 pins, side by side. The pins in one row are slightly offset from the pins in the other row. Because the pins are offset, they overlap slightly to fill in the gaps found in a seven- or nine-pin system.

Why you might need a dot matrix There are some things a dot matrix can do that laser cannot do. For instance, you can print on forms that use carbons or have multiple sheets. Some dot matrix printers have a wide carriage. Many spreadsheets, business inventory lists, and other business forms require 132-column sheets. Most laser printers are limited to 8½-inch by 11-inch sheets. Dot matrix printers can also print on odd sizes, shapes, and thicknesses of paper.

A dot matrix can use continuous sheets or forms. The print job can be started and then you can walk away. Thousands of sheets can be printed. The lasers use individual cut sheets, fed one at a time. Most of them have paper bins that hold 100 to 250 sheets. A dot matrix can print on low-cost paper or almost any kind of paper. Laser printers usually have to have a fairly good grade, which costs a bit more.

Some dot matrix printers use a multicolored ribbon to print color. By mixing the colors on the ribbon, all of the colors of the rainbow can be printed. It is a bit slow, but if you need color to jazz up a presentation or for accent, they are great.

Dot matrix printers can be very noisy. Enclosures are available that help reduce the noise, but they are a bit expensive. I used some packing foam under mine to reduce the noise. Several companies have designed new dot matrix printers that are very quiet.

Some vendors are selling laser printers for about the same price as dot matrix printers. The low cost of the lasers is forcing the dot matrix people to lower their prices. In addition to lower prices, many dot matrix companies are adding more features such as more memory and several fonts in order to attract buyers. If you can get by with a dot matrix printer, you should be able to find one at a very good price.

Daisywheel printers

The daisywheel has excellent letter quality. It has a wheel with all the letters of the alphabet on flexible "petals." To print a letter, the wheel spins, moving the selected letter beneath an electric solenoid hammer. The hammer hits the letter and presses it against a ribbon onto the paper. Daisywheel printers are very slow, cannot print graphics, and are quite noisy. They are practically obsolete.

Hewlett-Packard DeskJet Plus

The DeskJet Plus is a small printer that has quality almost equal to that of a laser. It uses a matrix of small inkjets instead of pins. As the head moves across the paper the ink is sprayed from the jets to form the letters. It comes with the Courier font, but it can use several other fonts that are available on plug-in cartridges. It has a speed of 1 to 2 pages per minute. It is small enough to sit on a desktop, is very quiet, and is relatively inexpensive with a street price of about $500. The inkjet wells are good for about 300 pages of text. They must then be replaced or refilled, which is relatively inexpensive and is easy to do.

Bubblejets

Canon manufactures a couple of printers based on the inkjet technology, but they call it bubblejet. Their BJ-10E is a small portable that sells for $309. Their desktop model—BJ-330e—is advertised for $610. The Diconix division of Kodak also makes a small portable inkjet-type printer. It is advertised for $341. These portables are ideal for attaching to laptops, providing excellent letter-quality print on the road.

Inkjet color

The Hewlett-Packard DeskJet 500C gives full color printing at a speed that is almost as fast as some laser printers. The system uses three small inkjets in a triangle with different colored inks. As the head moves across the paper, the ink is mixed and controlled by the software. It has a resolution of 300 × 300 dpi, the same as the standard laser, and can use many different types of paper and even transparent film. At this time the cost of the DeskJet 500C is about $700.

Canon color inkjet   Canon has an inkjet color printer. Their BJC-800 has some features not found on the HP DeskJet 500C. The Canon BJC can print on paper up to 11 by 17 inches. It has a resolution of 360 × 360 dpi, which is somewhat better than the HP DeskJet 500C.

Canon combination copier, printer, and scanner   Canon has developed the CJ10, a new all-around, do-everything color bubblejet copier/scanner/printer (see Fig. 14-2). This is an amazing machine that not only copies in color, but is also a color printer and scanner. With the available options, it can input graphics to a computer or copy and print from a still camera, a video camera, a video player, a 35mm film projector, an intelligent editor, and other devices. It can scan almost any kind of

14-2 A color copier, printer, and scanner all in one. Canon

color graphic into a computer, and can print out almost any color graphic or text from a computer or other input device.

The specifications include a flat-bed scanner with 400 dpi resolution for printing and scanning. It has eight-bit RGB color, using a four-color process. It can produce half-tones up to 256 gradations and has a magnification of 50 to 200 percent. This machine will satisfy just about all of the needs of an office. It can be used as a high-speed plotter, for presentations, for color brochures, and thousands of other colorful uses.

Laser printers

Hewlett-Packard developed the first laser printer, and they have remained in the forefront in laser technology. Hewlett-Packard is the IBM of the laser printer world, and like IBM, their products have always cost a bit more than other models. Because of their quality and the extras that HP lasers offered, they were well worth the extra cost.

Low-cost laser printers Hundreds of laser printers are now on the market. The competition has been a great benefit to consumers. It has driven down the prices of both lasers and dot matrix printers, and has forced many new improvements. Several new low-cost laser models have been introduced that print 8 ppm to 10 ppm instead of the 4 ppm to 6 ppm of the original models. They are smaller than the originals and can easily sit on a desktop. Most have 512K of memory with an option to add more. The discount price for some of these models is less than $600. I

14-3   A low-cost laser printer. Panasonic

recently bought a Panasonic KX-P4410 for $589 (see Fig. 14-3). A couple of years ago I bought an HP LaserJet III for $1650. They are still selling for about $1500.

The original 4-ppm to 6-ppm laser models have dropped from about $3500 to around $1500. Some are advertised for as little as $800. If you can afford to wait a few seconds, the 4-ppm to 6-ppm models will do almost everything the 8-ppm to 10-ppm models will do. For some applications, the 4-ppm models are almost as fast as the 8-ppm units. The prices will drop even more as the competition increases and the economies of scale in the manufacturing process become greater.

If you have used a high-end laser, such as the HP LaserJet III, you might be disappointed with the limited fonts provided in many of the low-cost lasers. But you can add font cartridges to them or use font software. Most of them let you use Adobe Type Manager (ATM), which comes bundled with OS/2 2.0, or True Type, which comes with Windows 3.1. Most of them also operate with Bitstream FaceLift fonts. With these fonts, you can scale the type on low-cost lasers. This gives you almost all of the benefits of an HP LaserJet III at about one-third the cost.

How lasers operate   Laser printers are a combination of copy machine, computer, and laser technology. On the down side, they have lots of moving mechanical parts and are rather expensive. Laser printers use synchronized, multifaceted mirrors and sophisticated optics to write the characters or images on a rotating, photosensitive drum. The drum is similar to those used in copy machines. A laser beam is swept across the spinning drum and is turned on and off to represent white and dark areas. As the drum spins, the laser writes one line across the drum, then rapidly returns and writes another. It is quite similar to the electron beam that sweeps across the face of a monitor.

The drum is sensitized by each point of light that hits it. The sensitized areas act like an electromagnet. The drum rotates through carbon toner, and the sensitized areas become covered with the toner. Paper is pressed against the drum, and the toner that was picked up by the drum is left on the paper. The paper is then sent through a heating element, where the toner is heated and fused to the paper. Except for the writing to the drum, this is the same thing that happens in a copy machine.

LED printers Some companies have developed LED systems to write on or sensitize a drum. Essentially, the LEDs do the same thing a laser beam does. The laser beam is a single beam that is swept across the drum by a complex system of rotating mirrors. The beam is switched on and off to sensitize areas of the drum. The LED system has a single row of tiny LEDs, at a density of 300 per inch. These LEDs are switched on and off, much like the laser beam. The end result from a laser or LED printer is about the same. But many more companies use the laser engine and it has become the standard.

Engine The drum and its associated mechanical attachments are called an engine. Canon is one of the foremost makers of engines. They manufacture them for their own laser printers and copy machines, and for dozens of other companies including Hewlett-Packard and Apple.

The Hewlett-Packard LaserJet was one of the first low-cost lasers. It was a fantastic success and became the de facto standard. Hundreds of laser printers are now on the market, and most of them emulate the LaserJet standard. Even IBM's laser printer emulates the HP standard.

Extras for lasers Don't be surprised if you go into a store to buy a laser printer that was advertised for $1000 and end up paying a lot more. The laser printer business is much like the automobile and the computer business. I have seen laser printer ads in the Los Angeles area for a very low price, but somewhere in the ad, in very small print, it says "w/o toner cartridge and cables." It might cost you $150 for the toner cartridge and up to $50 for a $5 cable." Extra fonts, memory, special controller boards, and software all cost extra. Some printers have small bin feeders. A large one might cost as much as $200.

Memory If you plan to do any graphics or desktop publishing, you need to have at least 1Mb of memory in your machine. Before it prints the first sheet, the printer loads the data into its memory and determines where each dot is placed on the sheet.

Not all lasers use the same memory configuration. For some machines, you must buy special plug-in boards. Check the type of memory you need before you buy. Several companies that offer laser memories include

ASP	(800) 445-6190
Elite	(800) 942-0018

Page description languages If you plan to do any complex desktop publishing, you need a page description language (PDL) of some kind. Text characters and graphics are two different things. Monitor controller boards usually have all of the alphabet and numeric characters stored in ROM. When you press the letter A on the keyboard, the computer dives into the ROM chip, drags out the A, and displays it in a precise block of pixels wherever the cursor is. These are called *bit- mapped* characters. If you wanted to display an A that is twice as large, you have to have a complete font set of that type in the computer.

Printers are very much like monitors and have the same limitations. They have a library of stored discrete characters for each font that they can print. My dot matrix printer has an internal font and two cartridge slots. Different font cartridges can be plugged into these slots, but it is limited to those fonts that happen to be plugged in.

With a good PDL, a printer can take one of the stored fonts and change it, or scale it, to any size you want. These are *scalable fonts*. With a bitmapped font, you have one type face and one size. With scalable fonts, you have one typeface with an infinite number of sizes. Most lasers printers can accept ROM cartridges that may have as many as 35 fonts. You can print almost anything you want with these fonts if your system can scale them.

Speed   Laser printers can print from 6 ppm to 10 ppm depending on the model and what they are printing. Some very expensive high-end printers can print over 30 ppm. A dot matrix printer is concerned with a single character at a time. Laser printers compose, then print, a whole page at a time. With a PDL, many different fonts, sizes of type, and graphics can be printed. But the laser must determine where every dot that makes up a character or image is to be placed before it is printed. This composition is done in memory. The more complex the page, the more memory is required and the more time is needed to compose the page. It might take several minutes to compose a complex graphic. Once composed, it prints out very quickly.

A PDL controls the laser and tells it where to place the dots on the sheet. Adobe's PostScript is the best known PDL. Several companies have developed their own PDLs, but of course, none of them are compatible with the others. This causes a major problem for software developers because they must try to include drivers for each of these PDLs. Several companies are attempting to clone PostScript, but it is doubtful they will achieve 100 percent compatibility. Unless you need to move your files from a machine that does not have PostScript to one that does, you might not need to be compatible. Hewlett-Packard includes their Printer Control Language (PCL) 5, a scalable system, on most of their printers.

Resolution   Almost all lasers printers have a 300 × 300 dpi resolution. This is very good, but not nearly as good as the 1200 × 1200 dpi used for typeset publications. Several companies have developed systems to increase resolution to 400 × 400 dpi or 600 × 600 dpi or more.

At 300 × 300 dpi, it is possible to print 90,000 dots in one square inch. On an 8½-by-11-inch paper, if you deduct a 1-inch margin from the top, the bottom, and both sides, you have 58.5 square inches × 90,000 dots = 5,265,000 possible dots.

Maintenance   Most laser printers use a toner cartridge that is good for 3000 to 5000 pages. The cost of a cartridge is about $100. Several small companies now refill spent cartridges for about $39. I have seen some advertised for as little as $29.95. Toner cartridges are sealed, so they last for some time on the shelf.

Most laser printers keep track of the number of sheets they print. If you have a LaserJet, the front panel buttons can be used to run a self-test. This test tells you the configuration, how much RAM is installed, the font cartridges installed, the type of paper tray, how many pages have been printed, and several other things. When the toner gets low, the HP LaserJet III displays a message on the digital readout window.

I had to install a new toner cartridge on my LaserJet III at exactly 4000 sheets. Unfortunately, I had not been keeping track of my usage and did not have a spare toner cartridge. You can guess what happened. The cartridge gave out on a weekend when I was facing a critical deadline (Murphy's Law). I finally found a store that was open on Saturday, but I had to drive about 50 miles to get there. (I have formulated a new law that I believe Murphy overlooked. If you need something, or there is a really good sale at a store, the store will always be located on the other side of town.) I now keep a spare cartridge on hand. If you remove the toner cartridge, turn it upside down, and shake it vigorously, sometimes you can get a few more copies out of it. This might help until you can get a new or refilled cartridge.

Of course, there are other maintenance costs. Because these machines are very similar to copy machines, they have a lot of moving parts that can wear out and jam up. Most of the larger companies give MTBF figures of 30,000 to 100,000 pages. Remember, these are only average figures and are not a guarantee. Most laser printers are expected to have an overall lifetime of about 300,000 pages.

Paper Many different types and weights of paper are available. Almost any paper will work in your laser, but if you use a cheap paper, it can leave lint inside the machine and cause problems in print quality. Generally speaking, any bond paper or a good paper made for copiers works fine. Colored paper made for copiers also works fine. You don't need to pay extra to get "laser" paper.

Most laser printers will accept any paper from 18-pound to 24-pound. I have even used 67-pound stock to make my own business cards. It is a bit heavy for wrapping around the drums, and it jams once in a while. Some lasers use a straight-through path, so heavier paper should not cause any problems.

Many laser printers are equipped with trays to print envelopes. Hewlett-Packard recommends envelopes with diagonal seams and gummed flaps. Make certain that the leading edge of the envelope has a sharp crease. Some companies also make address labels that can withstand the heat of the fusing mechanism in a laser printer. There are also other specialty supplies that can be used with your laser. Integraphix ((800) 421-2515) carries several different items that you might find useful. Call them for a catalog.

Sources There are just too many laser companies to list them all. Look for ads in the local papers and in any computer magazine for the nearest dealer.

Color Few color printers are available. They cost from $4000 to $15,000. These printers are often referred to as color laser printers, but they don't actually use the laser technology. They use a variety of thermal transfer technologies using wax or rolls of plastic polymer. The wax or plastic is brought into contact with the paper, heat is applied, and the melted wax or plastic material adheres to the paper. Very precise points, up to 300 dpi, can be heated. By overlaying three or four colors, all of the colors of the rainbow can be created. The cost of color printing ranges from about 5 cents a sheet to about 50 cents a sheet.

Most color printers have PostScript, or they emulate PostScript. The Tektronix Phaser CP can also use the Hewlett-Packard graphics language (HPGL) to emulate a plotter. These color printers can print out a page much faster than a plotter. A few of the companies that have color printers include

CalComp	(800) 225-2627
Howtek Pixelmaster	(603) 882-5200
NEC Technologies	(508) 264-8000
QMS ColorScript	(800) 631-2692
Seiko Instruments	(408) 922-5800
Tektronix	(800) 835-6100

Plotters

Plotters are devices that can draw almost any shape or design under the control of a computer. A plotter has from one to eight (or more) different colored pens. There are several different types of pens for various applications, such as writing on different types of paper or on film or transparencies. Some pens are similar to ballpoint pens, others have a fiber-type point. The points are usually made to a very close tolerance and can be very small so line thickness can be controlled. Line thickness can be very critical in some precise design work. The plotter arm can be directed to choose any one of the various pens. This arm is attached to a sliding rail and is moved from one side of the paper to the other. A solenoid lowers the pen at predetermined points on the paper so it can write. While one motor is moving the arm horizontally, a second motor moves the paper vertically beneath the arm. This motor moves the paper to predetermined points and the pen is lowered to write at that point. The motors are controlled by predefined X-Y coordinates. The pen and paper can be moved in very small increments, so almost any design can be drawn.

Plotters are ideal for such things as circuit board designs, architectural drawings, transparencies for overhead presentations, graphs, charts, and many CAD/CAM drawings. All of this can be done in as many as eight different colors.

Several different size plotters are available. Some desktop units are limited to only A- and B-sized plots. Other large floor-standing models can accept paper as wide as four feet and several feet long. A desk model costs as little as $200 to $2000. A floor-standing model costs from $4000 to $10,000. If you are doing very precise work, for instance, designing a transparency that will be photographed and used to make a circuit board, you want one of the more accurate and more expensive machines.

There are several manufacturers of plotters, but again, there are no standards. Just as with printers, each company has developed its own drivers. This is very frustrating for software developers who must try to include drivers in their programs for all the various brands. Hewlett-Packard is one of the major plotter manufacturers, and many of the other manufacturers now emulate the Hewlett-Packard drivers. Almost all of the software that requires a plotter includes a driver for Hewlett-Packard. If you are in the market for a plotter, try to make sure that it can emulate Hewlett-Packard. Houston Instruments is another major manufacturer of plotters. Their plotters are somewhat less expensive than the Hewlett-Packard plotters.

One of the disadvantages of plotters is that they are rather slow. There are now some software programs that allow laser printers to act as plotters. Laser printers are much faster than plotters, but except for the colored printers, they are limited to black and white.

Plotter sources   Here is a list of some of the plotter manufacturers. Call them for a product list and their latest prices.

AlphaMerics	(818) 999-5580
Bruning Computer	(415) 372-7568
CalComp	(800) 225-2667
Hewlett-Packard	(800) 367-4772
Houston Instrument	(512) 835-0900
Ioline Corp.	(206) 775-7861
Roland DG	(213) 685-5141

Plotter supplies   It is important that a good supply of plotter pens, special paper, film, and other supplies be kept on hand. Plotter supplies are not as widely available as printer supplies. A very high-priced plotter might have to sit idle if the supplies are not on hand. Most plotter vendors provide supplies for their equipment. One company that specializes in plotter pens, plotter media, accessories and supplies is

Plotpro, P.O. Box 800370, Houston, TX 77280   (800)223-7568

Installing a printer or plotter

Most IBM compatible computers allow for four ports—two serial and two parallel. No matter whether it is a plotter, or a dot matrix, daisywheel, or laser printer, it requires one of these ports. If you have a 286 or 386 computer, these ports might be built into the motherboard (see chapter 13 and the discussion on installing modems).

If you have built-in ports, you need a short cable from the motherboard to the outside. You also need a longer cable to your printer. If you don't have built-in ports, you have to buy an interface board.

Almost all laser and dot matrix printers use the parallel ports. Some of them can use serial and parallel ports. Many of the daisywheel printers and most of the plotters use serial ports. If the serial port is used, the printer can be up to 50 feet from the computer. If the parallel port is used, the printer can only be about 10 feet away. The serial printers use an RS-232C connector; the parallel printers use a Centronics-type connector. When you buy your printer, buy a cable from the vendor that is configured for your printer and your computer.

Printer sharing

Ordinarily a printer sits idle most of the time. Some days I don't even turn my printer on. There are usually several computers in most large offices and almost all of them are connected to a printer in some fashion. It is a waste of money if each one has a separate printer that is only used occasionally. It is fairly simple to make arrangements so that a printer or plotter can be used by several computers.

If there are only two or three computers, and they are fairly close together, it is not much of a problem. Manual switch boxes are available that cost from $25 to $150 that allow two or three computers to be switched online to a printer. If the computers use the parallel ports, the cables from the computers to the printer should be no more than 10 feet long. Parallel signals begin to degrade if the cable is longer than 10 feet, causing some loss of data. A serial cable can be as long as 50 feet.

If an office or business is fairly complex, then there are several electronic switching devices available. Some of them are very sophisticated and allow a large number of different types of computers to be attached to a single printer or plotter. Many of them have built-in buffers and amplifiers that allow cable lengths of up to 250 feet. They range in cost from $160 to $1400. Of course, there are also several networks that are available to connect computers and printers together. Many of them are very expensive to install.

One of the least expensive methods of sharing a printer is for the person to generate the text to be printed on one computer, record it on a floppy disk, walk it to a computer connected to a printer, and print it. If it is a large office, a single low-cost XT clone can be dedicated to running a high-priced laser printer.

Printer sharing device sources

Here are the names and phone numbers of some of the companies that provide switch systems. Call them for their product specs and current price list.

Altek Corp.	(301) 572-2555
Arnet Corp.	(615) 834-8000
Belkin Components	(310) 515-7585
Black Box Corp.	(412) 746-5530
Buffalo Products	(800) 345-2356
Crosspoint Systems	(800) 232-7729
Digital Products	(800) 243-2333
Extended Systems	(208) 322-7163
Fifth Generation	(800) 225-2775
Server Technology	(800) 835-1515
Quadram	(404) 564-5566
Rose Electronics	(713) 933-7673
Western Telematic	(800) 854-7226

15
Essential software

A SOFTWARE UPGRADE MIGHT BE ONE OF THE BETTER THINGS YOU CAN DO TO enhance your computer operations. There is more software, already written and immediately available, than you can use in a lifetime. Software companies are constantly revising and updating their products. Except for very unusual applications, the ordinary user should never have to do any programming. Off-the-shelf programs are available that can do almost anything you could ever want to do with a computer.

For most general applications, there are certain basic programs you will need. Speaking of basic, BASIC is one of them. GW-BASIC from Microsoft is more or less the standard. Before MS-DOS 5.0, GW-BASIC was included with all versions of DOS. It has been changed and is now called QBASIC. To run old BASIC programs, they have to be converted to QBASIC. Many applications still use BASIC. Even if you are not a programmer, BASIC is simple enough that anyone can design a few special applications with it.

There are several categories of programs you will need including a disk operating system (DOS), word processing, databases, spreadsheets, utilities, shells, communications, Windows, graphics, and computer-aided design. Depending on what you intend to use your computer for, there are hundreds of others for special needs.

Software can be more expensive than the hardware. The prices vary from vendor to vendor. It pays to shop around. I have seen software with a list price of $700 advertised by discount houses for as little as $350. Also remember that there are excellent free public domain programs that can do almost everything the high-cost commercial programs can do. Check your local bulletin board, user group, or the ads for public domain software in the computer magazines. Some excellent shareware programs are available that can be registered for a very nominal sum.

I can't possibly list all of the thousands of software packages available. Again, check the magazines listed in chapter 17. Most of them have detailed reviews of software in every issue. Briefly, here are some of the essential software packages that you will need.

Operating systems

DOS is to a computer is what gasoline is to an automobile. Without it, it won't operate. DOS is an acronym for disk operating system, but it does much more than just operate the disks. In recognition of this, OS/2 has dropped the D. If you are new to computers, DOS should be the first thing you learn. DOS has over 50 commands, but chances are you will never need to know more than 15 or 20 of them.

You can use any version of DOS on your computer. I don't know why anyone would want to, but you can even use MS-DOS 1.0. Of course, you will be severely limited in what you can do. I recommend you buy the latest version of MS-DOS, DR DOS, or OS/2.

When the operating system, config.sys, buffers, drivers, TSRs, and other functions are loaded into the 640K of available RAM, there is often not enough memory left to load other programs. OS/2, DR DOS 6.0, and MS-DOS 5.0 can take the operating system, TSRs, buffers, drivers, and other functions out of low memory and place them in memory above 640K. The older versions of DOS loaded everything into low memory.

There are many good commands in DOS, but there are some that, if not used properly, can be disastrous. Be very careful when using commands such as FORMAT, DEL, ERASE, COPY, and RECOVER. When invoked, RECOVER renames and turns all your files into FILE0001.REC, FILE0002.REC. . . . The disk might not be bootable and critical files might be garbled. Many experts say you should erase the RECOVER command from your disk files and leave it only on your original disks. It should only be used as a last resort. Norton Utilities, Mace Utilities, PC Tools, or one of the other utility programs is a much better choice to unerase or restore a damaged file.

COPY can cause problems if you copy a file onto a disk that has another file with the same name. The file with the same name on the disk will be replaced and gone forever. If you erase or delete a file, you might be able to recover it, but if it is copied over or written over, it is history. If you use a program like XTree for copying files, it asks if you want to replace the file with the same name before copying over it. WordStar also warns you of this problem before copying over a file with the same name.

MS-DOS

Bill Gates and Microsoft have come a long way since they first developed MS-DOS 1.0 for IBM. MS-DOS has gone through a lot of changes and has consistently improved. You can use any earlier version of MS-DOS on your system, but you will be severely limited in many ways. The present system, MS-DOS 5.0, has some excellent advantages over any previous version. If you are still using an older version, by all means, you should upgrade. It is really not that expensive.

DR DOS 6.0

The DR is for Digital Research, not doctor. The Digital Research Corporation ((800) 443-4200) was founded by Gary Kildahl, the developer of CP/M, the first operating system for personal computers. DR DOS 6.0 is completely compatible with MS-DOS. DR DOS 6.0 is the latest version, and it has several good features. One is FileLINK, which allows you to connect and transfer files over a serial cable. It also has ViewMAX to view, organize, and execute files and commands using only one or two keystrokes or a mouse. It has comprehensive online help, supports hard disk partitions up to 512Mb, has disk cache, a full-screen text editor, password protection, and many features not found in MS-DOS. If you work in a large office you might want to keep some of your nosy neighbors from snooping into your personal files. DR DOS 6.0 allows you to use a password to protect your files.

The ViewMAX shell feature lets DR DOS use icons to operate very much like Windows 3.1. You can use a mouse to quickly open files, copy, delete, and perform many of the other commands and functions. ViewMAX also has a clock that can run in a window of the screen. Another feature is a calculator for on-screen calculations.

DR DOS is very easy to install on a hard disk by just copying it onto the disk. There is no need to reformat your disk. If you have a previous version of DOS on your disk, DR DOS will copy over and replace the older version of DOS. It has the same commands and is fully compatible with DOS. DR DOS also comes bundled with SuperStor, a file compression program that allows you to double the capacity of your disks. If you bought the SuperStor program separately, it would cost over $100. The discount of DR DOS 6.0 plus SuperStor is less than $100. It is a real bargain!

Digital Research has merged with Novell, the network company. At the present time, they are developing new and more-powerful versions of DR DOS for both single users and high-end networks.

OS/2 2.0

OS/2 2.0 was introduced at the Spring COMDEX in April 1992. It comes complete with MS-DOS 5.0 and Windows 3.0. (They have promised to update to Windows 3.1 shortly.) OS/2 also has Adobe Type Manager that allows scalable fonts for Windows and for printing, as well as several other excellent utilities and goodies.

OS/2 2.0 breaks the 640K barrier and can seamlessly address over 4Gb of RAM. It can do true multitasking and run several programs at the same time. If one program crashes, the other programs are not affected. It can run all DOS software and any of the software developed for Windows. It even includes a few games, such as Solitaire and Chess, if you have nothing else to do.

IBM claims that OS/2 runs Windows applications better than Windows under MS-DOS. Many people bought Macintosh computers because they are easy to use and learn. IBM's OS/2 has many similarities with the Macintosh, and for some applications, it might be easier to use than the Macintosh.

At the present time there is very little software that can take advantage of OS/2's 32-bit capabilities. However, at the Spring COMDEX introduction, over 800 companies pledged to develop 32-bit software for OS/2.

One disadvantage of OS/2 is that it requires over 25Mb of hard disk space and about 6Mb of RAM. But hard disk and memory prices are dropping every day, so the advantages of its vast capabilities far outweigh the disadvantages of its being a memory hog. Also, it is very inexpensive. IBM gave away thousands of copies at COMDEX. They are also pricing it from $49 to $149. For this price you get MS-DOS 5.0, Windows 3.0, Adobe Type Manager, and many other utilities. My copy came on twenty-one 1.44Mb floppy disks. The 21 disks alone, even if they were blank, are worth $49.

Windows 3.1

Windows 3.0 was one of the most phenomenal successes of all time, but it has some flaws. Microsoft ((800) 426-9400) has extensively revised 3.1 and has added several new features. One added option is TrueType scalable fonts for the screen and for printing. They added an extensive list of printer drivers and it can print faster, and has a better SMARTDrive, with read and write caching.

One flaw in 3.0 was that it often caused the computer to hang-up with unrecoverable application errors (UAEs). When a UAE occurred, the whole system had to be rebooted. If you had work that had not been saved to disk or you had two or more windows open, everything was lost. The new 3.1 does away with UAEs. If there is an error, the program analyzes it, and gives you several options. Dr. Watson, a diagnostic utility, asks you to describe the details of what happened. These comments are saved as a record and can be useful to help Microsoft or other developers eliminate any problems. If the program does crash, only that operation goes down without affecting other open windows.

They added an object linking and embedding (OLE) utility. This allows data or graphics in one file to be imported and embedded in another. They also built in sound capabilities by using sound boards such as Sound Blaster ((408) 986-1461), Pro AudioSpectrum ((800) 638-2807), Soundcards ((213) 685-5141), and Multi-Sound ((717) 843-6916).

Windows NT   There are several other improvements in 3.1, but it is still a 16-bit system. At this moment Microsoft is working overtime to complete Windows NT (New Technology). It is a 32-bit system that will compete head-to-head with OS/2 2.0.

New Wave 4.0   Hewlett-Packard's New Wave adds several important features that make Windows 3.1 even better. It lets you use more than 11 characters to name a file. It lets you create objects, put them in folders, and manage them. You can use it to create multiple views of objects and macros to automate tasks, and it has several other very good utilities not found in Windows 3.1. It is an essential adjunct to Windows 3.1.

Norton Desktop for Windows 2.0   Norton Desktop for Windows has all of the utilities found in Norton Utilities for DOS plus several others. It also includes Norton Backup. It too is an essential adjunct to Windows 3.1.

DESQview

DESQview, from Quarterdeck Office Systems ((213) 392-9851), is similar to Windows in some respects. It runs on top of DOS, and it allows multitasking and multiusers. You can have up to 50 programs running at the same time and have as many as 250 windows open. It runs all DOS software, and is simple to learn and use. It is one of the better programs for managing DOS memory. It can load TSRs and other memory resident software into memory above 640K. DESQview seems to be able to find little niches and spaces above 640K that most other memory managers can't find or use.

DOS help programs

Learning DOS can be difficult, but several help programs are available. One such program is Doctor DOS from VMG ((405) 722-8244). The Phoenix Company ((617)

551-4000), one of the first developers of a clone BIOS, also has an excellent help program for learning DOS. There are many others, even some public domain programs. Look for ads in the computer magazines.

Word processors

The most used of all software is word processing. There are literally hundreds of word processor packages, each one slightly different from the others. It amazes me that they can find so many different ways to do the same thing. Most of the word processor programs come with a spell checker; some of them come with a thesaurus. They usually also include other utilities for such things as communications programs for your modem, outlining, desktop publishing, print merging, and others.

WordStar

I started off with WordStar 3.0 ((800) 227-5609) on my little CP/M Morrow with a hefty 64K of memory and two 140K single-sided disk drives. It took me some time to learn it. I have tried several other word processors since then and found that most of them require almost as much time to learn as WordStar did originally. WordStar does all I need, and I have been using it for so long, it is second nature to me. I can do most of the commands with my eyes closed and one hand tied behind my back. I am presently using version 7.0, which added many features. It allows the use of a mouse so you can point and click and easily control the position of the cursor. Version 7.0 is available for both DOS and Windows 3.1.

WordStar has an educational division that offers an excellent discount to schools, both for site licenses and for student purchases. The educational division can be reached at ((800) 543-8188.

WordPerfect

WordPerfect ((800) 225-5000) is one of the hottest selling word processors, so it must be doing something right. One thing they are doing right is giving free unlimited toll-free support. WordPerfect can select fonts by a proper name, has simplified printer installation, can do most desktop publishing functions including columns, and has many other useful functions and utilities. It also works with Windows.

Microsoft Word for Windows

This package was developed by the same people who gave us MS-DOS—Microsoft ((206) 882-8080). It lets you take advantage of all the features and utilities of Windows. It is among the best selling software in the country. If you have previously learned a different word processor, Word for Windows includes a manual that lists the differences in the most popular word processors. It can help you quickly become accustomed to Word for Windows.

PC-Write

PC-Write, from Quicksoft Inc. ((800) 888-8088), is the least expensive of all the word processors. It is shareware and is free if copied from an existing user. They ask for a $16 donation, and full registration with manual and technical support is $89. It is easy to learn and is an excellent personal word processor. Many other good word processors are available. Look for ads and reviews in the computer magazines.

Grammar checkers

You might be the most intelligent person alive, but you might not be able to write a simple intelligible sentence. Several grammar checking programs are available that work with most of the word processors. They analyze your writing and suggest ways to improve it. A couple of them include Right Writer, from Que Corp. ((800) 992-0244), and Grammatik, from Reference Software ((800) 872-9933).

Database programs

Database packages are very useful for business purposes, allowing you to manage large amounts of information. Most programs allow you to store information, search it, sort it, do calculations, make up reports, and several other very useful features. There are almost as many database programs as there are word processors. Few of them are compatible with each other. A strong effort is underway in the industry to establish some standards under the Structured Query Language (SQL) standard. Several of the larger companies have announced their support for this standard.

dBASE IV

Ashton-Tate, with their dBASE II, was one of the first companies to develop a database program for the personal computer. It is very powerful and has hundreds of features. It is a highly structured program and can be a bit difficult to learn. dBASE IV is much faster than dBASE III, has a built-in compiler, SQL, and an upgraded user interface, along with several other enhancements. Ashton-Tate is now a division of Borland ((408) 438-5300).

askSam

This funny looking name is an acronym for access knowledge via stored access method. It is a free-form, text-oriented database management system. It is almost like a word processor. Data is typed in randomly, then sorted and accessed. Data can also be entered in a structured format for greater organization. It is not quite as powerful as dBASE IV, but is much easier to use. It is also much less expensive, and is ideal for personal use and for the majority of business needs.

Seaside Software ((800) 327-5726) has a discount program for students. Students can buy the $295 program for only $45 when the order is placed by an instructor. Any instructor who places an order for 10 or more copies gets a free copy.

R:BASE 3.1

R:BASE has been around for a long time. It has recently been revised and updated. It now has pull-down menus, mouse support, is fully relational for multitable tasks, and has an English-like procedural language. It is one of the more powerful and more versatile of the database programs. Microrim ((206) 885-2000) is so sure you like the program, they offer an unlimited, no-questions-asked, 90-day, money-back guarantee.

FoxPro

FoxPro, from Fox Software ((800) 426-9400), is very easy to use. It has windows and can be controlled by a mouse or the keyboard. The View window is the master control panel to create databases, open files, browse, set options, and other functions. You don't have to be a programmer to type commands into the Command window. The Browse window lets you view, edit, append, or delete files. It also has memo fields and a built-in editor, allows you to create macros, has extensive context-sensitive help, and much more. FoxPro is now a division of Microsoft.

Paradox

Paradox is fairly easy to learn and use, and is fast and powerful. It is designed for both beginners and expert users. It is a full-featured relational database that can be used on a single PC or on a network. The main menu has functions like view, ask, report, create, modify, image, forms, tools, scripts, and help. Choosing one of these items brings up options that are associated with that item. Extensive use is made of the function keys. The query by example is very helpful for beginners and experts alike. Paradox also has a very powerful programming language, PAL. Experienced programmers can easily design special applications. Paradox is one of the Borland ((408) 438-5300) family of products.

Spreadsheets

Spreadsheets are primarily number crunchers. They have a matrix of cells in which data is entered. Data in a particular cell can be acted on by formulas and mathematical equations. If the data in the cell that is acted on affects other cells, recalculations are done on them. Several of the tax software programs use a simple form of spreadsheet. Your income and all your deductions are entered. If an additional deduction is discovered, it is entered and all the calculations are done over automatically.

In business, spreadsheets are essential for inventory, expenses, accounting, forecasting, charting, and dozens of other vital business uses. A large number of spreadsheet programs are available. Here are just a few.

Lotus 1-2-3

Lotus was one of the first and most popular spreadsheets. It is now available in a Windows version.

Excel

Excel, from Microsoft ((206) 882-8080), is a very powerful spreadsheet program with pull-down menus, windows, and dozens of features. It can even perform as a database.

Quattro Pro

The Quattro Pro spreadsheet, another Borland ((408) 438-8400) product, looks very much like Lotus 1-2-3, but it has better graphics capabilities for charts, calculates faster, has pull-down menus, can print sideways, and has several other features not found in Lotus 1-2-3. One of the better features is the price, about $99.

SuperCalc5

SuperCalc, introduced in 1981, was one of the pioneer spreadsheets. It has never enjoyed the popularity of Lotus, though it has features not found in Lotus. It is compatible with Lotus 1-2-3 files, and can link to dBASE and several other files. It is an excellent spreadsheet. Computer Associates ((408) 432-1727) has also developed several excellent accounting packages costing from $595 to $695. There are many other spreadsheet programs. Check the ads and reviews in the computer magazines.

Utilities

Utilities are essential tools that can unerase a file, detect bad sectors on a hard disk, diagnose, unfragment, sort, and do many other things. Norton Utilities was the first, and is still the foremost, in the utility department. Mace Utilities has several functions not found in Norton. Mace Gold is an integrated package of utilities that includes POP (a power-out protection program), a backup utility, TextFix, and dbFix for data retrieval. PC Tools has even more utilities than Norton or Mace.

Ontrack, the people who have sold several million copies of Disk Manager for hard disks, also have a utility program called DOSUTILS. It provides tools to display and modify any physical sector of a hard disk, to scan for bad sectors, and to diagnose and analyze the disk.

Steve Gibson's SpinRite, Prime Solution's Disk Technician, and Gazelle's OPTune are excellent hard disk tools for low-level formatting, for defragmenting, and for detecting potential bad sectors on a hard disk.

Norton Utilities

This is a program everybody should have. Norton also has Norton Commander, a shell program, and Norton Backup, a very good hard disk backup program. The Norton Company ((213) 453-2361) has recently merged with Symantec.

Mace Utilities

Mace Utilities was developed by Paul Mace, and was recently acquired by Fifth Generation Systems ((504) 291-7221), the people who developed FastBack, the leading backup program.

PC Tools

This is an excellent program from Central Point Software ((503) 690-8090) that just about does it all. It has data recovery utilities, hard disk backup, a DOS shell, a disk manager, and more.

SpinRite II

This software, from Gibson Research ((714) 362-8800), can check the interleave and reset it for the optimum factor, and can do it without destroying your data. It can also test a hard drive and detect any marginal areas. SpinRite can maximize hard disk performance and prevent hard disk problems before they happen. Steve Gibson, the developer of SpinRite, writes a very interesting weekly column for *InfoWorld*.

Disk Technician

Disk Technician, from Prime Solutions ((619) 274-5000), does essentially the same things SpinRite does, and a bit more. It has several automatic features and can now detect most viruses. It can be installed as a TSR and work in the background to detect errors as they happen when writing to a hard disk.

OPTune

Optune is another utility that can maximize hard disk performance. It is similar to SpinRite and Disk Technician. Gazelle Systems ((800) 233-0383) also developed QDOS 3, an excellent shell program, and Back-It 4, a very good hard disk backup program.

CheckIt Pro

This program, from Touch Stone Software ((800) 531-0450), quickly checks and reports on your computer's configuration, the type of CPU, the amount of memory, and the installed drives and peripherals. It runs diagnostic tests of the installed items and can do performance benchmark tests.

Directory and disk management programs

There are dozens of disk management programs to help you keep track of files and data on your hard disk, with features such as find, rename, view, sort, copy, delete, and many other useful utilities. These can save an enormous amount of time and make life a lot simpler.

XTreePro Gold

Executive Systems ((800) 634-5545) XTree was one of the first and is still one of the best disk management programs. It has recently been revised and is now much faster and has several new features. It now has a Windows version.

QDOS III

This disk management program, from Gazelle Systems ((800) 233-0383), is similar to XTree. It does not have quite as many features as XTree, but it is less expensive.

Tree86 3.0

This is a low-cost disk management program from Aldrige Company ((713) 953-1940). It is similar to XTree.

Wonder Plus 3.08

Wonder, or 1DIR, was one of the early disk management shells. Bourbaki ((208) 342-5849) revised and updated it.

Search utilities

I have about 3000 files on my hard disk in several subdirectories. You can imagine how difficult it is to keep track of all of them. I sometimes forget in which subdirectory I filed something. There are a couple of programs that can search your directories and look for a file by name. Several other programs are available that can search through your files and find almost anything you tell them to. You don't even have to know the full name of what you are looking for. They can accept wild cards and tell you where there are matches.

Magellan 2.0

Magellan 2.0, from Lotus ((800) 233-1662), is a very sophisticated program that can navigate and do global searches through files and across directories. It finds text and lets you view it in a window. It also lets you compress files, backup, compare, undelete, and several other excellent utilities. Other search programs are available that are not quite as sophisticated as Magellan. There are also public domain and shareware search programs.

Computer-aided design
AutoCAD

AutoCAD, from Autodesk ((800) 228-3601) is a high-end, high-cost design program. It is quite complex, with an abundance of capabilities and functions. It is also rather expensive at about $3000. Autodesk is the IBM of the CAD world and has established the standard for the many clones that have followed.

Generic CADD

Autodesk has several modules and other programs that cost less than the full-blown AutoCAD. One of them is Generic CADD 6.0.

Home Series

Autodesk has a set of five low-cost programs they call the Home Series, which include home, kitchen, bathroom, deck, and landscape. The programs let you design your dream home, an up-to-date kitchen, a bathroom, or a deck, or plan your landscape. Each of the five programs has a list price of $59.95. The programs come with a library of professional symbols such as doors, outlets, furniture, fixtures, and appliances that you import and place in your drawing. The program tracks the materials specified in your drawing and automatically creates a shopping list. I recommend these programs for anyone who plans to design their own home or do any remodeling on an older home. They can save you hours of time and lots of money.

DesignCAD 2D and DesignCAD 3D

These CAD programs, from American Small Business Computers ((918) 825-4844), do just about everything AudoCAD can do at about one-tenth the cost. DesignCAD 3D allows you to make three-dimensional drawings. Several other companies offer CAD software. Check the computer magazines for ads and reviews.

Miscellaneous

Many programs are available for things such as accounting, statistics, finance, and many other applications. Some are very expensive, some are very reasonable.

Money Counts

This is a very inexpensive program from Parsons Technology ((800) 233-6925) that can be used at home or in a small business. With it you can set up a budget, keep track of your expenses, balance your checkbook, and several other functions. It costs $40.

It's Legal

This is another program from Parsons Technology. It helps you create wills, leases, promissory notes, and other legal documents.

WillMaker 4.0

A low-cost program from Nolo Press ((415) 549-1976) helps you create a will. A will is an important document. Everyone should have a will, no matter what their age or how much they own. Many people put off writing a will because they don't want to take the time, or they don't want to pay a lawyer a large fee. This inexpensive software helps you create a legal will.

The Random House Encyclopedia

Microlytics ((716) 248-9150) put a whole encyclopedia on disk. You can find any subject very quickly.

ACT!

This program from Contact Software ((800) 228-9228) lets you keep track of business contacts, schedules, and business expenses, write reports, and about 30 other features.

Form Express

Most businesses have dozens of forms that must be filled out. Quite often, the information is transferred to a computer. Forms Express ((415) 382-6600) lets you design and fill in almost any kind of form on a hard disk. If necessary, the form can then be printed out.

Summary

I can't possibly mention all of the fantastic software that is available. There are thousands and thousands of ready-made software programs that allow you to do almost anything with your computer. Look through the computer magazines for reviews and ads. You should be able to find programs for almost any application.

16
Other enhancements

IN PREVIOUS CHAPTERS I TALKED ABOUT JUST A FEW OF THE THOUSANDS OF things you can add to your computer to upgrade and enhance it. I also discussed a few of the things you can do with your computer. There are many, many ways to make your computer more useful and get more out of it. I can't possibly list them all, but here are just a few other uses for your computer:

Home office

Many businesses can be operated from a home office. Several advantages in having a home office include no commuting, no high office rent, no need for day care, and setting your own hours.

Deducting the cost of your computer

If you have a home office, you might be able to deduct part of the cost of your computer from your income tax. You might even be able to deduct a portion of your rent, telephone bills, and other legitimate business expenses.

Some IRS rules

I can't give you all the IRS rules for a home office, but there are several deductions available if you use a portion of your home exclusively and regularly to operate your business. These deductions might include portions of your real estate taxes, mortgage interest, operating expenses (such as home insurance premiums and utility costs), and depreciation allocated to the area used for business. You might even be able to deduct a portion of the cost of painting the outside of your house or repairing the roof.

Before you deduct any expenses, I recommend you buy the latest tax books and consult with the IRS or a tax expert. There are many, many rules and regulations, and they change frequently. For more information, call the IRS and ask for publication #587, *Business Use of Your Home*. Look in your telephone directory for the local or 800 number for the IRS.

Home office as a tax preparer

Congress and the IRS change the tax rules every year, and every year they become more and more complicated. It is almost impossible for the ordinary person to be aware of and understand all the rules and regulations. Some of the rules are even difficult for the IRS to understand. If you call several IRS offices with a complicated question, about 50 percent of the answers you get will be wrong.

If a person works at a single job and has a single source of income, the forms are fairly simple. But if you have several sources of income or a small business, preparing your taxes can be a nightmare. It is an impossible task for some people and they must hire a tax preparer.

Being a tax preparer is almost like having a guaranteed income. If you have any aptitude for accounting or tax preparation, you might consider taking a course. Many community colleges offer courses in accounting, and H & R Block is probably the best place to learn tax preparation. They conduct classes throughout the year in various locations. Many tax preparers charge from $50 to $100 dollars an hour.

Tax programs

Because you have a computer, it might not be necessary for you to pay a tax preparer to do your taxes. Several tax programs are available that can do the job for you. Unless you have a very complicated income, your taxes can be done quickly and easily. In many cases, the cost of the program is less than the cost of having a tax preparer do your taxes.

Besides doing your own taxes, most of these programs allow you to set up files and do the taxes of others. Of course, the software vendors would like each person to buy a separate copy of the program, especially if you are in the tax preparation business. Many companies offer programs for professional tax businesses, but they usually cost more.

All of the programs operate like a spreadsheet, in that the forms, schedules, and worksheets are linked together. When you enter data in one place, other affected data is automatically updated. Some of the programs are simply templates for Lotus 1-2-3 or Symphony and require those programs to run. Most of them have a built-in calculator so you can do calculations before entering figures. Many of them allow "what if" calculations to show what your return will look like with various inputs. Some of them offer modules for some of the larger states, such as New York and California. Most of them allow you to print IRS acceptable forms.

Andrew Tobias' Taxcut

This program, from Meca Ventures ((203) 222-9150), handles most average returns. It can be interfaced with Andrew Tobias' Managing Your Money, which is an excellent personal financial program.

TurboTax

TurboTax, from ChipSoft Inc. ((619) 453-8722), is unique in that it offers modules for 41 states. It has an excellent manual, and is fairly easy to install and learn. It starts out with a personal interview about your financial situation for the past year. It then lists the forms you might need. Based on your present-year taxes, it can estimate what your taxes will be next year.

J.K. Lasser's Your Income Tax

This program has several state modules, a scratch pad, a calculator, and next-year tax planning. The popular *J.K. Lasser's Tax Guide* is included with the package. It can be ordered by calling (800) 624-0023.

TaxView

TaxView, from SoftView Inc. ((800) 622-6829) is the PC version of MacInTax, the foremost tax program for the Macintosh. It runs under Windows (a run-time version is included), and it is recommended that it be used with a mouse. It is very easy to learn and use, has a calculator, allows "what ifs," and supports a large number of IRS forms.

EasyTax

This program, from Valley Management Consultants ((215) 947-4610), has modules for several states.

Electronic filing

The IRS is now accepting electronic filing from certain tax preparers and companies. Eventually you should be able to complete your taxes with a tax preparation program and use your modem to send it directly to the IRS. This will save you a lot of time and will save the IRS even more. Ordinarily the IRS has to input the data from your return into their computers by hand. Can you imagine the amount of time saved if they receive it directly into their computers. Electronic filing also offers advantages including:

- Faster refunds (up to three weeks faster).
- Direct deposit of your refund.
- More accurate returns resulting in fewer errors.
- IRS acknowledges receipt of your return.
- Reduced paperwork.
- Saves IRS labor, and taxpayers money.

However, there are still some limitations. For more information call ((800) 829-1040) and ask for the electronic filing coordinator. Or check with your local IRS office to see if electronic filing is possible in your area.

Other tools of the trade

The following items are some other tools that can be used with your computer for business uses.

Point of sale terminals

Point of sale (POS) terminals are usually a combination of a cash drawer, a computer, and special software. They provide fast customer checkout, credit card handling, audit and security, reduced paperwork, and efficient accounting. By keying in codes for various items, the computer can keep a running inventory of everything that is sold. The store owner immediately knows when to reorder certain items. A POS system provides instant sales analysis data as to which items sell best, buying trends, and profit or loss.

Several POS systems are available. A simple cash drawer with a built-in 40-column receipt printer, costs as little as $500. More complex systems cost $1500 and more, and software costs from $175 to $1000, but these systems can replace a bookkeeper and accountant. In a successful business that sells goods, a POS system can easily pay for itself. Here are a few POS hardware/software companies:

Alpha Data Systems	(404) 499-9247
CA Retail	(800) 668-3767
CompuRegister	(314) 365-2050
Computer Time	(800) 456-1159
Datacap Systems	(215) 699-7051
Indiana Cash Drawer	(317) 398-6643
Merit Digital Systems	(604) 985-1391
NCR Corp.	(800) 544-3333
Printer Products	(617) 254-1200
Synchronics	(901) 761-1166

Bar codes

Bar codes are a system of black-and-white lines arranged in a system much like the dots and dashes of Morse code. By using combinations of wide and narrow bars and wide and narrow spaces, any number or letter of the alphabet can be represented.

Bar codes were first adopted by the grocery industry. A central office was set up that assigned a unique number, a universal product code (UPC), for just about every manufactured and prepackaged product sold in grocery stores. Different sizes of the same product have a different and unique number assigned to them. The same type products from different manufacturers also have unique numbers.

When the clerk runs an item across the scanner, the dark bars absorb light and the white bars reflect light. The scanner decodes the bar code and sends the number to the main computer. The computer then matches the number to the numbers stored on its hard disk. Linked to the number on the hard disk is the price of the item, the description, the amount in inventory, and several other pieces of information about the item. The computer sends back the price and the description of the item to the cash register, where it is printed out. The computer then deducts that item from the inventory and adds the price to the cash received for the day.

A store might have several thousand items with different sizes and prices. Without a bar-code system, the clerk must know most of the prices, and enter them in the cash register by hand. Many errors are committed. With bar codes, the human factor is eliminated, the transactions are performed much faster and with almost total accuracy.

At the end of the day, the manager can look at the computer output and immediately know such things as how much business was done, what inventories need to be replenished, and what items were the biggest sellers. With the push of a button, the manager can change any or all of the prices in the store. Bar codes can be used to increase productivity, to keep track of time charged to a particular job, to track inventory, and in many other ways. There are very few businesses, large or small, that could not benefit from the use of bar codes.

There are several different types of bar-code readers or scanners. Some are actually small portable computers that store data and download it into a larger computer. Some systems require their own interface card, which must be plugged into one of the slots on the motherboard. Some companies have devised systems that can be inserted in series with the keyboard so no slot or other interface is needed. Key-Tronic has a keyboard with a bar-code reader as an integral part of the keyboard.

If you are interested in bar-code and automatic identification technology, there are two magazines available that are sent free to qualified subscribers:

- *ID Systems*, 174 Concord St., Peterborough, NH 03458.
- *Automatic I.D. News*, P.O. Box 6158, Duluth, MN 55806-9858.

Write for subscription qualification forms. Almost everyone who has any business connections can qualify.

Bar code printers   Special printers have been designed for printing bar-code labels. Labels can also be printed on the better dot matrix printers and on laser printers. Several companies specialize in printing labels to your specifications.

Radio frequency ID

Another system of identification uses small tags that are read by a radio frequency identification (RFID) system. These systems can be used on production lines and in places that are difficult to access.

An RFID system is being used in California for toll-bridge collection. You buy a small tag that is good for a month of tolls. The tag is placed in the window of your car and is automatically read as you pass through the toll gate. You don't even have to slow down.

RFID-type systems can also be used in stores, libraries, and many other places. Many clothing stores use a system that has detectors at the exits. If someone tries to walk through with an item that has not had the tag removed, an alarm goes off.

Computer vision

Many companies have set up cameras on their production lines to control them in a variety of ways. One use is to inspect items as they come off the assembly line. For instance, the image of a circuit board that is perfect with respect to component placement and appearance is digitized and stored in the computer. Each time a circuit board comes off the assembly line, the camera focuses on it and the computer compares it to the stored image. If the two images match, the board is sent on for further assembly or electronic testing. The computer can check the circuit board much faster than a human being, and do it better and more consistently.

CD-ROM

New information is being published and disseminated at an ever-increasing rate. We are being inundated in a flood of information that makes Noah's flood seem like an April shower. I subscribe to over 50 computer magazines, but I have a difficult time trying to keep up. I have recently subscribed to the Ziff-Davis ((212) 503-4400) Computer Library on CD-ROM. Subscribers get a new CD-ROM disk filled with articles from over 140 magazines. One big advantage to having the articles on CD-ROM is that I can quickly search for items that are of interest. I can also cut and paste items into other files on my hard disk. The subscriptions are rather expensive however, at about $900. Several other vendors provide hundreds of educational and scientific programs, data, and information on CD-ROM. One is the Bureau of Electronic Publishing at (800) 828-4766.

Several companies sell public domain software and shareware on CD-ROM. One is PC-SIG ((800) 245-6717), another is Alde Publishing ((612) 835-5240). A CD-ROM might contain over 3000 different programs, just about everything that you would ever need.

The CD-ROM drives are now very reasonable and cost from $250 to $500. There are external types that sit on your desk and internal types that can be installed in a standard half-height bay. A CD-ROM is very much like a compact audio disk except that the CD-ROM is for digital data. One CD-ROM can store the same amount of data as about 1500 floppies.

Several advances have been made in the technology in the last few years. At one time it wasn't practical to store video images on CD-ROM. One frame might require over 25Mb. But with digital video interactive (DVI) and other compression technologies, it is now practical to store all sorts of graphic images and video on CD-ROM. One way they use less memory for is to use the same elements that do not change in the next frame. For instance, if you have a tiger in a jungle scene and the tiger is moving, but the background scenery does not change, only those elements that depict the tiger moving have to be stored. The same background can be used and only those elements that change need to be updated. This is one way that black-and-white movies are colorized.

Choosing a CD-ROM drive

There are many drives on the market. Some of them are very slow and do not have many multimedia capabilities. It might cost a bit more, but try to get a drive that uses a SCSI interface. Also make sure it has an audio output capability.

Multimedia

Windows 3.1 now supports both sound and video. Many new programs are being developed to take advantage of this capability. Multimedia is one of the hottest buzzwords around. It is an all-encompassing term that includes just about everything you can attach to or do with a computer. This includes items such as audio, video, and musical instrument digital interface (MIDI).

You can attach a musical keyboard to a computer, and with the proper software and plug-in boards, you can make or compose your own music. It is as simple as typing in the notes from your computer keyboard. The composition is recorded on your hard disk as a file. If you don't like the results of your composition, you can delete notes, change them, or do just about anything to the file that you can do to text with a word processor. Some software packages let you use the mouse to arrange and sequence the notes. With the proper software, a plug-in board, and a speaker system, you can make music that sounds like a 100-piece orchestra. One of the most popular plug-in boards for sound and multimedia is the Sound Blaster Pro from Creative Labs ((408) 986-1461).

Many CD-ROM players are now capable of audio output. This is not surprising, because they are basically the same as a high-fidelity compact disk player. Many CD-ROM disks have interactive sound to annotate the text or graphics.

These new capabilities make CD-ROM a great tool for teaching and learning. There are hundreds of disks available such as Microsoft Bookshelf and Grolier's Encyclopedia, disks with clip art, nature and animal disks, and educational and training disks.

The labor and cost required to create a CD-ROM disk can be tremendous. For instance, Adam Software is creating a disk that has comprehensive drawings of the human body. It shows in great detail slices through the body at almost any point, and shows the various tissues, muscles, nerves, bones, and other anatomical features. It will have the most complete drawings of the human body that have ever been done. This disk can be used to teach anatomy or surgery, and will be more beneficial than using cadavers for training. Because it entails so many drawings and so much detail, it will initially cost almost $4000 for each disk.

If you are just getting started in multimedia, the Media Vision Company ((510) 770-8600) offers a complete bundle of 16 different items to get you started. The bundle includes a CD-ROM, a sound card, several CD-ROM disks, and several software packages. IBM has a package they call Ultimedia that includes several products for PS/2 computers. These products and several others for the PC are carried by the MultiMedia Direct Company ((800) 354-1354).

Hundreds of other multimedia products are available. *NewMedia* lists many of them. They have put together a multimedia reference guide they call *Source '92*. It lists more than 2000 multimedia services, suppliers, manufacturers, producers, and consultants. Call (800) 832-3513 for more information. *NewMedia* is a new magazine devoted to multimedia. It is a free magazine to qualified subscribers. If you are interested in multimedia, you need this magazine. For a qualification form, write to them at:

NewMedia, P.O. Box 1771, Riverton, NJ 08077-7331.

Here are some other multimedia sources:

Broderbund Software	(415) 382-4400
Bureau of Electronic Publishing	(800) 828-4766
Compton's New Media	(619) 259-0444
DAK Industries	(800) 888-7808
DeLorne Mapping Street Atlas	(207) 865-1234
Dr. T's Music Software	(617) 455-1454
E-Book Electronic Library of Art	(408) 262-0502
Educorp Computer Services	(619) 536-9999
Metatec's Nautilus	(614) 761-2000
Newsbytes News Network	(415) 550-7334
Quanta Press, Inc.	(612) 379-3956
The Voyager Company	(310) 451-1383
World Library, Inc.	(714) 748-7197
Ziff-Davis Computer Library	(212) 503-4400

With a subscription to Metatec's Nautilus and the Ziff-Davis Computer Library you get a monthly disk. Many of the items on the Nautilus disks are low-cost shareware. The annual subscription is $137. The Ziff-Davis Computer Library is a collection of articles from all the computer magazines. The subscription for this service is about $900.

VGA-to-video adapters

Several companies have developed special VGA adapters that can transform VGA output to a television signal. This NTSC signal can then be recorded on a VCR or displayed on a TV screen. These adapters can be used to create presentations or computerized special effects. The US Video company ((203) 964-9000) has several adapters. Their TVGA card can drive a monitor up to 1024 × 768 and also output NTSC signals. They also have several other cards for special effects. Other companies who have similar products include Jovian Logic Corp. ((415) 651-4823) and Willow Peripherals ((212) 402-0010).

Local area networks

If you have a small business with several computers, you might consider connecting them into a network. The 486 is excellent as a server for local area networks (LANs). You can attach several terminals or smaller computers to your 486. The 486 can have very large databases, files, information, and software that can be accessed and shared by these other terminals. This gives the less-expensive computers most of the benefits of the 486. A LAN allows multitasking, multiusers, security, centralized backup, and shared resources such as printers, modems, fax machines, and other peripherals.

There are three main types of LAN systems: Ethernet, Token Ring, and ARCnet. In addition, there are several proprietary systems. A good network system can support as many as 100 terminals or stations. Those terminals can be very inexpensive PCs, or a combination of PCs, 286s, and 386s. Of course, the larger the network and the more complex it is, the more expensive it will be. If you have a small business, you might not need a large network or one that is very sophisticated. A LAN can be two or more computers tied together so that they share and process the same files. This is called a *shared CPU* system, because all the terminals share the same CPU. This works well if there are only a few terminals online, but if there are several vying for attention at the same time, there is usually some delay.

Equipment needed for LANs

Besides the terminals, other equipment needed to form a LAN includes plug-in boards, cables, and software. Most systems require a plug-in board in each terminal and a master board in the server. The boards cost from $100 to $1000 each.

Several types of cable can be used, such as inexpensive twisted telephone cables, coaxial shielded cables, and fiber-optic cables. The type of system installed dictates the type of cable needed. A simple system might require only standard telephone cables. A sophisticated system might need shielded coaxial or fiber-optic cable.

Besides the plug-in boards, the system needs special drivers and LAN software to control and manage the network. Some companies supply special software to match their hardware. Many companies, such as Novell and Microsoft, develop network software for several types of network hardware. Most software is sold with the explicit understanding and agreement that it will be used on a single computer by a single user. If it is to be used on a network, it usually costs more.

Low-cost switches and LANS

You might have just a couple of computers and want them to share a printer or switch from a laser printer to a dot matrix printer. This can be done very easily with mechanical switch boxes. Some switch boxes can handle the switching needs for four or five systems. These boxes cost from $50 to $500. Check the ads in the computer magazines.

Some electronic switch boxes are a bit more sophisticated and have more capabilities and functions, including buffers and spooling. Computone Products ((800) 241-3946) has an ATCC cluster controller that can control up to 64 terminals. Here are a few other vendors:

Aten Research	(714) 992-2836
Interex Computer	(316) 524-4747
Protec Microsystems	(800) 363-8156
Rose Electronics	(713) 933-7673
Total Technology	(714) 241-0406
Western Telematic	(714) 586-9950

Zero slot LANs

Several companies provide low-cost LANs that use the RS-232 serial port. They don't require the use of a slot. Here are just a few:

Amica Company, PC-Hooker Turbo	(800) 888-8455
Applied Knowledge	(408) 739-3000
Artisoft, LANtastic Z	(602)293-6363
Fifth Generation System, Brooklyn Bridge	(800) 873-4384
GetC, File Shuttle Express	(800) 663-8066 or (604) 684-3230
Traveling Software, LapLink	(800) 662-2652 or (206) 483-8088

LAN magazine

Most of the computer magazines carry articles on networking, and there are several magazines devoted entirely to LANs. Check the list of magazines in chapter 17.

Books on LANs

If you would like to learn more about networks, you should read *Build Your Own Network And Save A Bundle*, published by TAB/McGraw-Hill and written by Aubrey Pilgrim. I recommend it highly. Several other books on networking are available. Here are some from Windcrest/McGraw-Hill:

- *TOPS: The IBM/Macintosh Connection*, S. Cobb and M. Jost, No. 3210
- *Networking with the IBM Token-Ring*, C. Townsend, No. 2829
- *Networking with Novell NetWare, A LAN Manager's Handbook*, Paul Christiansen, Steve King, and Mark Munger, No. 3283
- *Networking with 3 + Open*, Stan Schatt, No. 3437

You can order from TAB/McGraw-Hill, Blue Ridge Summit, PA 17294-0850, or call (800) 822-8138.

Desktop publishing software

Desktop publishing (DTP) covers a lot of territory. A desktop publishing system could be just a PC with a word processor and a dot matrix printer. Or it could be a full-blown system with laser printers with PostScript and lots of memory, scanners, 286 or 386 computers with many, many megabytes of hard disk space, sophisticated software, and other goodies.

The type of system you need depends on what you want it to do, and of course, how much money you want to spend. Desktop publishing can be used for newsletters, ads, flyers, brochures, sales proposals, sophisticated manuals, and all sorts of printed documents.

If your project isn't too complex, you can probably do a fairly good job with a laser printer and a good word processing program. WordStar 7.0 has page preview, scalable fonts, and several other functions that can be used in desktop publishing. Microsoft Word for Windows, WordPerfect, AMI, and several other programs can also be used. Most of the more sophisticated word processors let you add graphics and flow the text around them.

If you are doing a more complicated and professional type of DTP, with a lot of graphics and different types and fonts, you should use a high-end software package. The premier high-end packages are Ventura from Xerox ((800) 822-8221) and Page-Maker from Aldus ((206) 622-5500). There are many other desktop publishing packages available ranging from $89 to $15,000. Here are just a few of the companies that supply page layout software:

IMSI Publisher	(415) 454-7101
Microsoft Publisher for Windows 1.0	(800) 426-9400
Power Up Software, Express Publisher	(800) 851-2917
Timeworks, Publish It 2.0	(800) 323-7744
Unison World Software, Avagio	(800) 444-7553

Books for desktop publishing

If you are serious about desktop publishing several books are available on the subject. Here are a few from TAB/McGraw-Hill:

- *Mastering PageMaker*, G. Keith Gurganus, No. 3176
- *Ventura Publisher*, Elizabeth McClure, No. 3012
- *The Print Shop Companion*, P. Seyer and H. Leitch, No. 3218
- *IBM Desktop Publishing*, G. Lanyi and J. Barrett, No. 3109
- *Desktop Publishing & Typesetting*, M.L. Kleper, No. 2700

You can order these and many other computer books from TAB/McGraw-Hill, Blue Ridge Summit, PA 17294-0850 or call (800) 822-8138. Osborne/McGraw-Hill ((800) 227-0900) and Microsoft Press ((800) 888-3303) also publish books on destop publishing and many other computer subjects.

Desktop Publishing

Several magazines are devoted exclusively to desktop publishing. Almost every computer magazine carries desktop publishing articles. Check the list of magazines in chapter 17.

Clip art

Several software packages are available with images you can import and place in your page layout. The software lets you move the images around, rotate, size, or revise them. The images include humans, animals, business, technical, industrial, borders, enhancements, etc. Most of the companies have the images set up in modules on floppies, and most have several modules with hundreds or even thousands of images. The cost of each of the modules ranges from $15 to $200. Contact the following companies for more information:

Antic Cyber Design, Architecture	(800) 234-7001
Artware System Artware, Varied	(800) 426-3858
CD Designs Graphics, Varied	(800) 326-5326
EMS Shareware DTP Library, Varied	(301) 924-3594
Kinetic Corp., U.S. maps	(502) 583-1679
Metro ImageBase PicturePak, Varied	(800) 525-1552
Micrografx Clip Art, Varied	(800) 272-3729

Micrografx has four different packages that allow you to create almost any kind of art or line drawing for your desktop publication.

17
Component sources

HOW MUCH YOU SAVE BY DOING IT YOURSELF DEPENDS ON WHAT COMPONENTS YOU buy and who you buy them from. You have to shop wisely and be fairly knowledgeable about the components in order to take advantage of bargains.

Computer swaps

I have done almost all of my buying at computer shows and swap meets. There is at least one computer show or swap almost every weekend in the larger cities. If you live in or near a large city, check your newspaper for ads. In California, there are several computer magazines, such as *MicroTimes* and *Computer Currents*, that list coming events.

One of the best features of a swap meet is that almost all of the components you need are on display in one place. Several booths will have the same components. I usually take a pencil and pad with me to the shows. I walk around, writing down the prices of the items I want to buy, and comparing prices at the various booths. There can be quite a wide variation in the prices. I bought a good printer at a show where one dealer was asking $995 for it, and about 50 feet away, another dealer was offering the same printer for $695. You can also haggle with most of the dealers at these shows, especially when it gets near closing time. Rather than pack up an item and lug it back to their store, many will sell it for a lower price.

The Interface Company puts on the biggest computer shows in the country. They have a Spring Computer Dealers Exposition (COMDEX) in Atlanta or Chicago and a Fall COMDEX in Las Vegas. They usually attract over 120,000 visitors to the Las Vegas show.

Your local store

I consider myself to be fairly knowledgeable about electronics and computers. I hate to admit it, but a few times in the past, I have been sold inferior and shoddy merchandise. Times have changed and most of the boards and components today have been around long enough that the bugs have been found and eliminated.

Most of the vendors at computer swaps are local business people. They want your business and don't want to risk losing you as a customer. However, there might be a few vendors from other parts of the country. If you buy something from a vendor who does not have a local store, be sure to get their name and address. Most components are reliable, but there is always a chance that something might not work. You might need to exchange it or get it repaired, or you might need to ask questions or need some support to get it working.

Once you have all of the components, it should take less than an hour to assemble your computer. Most components are now fairly reliable, but there is still a possibility that a new part could be defective. Most dealers will give you a warranty of some kind and will replace defective parts. So if at all possible, try to deal with a knowledgeable vendor who will support you and help you if you have any problems.

Mail order

Every computer magazine carries pages and pages of ads for compatible components and systems that can be sent to you through the mail. If you live in an area where there are no computer stores or shows, you can buy by mail. Another reason to use mail order is because it is usually less expensive than local vendors. Most local vendors have to buy their stock from a distributor. The distributor buys it from the manufacturer or a wholesaler. By the time you get the product, it has passed through several companies each of whom have made some profit. One reason IBM and Apple computers are more expensive is that they have several middlemen. Most of the direct marketers have cut out the middlemen and passed their profit on to you as discount prices.

Ads are the lifeblood of magazines. The subscription price of a magazine does not even pay the mailing costs, so they must have ads. A few bad advertisers can ruin a magazine, so the magazines have formed the Microcomputer Marketing Council (MMC) of the Direct Marketing Association, 6 East 43rd St., New York, NY 10017. They have an action line at (212) 297-1393. If you have problems with a vendor that you cannot resolve, they might be able to help. They police their advertisers fairly closely.

You should be sure of what you need and what you are ordering. Some of the ads aren't written very well and might not tell the whole story. Ads are expensive so they abbreviate or leave out a lot of important information. If possible, call the vendor and ask any questions you have about a product. Ask what their return policy is for defective merchandise. Also ask how long before the item will be shipped, and ask for the current price. The ads are usually placed about two months before the magazines are delivered. The way prices change, there could be quite a difference in cost by the time you place your order. A \$2 or \$3 phone call can save you a lot of time, trouble, grief, and maybe even some money.

Ten rules for ordering by mail

Here are some brief rules that you should follow when ordering by mail:

Rule 1—look for a street address Make sure the advertiser has a street address. In some ads, they give only a phone number. If you decide to buy from a vendor, call and verify that there is a person on the other end with a street address. Before you send any money, do a bit more investigation. If possible, look through past issues of the same magazine for previous ads. If the vendor has been advertising for several months, then it is probably okay.

Rule 2—compare other vendors' prices Check through the magazines for other vendors' prices for the same product. The prices should be fairly close. If it appears to be a bargain that is too good to be true, then . . . you know the rest.

Rule 3—buy from MMC members Buy from a vendor who is a member of the Microcomputer Marketing Council of the Direct Marketing Association or other recognized association. There are now about 10,000 members who belong to marketing associations. They have agreed to abide by the ethical guidelines and rules of their associations. Except for friendly persuasion and the threat of expulsion, the associations have little power over their members, but most members realize what is at stake and put a great value on their membership. Most advertisers in the major computer magazines are members. The U.S. Post Office, the Federal Trade Commission, magazines, and legitimate businesspeople who advertise have taken steps to try to stop the fraud and scams.

Rule 4—do your homework Read the ads carefully. Advertising space is very expensive, and many ads use abbreviations. Some ads might not be entirely clear; if in doubt, call and ask. A \$2 telephone call might save you a lot of time and prevent a lot of frustration. Know exactly what you want; state precisely the model, make, size, component, and any other pertinent information. Tell them which ad you are ordering from, and ask them if the price is the same, if the item is in stock, and when you can expect delivery. If the item is not in stock, indicate whether you will accept a substitute or want your money refunded. Ask for an invoice or order number. Ask the person's name. Write down all of the information—the time, the date, the company's address and phone number, a description of the item, and the promised delivery date. Save any and all correspondence.

Rule 5—ask questions Ask if the advertised item comes with all the necessary cables, parts, accessories, software, etc. Ask what the warranties are. Ask about the seller's return and refund policies. Ask with whom you should correspond if there is a problem.

Rule 6—don't send cash You will have no record if you send cash. If possible, use a credit card. If you have a problem, you can possibly have the bank refuse to pay the amount. A personal check might cause a delay of three to four weeks while the vendor waits for it to clear. A money order or credit card order should be filled and shipped immediately. Keep a copy of the money order.

Rule 7—ask for a delivery date   If you have not received your order by the promised delivery date, notify the seller.

Rule 8—try the item as soon as you receive it   If you have a problem, notify the seller immediately by phone, then in writing. Give all details. Don't return the merchandise unless the dealer gives you a return material authorization (RMA). Make sure to keep a copy of the shipper's receipt or packing slip, or some evidence the material was returned.

Rule 9—double check defective products   If you believe the product is defective or you have a problem, reread your warranties and guarantees. Reread the manual and any documentation. It is very easy to make an error or misunderstand how an item operates if you are unfamiliar with it. Before you go to a lot of trouble, try to get some help from someone else. At least get someone to verify that you have a problem. Many times a problem will disappear and the vendor will not be able to duplicate it. When you call, try to have the item in your computer and be at the computer so you can describe the problem as it occurs.

Rule 10—try to work out any problems with the vendor   If you cannot, write to the consumer complaint agency in the seller's state. You should also write to the magazine and to the DMA, 6 E. 43rd St., New York, NY 10017.

Federal Trade Commission rules

Here is a brief summary of the FTC's mail-order rules:

Rule 1—shipment within 30 days   The seller must ship your order within 30 days unless the ad clearly states that it will take longer.

Rule 2—right to cancel   If it appears that the seller cannot ship when promised, he must notify you and give a new date. You must be given the opportunity to cancel your order and receive a refund of your money if you desire.

Rule 3—must notify you if the order can't be filled   If the seller notifies you that he cannot fill your order on time, he must include a stamped self-addressed envelope or card so that you can respond to his notice. If you do not respond, he can assume that you agree to the delay. He must ship within 30 days of the end of the original 30 days, or cancel your order and refund your money.

Rule 4—right to cancel if delayed   Even if you consent to a delay, you still have the right to cancel at any time.

Rule 5—must refund your money if the order is cancelled   If you cancel an order that has been paid for by check or money order, the seller must refund your money. If you paid by credit card, your account must be credited within one billing cycle. Store credits or vouchers in place of a refund are not acceptable.

Rule 6—no substitutions   If the item you ordered is not available, the seller cannot send you a substitute without your express consent.

Online services

If you have a modem, there are several bulletin board services and online companies that offer all kinds of shopping services. You can call from your computer and buy such things as airline tickets, furniture, clothing, toys, electronics, computers, and just about anything else you can imagine. Online services offer some advantages over mail order. The prices quoted in some magazines might be two or three months old by the time the magazine is published. The prices quoted by the online services are the latest up-to-the-minute prices. Here are just a few of the bulletin board services that offer online buying:

First Capitol Computer
16 Algana
St. Peters, MO 63376
(314) 928-9889
BBS line (314) 928-9228

Leo Electronics
P.O. Box 11307
Torrance, CA 95124
(213) 212-6133
BBS line (213) 212-7179

JDR Microdevices
2233 Branham Ln.
San Jose, CA 95124
(408) 559-1200
BBS line (408) 559-0253

Swan Technologies
3075 Research Dr.
State College, PA 16801
(815) 234-2236
BBS line (814) 237-6145

Here are some other online companies:

CompuServe	(800) 848-8990
Delphi	(800) 544-4005
Genie	(800) 638-9636
Prodigy	(800) 776-3449

Sources of knowledge

Many good magazines are available that can help you gain the knowledge needed to make sensible purchases and to learn more about computers. These magazines carry some very interesting and informative articles and reviews of software and hardware. They also have many ads for computers, components, and software. Some of the better magazines that you should subscribe to include *Computer Shopper*, *PC Sources*, *Byte*, *Infoworld Direct*, *Computer Monthly*, *PC World*, and *PC Magazine*. Most of these magazines are available on local magazine racks. But you will save money with a yearly subscription, and they will be delivered to your door.

If you need a source of components, you only have to look in any of the magazines to find hundreds of them. If you live near a large city, there are probably several vendors who advertise in your local paper. Many of the magazines have a section that lists all of the products advertised in that particular issue. The components and products are categorized and listed by page number. This makes it very easy to find what you are looking for. Another source of computer information can be found in the many good computer books published by TAB/McGraw-Hill.

Computer magazines

Here are just a few of the magazines that will help you keep abreast to some degree.

Byte
P.O. Box 558
Highstown, NJ 08520

Compute!
P.O. Box 3244
Harlan, IA 51593-2424

Computer Currents
5720 Hollis St.
Emeryville, CA 945608

Computer Graphics World
P.O. Box 122
Tulsa, OK 74101-9966

Computer Monthly
P.O. Box 7062
Atlanta, GA 30357-0062

Computer Shopper
P.O. Box 51020
Boulder, CO 80321-1020

Data Based Advisor
P.O. Box 3735
Escondido, CA 92025-9895

Home Office Computing
P.O. Box 51344
Boulder, CO 80321-1344

LAN
P.O. Box 50047
Boulder, CO 80321-0047

MicroTimes
5951 Canning St.
Oakland, CA 94609

PC Computing
P.O. Box 50253
Boulder, CO 80321-0253

PC Magazine
P.O. Box 51524
Boulder, CO 80321-1524

PC Sources
P.O. Box 50237
Boulder, CO 80321-0237

PC Today
P.O. Box 85380
Lincoln, NE 68501-9815

PC World
P.O. Box 51833
Boulder, CO 80321-1833

Personal Workstation
P.O. Box 51615
Boulder, CO 80321-1615

Publish!
P.O. Box 51966
Boulder, CO 80321-1966

Unix World
P.O. Box 1929
Marion, OH 43306

Free magazines

The magazines listed in this section are sent free to qualified subscribers. *PC Week* and *InfoWorld* are excellent magazines. They are so popular that the publishers have to limit the number of subscribers. They cannot possibly accommodate all the people who have applied. The publishers have set standards which have to be met in order to quality. They do not publish the standards, so even if you answer all of the questions on the application, you still might not qualify.

To get a free subscription, you must write to the magazine for a qualifying application form. The form asks several questions such as how you are involved with computers, the company you work for, whether you have any influence in purchasing the computer products listed in the magazines, and several other questions that give them a profile of their readers.

This list of magazines is not nearly complete. Hundreds of different trade magazines are sent free to qualified subscribers. The Cahners Company alone publishes 32 different trade magazines. Many of the trade magazines are highly technical and narrowly specialized.

Automatic I.D. News
P.O. Box 6158
Duluth, MN 55806-9870

California Business
P.O. Box 70735
Pasadena, CA 91117-9947

Communications Week
P.O. Box 2070
Manhasset, NY 11030

Computer Design
P.O. Box 3466
Tulsa, OK 74101-3466

Computer Products
P.O. Box 14000
Dover, NJ 07801-9990

Computer Reseller News
P.O. Box 2040
Manhasset, NY 11030

Computer Systems News
600 Community Dr.
Manhasset, NY 11030

Computer Technical Review
924 Westwood Blvd., #65
Los Angeles, CA 90024

Designfax
P.O. Box 1151
Skokie, IL 60076-9917

Discount Merchandiser
215 Lexington Ave.
New York, NY 10157

EE Product News
P.O. Box 12982
Overland Park, KS 66212

Electronic Manufacturing
P.O. Box 159
Libertyville, IL 60048

Electronic Publish & Print
650 S. Clark St.
Chicago, IL 60605-9960

Electronics
P.O. Box 985061
Cleveland, OH 44198

Federal Computer Week
P.O. Box 602
Winchester, MA 01890

ID Systems
P.O. Box 874
Peterborough, NH 03458

Identification Journal
2640 N. Halsted St.
Chicago, IL 60614-9962

InfoWorld
1060 Marsh Rd.
Menlo Park, CA 94025

InfoWorld Direct
401 Edgewater Pl., #630
Wakefield, MA 01880

Lan Times
122 East, 1700 South
Provo, UT 84606

Lasers & Optronics
301 Gibraltar Dr.
Morris Plains, NJ 07950

Machine Design
P.O. Box 985015
Cleveland, OH 44198-5015

Manufacturing Systems
P.O. Box 3008
Wheaton, IL 60189-9972

Medical Equipment Designer
29100 Aurora Rd., #200
Cleveland, OH 44139

Mini-Micro Systems
P.O. Box 5051
Denver, CO 80217-9872

Modern Office Technology
1100 Superior Ave.
Cleveland, OH 44197-8032

NewMedia
P.O. Box 1771
Riverton, NJ 08077-7331

Office Systems 90
P.O. Box 3116
Woburn, MA 01888-9878

Office Systems Dealer 90
P.O. Box 2281
Woburn, MA 01888-9873

PC Week
P.O. Box 5920
Cherry Hill, NJ 08034

Photo Business
1515 Broadway
New York, NY 10036

The Programmer's Shop
5 Pond Park Rd.
Hingham, MA 02043-9845

Quality
P.O. Box 3002
Wheaton, IL 60189-9929

Reseller Management
Box 601
Morris Plains, NJ 07950

Robotics World
6255 Barfield Rd.
Atlanta, GA 30328-9988

Scientific Computing
301 Gibraltar Dr.
Morris Plains, NJ 07950

Surface Mount Technology
P.O. Box 159
Libertyville, IL 60048

Unix Review
P.O. Box 7439
San Francisco, CA 94120

Public domain and shareware software

Several companies provide public domain, shareware, and low-cost software. They also publish catalogs listing their software. Some charge a small fee for their catalog.

The Computer Room	(703) 832-3341
Computers International	(619) 630-0055
International Software Library	(800) 992-1992
MicroCom Systems	(408) 737-9000
Micro Star	(800) 443-6103
National PD Library	(619) 941-0925
PC Plus Consulting	(818) 891-7930
PC-Sig 1030D	(800) 245-6717
Public Brand Software	(800) 426-3475
Selective Software	(800) 423-3556
Shareware Express	(800) 346-2842
Software Express/Direct	(800) 331-8192
Softwarehouse	(408) 748-0461

Computer books

Several companies publish computer books. One of the larger companies is TAB Books, a division of McGraw-Hill, Blue Ridge Summit, PA 17294-0850, (800) 822-8138. Call or write them for a catalog listing of the many books that they publish.

18

Troubleshooting and repairing your PC

THIS IS THE LONGEST CHAPTER IN THE WHOLE BOOK. IT COULD BE TEN TIMES AS long and still not cover every possible problem, but this chapter covers most of the problems you might experience.

The importance of documentation

You should have documentation for all your computer components. You should have a written record of the switch and jumper settings for each of your boards. It is also very important that you have the drive type and the CMOS information for your hard disk drives. If your system fails, you might not be able to access your hard drive and its data if you don't know the drive type listed in your CMOS configuration. You should know what components are inside your computer and how they are configured. Norton Utilities 6.01 has a SysInfo file that does a complete check of your system, and lets you print it out. This gives you an excellent report on what is in your system. You should also have a bootable backup disk that contains your autoexec.bat and config.sys files.

The number one cause of problems

If you add something to your computer or do some sort of repair and the computer is not up and running, there is always the possibility that something was not plugged in correctly or some minor error was made in the installation. I have a friend who works for a large computer mail-order firm. His job is to check and repair the components that are returned by customers. I asked him what the biggest problem was, and his answer was, "People just don't read and follow the instructions or they make errors and don't bother to check their work." By far the greatest problem in assembling a unit, or adding something to a computer, or installing software, is not following the instructions. Quite often it is not necessarily the fault of the person trying to follow the instructions. I am a member of Mensa and have worked in the electronic industry for over 30 years, but sometimes I have great difficulty trying to decipher and follow the instructions in some manuals. Sometimes a very critical instruction or piece of information is inconspicuously buried on page 300 of a 450-page manual.

If you have just added something to your computer, recheck all the cables and any boards. Make sure the boards are configured properly and that they are properly seated. Read the instructions again, then turn on the power. If it works, put the cover on and button it up.

What to do if it is completely dead

Several diagnostic programs are available, and they are great. But if the computer is completely dead, software won't do you any good. If it is completely dead, the first thing you should do is check the power. If you don't have a voltmeter, plug a lamp into the same socket and see if it lights. Check your power cord. Check the switch on the computer. Check the fan in the power supply. Is it turning? If the fan is not turning, then the power supply is probably defective. However, the fan can operate even though the power supply is defective. Do any of the panel lights come on when you try to boot up? Does the hard drive motor spin? Most power supplies have a small glass fuse. Remove it and check it with an ohmmeter. If the fuse is good, but you still get no power to the disk drives and panel lights, replace the power supply.

If you hear the fan motor and the panel lights come on, but the monitor is dark, check the monitor's power cord, its fuses, and its adapter. You should also check the monitor's brightness and contrast controls. If you just installed the monitor, check the motherboard or adapter for any switches or jumpers that should be set. Check your documentation. You should also check your CMOS setup to make sure the BIOS knows what type of monitor you have.

If you add a board or some accessory and your computer doesn't work, remove the item and try the computer again. If the computer works without the board, then you know it must be the board. A short in a board or a peripheral can prevent the computer from working. Remove all of the boards except for the monitor adapter and disk controller, and disconnect all peripherals. If the system works, add the boards back until it stops working. Be sure to turn off the power each time you add or remove a board or cable. If you have spare boards, swap them with suspected boards in your system.

Config.sys and autoexec.bat files

If you add a new piece of software and your system doesn't work or it doesn't work the way it should, check your autoexec.bat and config.sys files. Many programs change these files as they are being installed. These files might have commands and statements that conflict with your new software or system. I try a lot of different software and systems, and I have had problems when a statement or command was left in the autoexec.bat or config.sys file from a system no longer being used. Check these files often and clean them up. You can use the DOS 5.0 Edit command to check and revise these files.

You might get an error message that says, "Unrecognized command in config.sys." You might then get an additional message saying, "Bad or missing file, driver, or path." You might have a misspelled word in your config.sys file, or you might have left out a backslash or some other character. The structure of the config.sys file is rather strict and doesn't provide much room for error.

Whenever you make a change to your autoexec.bat or config.sys files, always keep the old one as a backup. You can rename them with the RENAME command. If your new autoexec.bat or config.sys files don't work, you can always go back and give the old files their original names.

If you have a long autoexec.bat file that doesn't work, you might try editing out parts of it, then reboot and retry it. I had a very long autoexec.bat file and I decided to trim it down and clean it up. After I did, it would not boot at all. I had to use a floppy and add parts of the file back until it worked.

Multiple config.sys files

There are times when it might be necessary to have more than one config.sys file. I have one computer that has a lot of TSR programs on it. They take up a lot of my 640K of memory. If I want to run Prodigy, I need about 500K of free RAM. When I try to run Prodigy, I get the message, "Insufficient memory." I made up a couple of config.sys files on bootable floppy disks. Instead of booting up from my hard disk, I boot up from these floppies and load whatever config.sys I want. Several public domain and some commercial programs let you have as many as 15 or 20 different config.sys files on your hard disk. You can point to the one you want, reboot your system, and you are ready to go. DOS 6.0 allows you to load parts of a config sys file.

Power on self-test

Every time a computer is turned on, or booted up, it does a power on self-test (POST). It checks the RAM, the floppy drives, the monitor, the printer, the keyboard, and other peripherals. If everything is okay, it gives a short beep then boots up. If a unit is not found, or if the unit is not functioning correctly, it beeps and displays an error code. It might beep two or more times depending on the error, or if the power supply or the motherboard is defective, it might not beep at all.

The codes start with 100 and go up to 20,000. Ordinarily the codes are not displayed if there is no problem. If there is a problem, the last two digits of the code will be something other than 00. Each BIOS manufacturer develops their own codes so there are some slight differences, but most of them are similar to ones shown in Table 18-1.

Table 18-1. POST codes

101	Motherboard failure
109	Direct memory access test error
121	Unexpected hardware interrupt occurred
163	Time and date not set
199	User indicated configuration not correct
201	Memory test failure

Table 18-1. Continued.

301	Keyboard test failure or a stuck key
401	Monochrome display and/or adapter test failure
432	Parallel printer not turned on
501	Color graphics displayed and/or adapter test failure
701	Math coprocessor test error
901	Parallel printer adapter test failure
1101	Asynchronous communications adapter test failure
1301	Game control adapter test failure
1302	Joystick test failure
1401	Printer test failure
1701	Fixed disk drive and/or adapter test failure
2401	Enhanced graphics display and/or adapter test failure
2501	Enhanced graphics display and/or adapter test failure

The list in Table 18-1 is very brief. If you would like to see an extensive listing of these codes, I recommend that you get Scott Mueller's *Upgrading and Repairing PCs, 2nd Edition*, published by QUE.

Beep error codes   Besides the POST codes, IBM and most compatible systems give a series of audible beeps from the speaker for certain errors. If the POST is performed and everything is okay, there should be one short beep. If there is no beep, there is probably no power to the system, or possibly the CPU or some other critical IC has failed.

There are several other beep error codes in the system BIOS. Each BIOS manufacturer uses slightly different codes. Some of the beep codes are for fatal errors that cause the system to hang up completely. You can check the beep system by holding a key down while the system is booting. You might hear a continuous beep. After the boot is complete, the system gives two short beeps and displays the message, "Keyboard error. Press F1 to continue."

POST cards   Several companies have developed diagnostic cards or boards that can be plugged into a slot on the motherboard to display the POST codes (see Fig. 18-1). If there is a failure in the system, it can tell you what is wrong immediately.

Advanced Software ((800) 835-2467) has an inexpensive POST card that can be used on all ISA machines. Advanced Software is also a vendor of upgrade BIOS chips for most major manufacturers. They also sell several other computer components.

POST-Probe   If the computer is completely dead, it cannot run the power on self-test. If you have tried all of the earlier suggestions and your computer is still dead, then you might have some serious problems. You might need some high-level troubleshooting. You can take it in to a shop and have a professional work on it, or you can use a diagnostic card such as the POST-Probe from Micro 2000 ((818) 547-0125) (see Fig. 18-2).

If you have eliminated the possibility of a defective plug-in board or peripheral, then the problem is probably in your motherboard. If the power supply is okay, you

18-1 A POST card from Advanced Software.

18-2 The POST-Probe diagnostic card from Micro 2000. Note that it also has an MCA adapter board. It will work on PS/2 machines as well as ISA and EISA computers.

can plug the POST-Probe into a slot and it will test and check each chip and component on the motherboard. It has a small digital display that shows the condition of each component. The POST-Probe works on any ISA or EISA machine, XT, 286, 386, or 486. It also comes with an MCA adapter so it can be used on IBM PS/2 systems.

The POST-Probe is something that every professional repair shop should have. But it might also be well worth the money for an individual to buy one. If you have to take your computer to a repair shop, at $50 to $100 an hour, the repair could be rather expensive. You also have to give up some of your time and go to the trouble of taking the computer to the shop. If the shop is busy, it might be some time before you get your computer back. If your computer is critical to your business, then it might be a good idea to have a POST-Probe on hand just in case of a failure.

Spares   It might be a good idea to have a few spare boards and components on hand, especially if your computer is critical to your business and you cannot afford down time. I suggest that you have a spare floppy drive, a floppy drive controller board, and a keyboard. These items are all fairly inexpensive. Depending on how critical your business is and how important your computer is to it, you might even want to have spares of all your components, such as a motherboard, power supply, and plug-in boards.

Electricity—the lifeblood of the computer

Troubleshooting is a little easier if you know just a little of the electronic basics. Computers are possible because of electricity. An electric charge is formed when there is an imbalance or an excess amount of electrons at one pole. The excess electrons flow through whatever path they can find to get to ground or to the other pole. It is much like water flowing downhill to find its level.

Most electric or electronic paths have varying amounts of resistance so that heat is created when the electrons pass through. For instance, if a flashlight is turned on, electrons pass through the bulb, which has a resistive filament. The heat generated by the electrons passing through the bulb causes the filament to glow and create light. If the light is left on for a period of time, all of the excess electrons from the positive anode of the batter pass through the bulb to the negative pole of the battery. The amount of electrons at the negative and positive poles are then the same, and the battery is dead.

A computer is made up of circuits and boards that have resistors, capacitors, inductors, transistors, motors, and many other components. These components perform useful functions when electricity passes through them. The circuits are designed so that the path of the electric current is divided, controlled, and shunted to do the work we want done. Occasionally, too many electrons find their way through a weakened component and burn it out, or for some reason the electrons are shunted through a different path. This can cause an intermittent, a partial, or a complete failure.

The basic components of a computer

The early IBM PC had an 8088 CPU and four other basic support chips—the 8259 interrupt controller, the 8237 DMA controller, the 8253/8254 programmable interval timer, and the 8255 programmable input/output controller. These same chips are found in the 8086, the 286, the 386, and the 486. You will find two DMA and two interrupt controllers in the 286, 386, and 486. You might not be able to see these chips on the modern motherboards because they are usually contained in a VLSI package.

The CPU is the brain of the computer. It controls the basic operation by sending and receiving control signals and memory addresses. It sends and receives data along the bus to and from other parts of the system. It carries out computations, numeric comparisons, and many other functions in response to software programs.

The 8259 programmable interrupt controller responds to interrupt requests generated by the system hardware components. These requests can be from such components as the keyboard, disk drive controller, and system timer. The 8237 DMA controllers transfer data to and from the computer's memory without passing it through the CPU. This allows input and output from the disk drives without CPU involvement. The 8253/8254 programmable interval timer generates timing signals for various system tasks, and the 8255 input/output controller provides an interface between the CPU and the I/O devices.

Of course, several other chips are interrelated to each of these main chips, and all of the main chips are interrelated. Because they are all so intimately interrelated, a failure in any chip can cause the whole circuit to fail. The actual defect can be very difficult to pinpoint.

Fewer bugs today

In the early days there were lots of bugs and errors in the clone computers. The Far East manufacturers didn't spend a lot of money on quality control and testing. Most computer manufacturers have now been making the parts long enough that the designs have been firmed up. They now know what works best and most of the earlier bugs have been eliminated.

Document the problem—write it down

Chances are, if a computer is going to break down, it will do it at the most inopportune time. This is one of the basic tenets of Murphy's immutable and inflexible law. If it breaks down, try not to panic. Ranting, cussing, and crying might make you feel better, but it won't solve the problem. Instead, get out a pad and pencil and write down everything as it happens. Write down all the particulars, how the cables were plugged in, the software that was running, and anything that might be pertinent. If you get error messages on your screen, use the PrtSc key to print out the messages.

If you can't solve the problem, call your vendor for help. If you have all the information written before you, it will help. Try to call from your computer, as it is acting up.

DOS error messages

DOS has several error messages if you try to make the computer do something it can't do. But many of the messages are not very clear. The DOS 5.0 manual has over

650 pages, but according to the index, there are only two very brief mentions of *error* in the manual.

Several books about DOS are available. Kris Jamsa has written several for Osborne/McGraw-Hill ((800) 227-0900). His *DOS Secrets, Solutions, Shortcuts* is one of the better books. He explains DOS commands in great detail, and his is one of the few books that also explains the DOS error messages and what to do about them. This is definitely one reference book that should be in your library.

Common DOS error messages

Access denied   You tried to write on or erase a file that was protected. The file might be protected by an ATTRIBUTE command. Use the ATTRIBUTE Command to unprotect it.

Bad command or file name; File not found   You made a mistake in typing in the command, or the command or file does not reside in the current directory.

CHKDSK errors   You should run CHKDSK often. Some people put CHKDSK/F in their autoexec.bat so that it is run every time the system is booted up. CHKDSK might give you an error message that says, "*nnn* lost clusters found in *n* chains. Convert lost chains to files Y/N." You might try Norton's Disk Doctor to repair clusters or reinvoke CHKDSK with the /F (for fix) and the lost clusters will be converted to FILE0000.CHK. These are usually incomplete files. When you delete a file, sometimes portions of it are left in a sector, or something might have caused an error in the FAT.

General failure reading or writing drive n, Abort, Retry, Fail   The disk might not be formatted. It is also possible that track 0 on the disk, which stores the FAT, has become defective. It might be possible to restore the disk by using Norton's Disk Doctor on it.

Invalid directory   If you do a change directory from the root directory, all you have to type is cd and the directory name. If you happen to be in the WordStar directory and you type cd Norton, it will say that it is an invalid directory. If you are in any directory except the root directory, you have to type cd\ and the directory name. If you type cd/norton, using the forward slash instead of the backslash, you will get the same message.

Nonsystem disk or disk error. Replace and strike any key when ready.   You had a nonbootable disk in drive A.

Not ready error reading drive A:, Abort, Retry, Fail   You asked the computer to go to drive A and it was not ready or there was no disk in the drive.

Power supply

The power supply is one of the most frequent causes of problems. Most of the components in your computer are fairly low power and low voltage. The only high voltage in your system is in the power supply, and it is pretty well enclosed, so there is no danger of shock if you open your computer and put your hand inside it. However, you should never ever connect or disconnect a board or cable while the power is on. Fragile semiconductors can be destroyed if you do so.

Most of the power supplies have short-circuit protection. If too much of a load is placed on them, they drop out and shut down, similar to what happens when a circuit breaker is overloaded. Most power supplies are designed to only operate with a load. If you take one out of a system and turn it on without a load, it probably won't work. You can plug in a floppy drive to act as a load if you want to check the power supply voltages when it is not plugged into the motherboard.

Semiconductors have no moving parts, and if the circuits are designed properly, the semiconductors should last indefinitely. Heat is an enemy and can cause semiconductor failure. The fan in the power supply should provide adequate cooling. All of the openings on the back panel should have fillers, and the holes on the bottom of the chassis should be covered with tape. This forces the fan to draw air in from the front of the computer, pull it over the boards, and exhaust it through the opening in the power supply case. Nothing should be placed in front of or behind the computer that will restrict air flow. If you don't hear the fan when you turn on your computer, or if the fan isn't running, then the power supply could be defective.

Table 18-2. Power supply connections

Disk drive power supply connections

	Pin	Color	Function
	1	Yellow	+12-V dc
	2	Black	Ground
	3	Black	Ground
	4	Red	+5-V dc

Power supply connections to the motherboard

P8	Pin	Color	Function
	1	White	Power good
	2	No connection	
	3	Yellow	+12-V dc
	4	Brown	–12-V dc
	5	Black	Ground
	6	Black	Ground

P9	Pin	Color	Function
	1	Black	Ground
	2	Black	Ground
	3	Blue	–5-V dc
	4	Red	+5-V dc
	5	Red	+5-V dc
	6	Red	+5-V dc

The eight-bit slotted connectors on the motherboard have 62 contacts; 31 on the A side and 31 on the B side. The black ground wires connect to B1 of each of the eight slots. B3 and B29 have +5-volts dc, B5 has –5-volts dc, B7 has –12 volts dc, and B9 has +12-volts dc. See Table 18-2. These voltages go to the listed pins on each of the eight plug-in slots. I won't list the functions of the other contacts on the slots.

Most of them are for address lines and data input/output lines. They usually are not a problem.

Batteries

The early PC and XT did not have an on-board battery. Every time you booted up, the computer asked for the time and date. Several companies made fortunes designing plug-in boards, usually multifunction boards, with a clock and battery for these machines. When the AT 286 was introduced, it came with a battery and an on-board clock. The new 286 also had a CMOS setup that had all of the system configuration. The battery was able to keep the CMOS setup alive when the computer was turned off. The battery was usually a nickel-cadmium or alkaline battery that had to be replaced about every two years. If you have one of these older computers, and you have to input the date and time every time you turn on your computer, you probably need a new battery. Most of the newer systems use a lithium battery that is soldered onto the motherboard. They have a lifespan of about 10 years.

Instruments and tools

For high-level troubleshooting, you need some rather sophisticated and expensive instruments to do a thorough analysis. You need a good high-frequency oscilloscope, a digital analyzer, a logic probe, and several other expensive pieces of gear. You also need a test bench with a spare power supply, spare disk drives, and spare plug-in boards. You should also have a diagnostic card, such as the POST-Probe, and several of the diagnostic and utility software programs. It might also be a good idea to have a known good computer with some empty slots so that you can plug in suspect boards and test them.

You also need a volt-ohmmeter, some clip leads, side-cutting dikes, long-nose pliers, various screwdrivers, nut drivers, a soldering iron, and solder. You need a good work bench with plenty of light, and a flashlight or a small light to light up the dark places in the computer case. And most importantly, you need quite a lot of training and experience. But for most problems, just a little common sense will tell you what is wrong.

Common problems

For most of the common problems you won't need a lot of test gear. Often a problem can be solved by using your five senses—sight, hearing, smell, touch, and taste. Actually, you won't be using taste very often.

If you look closely, you can see a cable that is not plugged in properly, or a board that is not completely seated, or a switch that is not set right, or many other obvious things. You can use your ears to listen for unusual sounds. The only sound from your computer should be the noise of your drive motors and the fan in the power supply. If you have ever smelled a burned resistor or capacitor, you will never forget it. If you smell something unusual, try to locate where it is coming from. If you touch a component and it seems unusually hot, it could be the cause of your problem. Except for the inside of your power supply, there should not be any voltage above 12 volts in your computer. It should be safe to touch the components.

Electrostatic discharge (ESD)

Before you touch any of the components or handle them, you should ground yourself and discharge any static voltage you have built up. You can discharge yourself by touching an unpainted metal part on the case of the computer or any device that is plugged in. It is possible for a person to build up a static charge of 4000 volts. If you walk across a carpet and touch a brass door knob, you can sometimes see a spark fly and you get a shock. On most electronic assembly lines, the workers wear a ground strap whenever they are working with any ESD-sensitive components.

Recommended tools

Here are some tools that you should have around, even if you never have any computer problems. You should have several sizes of screwdrivers. A couple of them should be magnetic for picking up and starting small screws. You can buy magnetic screwdrivers, or you can make them yourself. Just take a strong magnet and rub it on the blade of the screwdriver a few times. The magnets on cabinet doors will do, or the voice coil magnet of a loudspeaker. Be very careful with any magnet around your floppy disks. It can erase them. You should also have a small screwdriver with a bent tip that can be used to pry up ICs. Some of the larger ICs are very difficult to remove. One of the fillers for the slots on the back panel also makes a good prying tool.

You should have a couple of pliers. You should have at least one long-nose pliers. You need side-cutting dikes for cutting leads of components and cutting wire. You can buy cutters that also have wire strippers.

You need a soldering iron and some solder. You shouldn't have to do much soldering, but you never know when you might need to repair a cable or do some other minor job. You also need cable crimpers if you build your own cables.

By all means buy a volt-ohmmeter. There are dozens of uses for a volt-ohmmeter. They can be used to check the wiring continuity in your cables, phone lines, switches, etc., as well as the proper voltages in your computer. There are only four voltages to check for: +12 volts, –12 volts, +5 volts, and –5 volts. You can buy a relatively inexpensive volt-ohmmeter at any Radio Shack or electronics store.

You should have several clip leads, which you can buy at Radio Shack or any electronics store. And finally, you need a flashlight for looking into the dark places inside your computer or at the cable connections behind your computer.

How to find the problem

Spare swapping

If a computer is down and you suspect a board, if you have a spare that is the same, swap it. If you don't have a spare, maybe you can borrow one from another computer. If you suspect a board, but don't know which one, take the boards out to the barest minimum, then add them back until the problem develops.

CAUTION! Always turn off the power when plugging in or unplugging a board or cable.

Chip problems

If you install memory chips or other ICs and get errors, check that they are seated properly and that all the pins are in the sockets. If you swap an IC, make a note of how it is oriented before removing it. There should be a small dot of white paint or a U-shaped indentation at the end that has pin 1. If you forgot to note the orientation, look at the other ICs. Most boards are laid out so that all the ICs are oriented the same way. The chrome fillers that are used to cover the unused slots on the back of the case make very good tools for prying up ICs.

Chips also have a tendency to creep out of their sockets due to environmental changes, vibration, and other factors. Make sure they are all seated properly. I once added a second hard drive to a computer. I had to remove a board that had several chips on it so I could install the hard drive. When I plugged the board back in, the system did not work. I finally discovered that some of the chips were not completely seated. Over a period of time they had crept out of their sockets. In removing the board, I must have flexed it enough to cause some of the chips to lose contact. I pressed the chips back in and the system worked perfectly.

Intermittent problems

Intermittent problems can be most frustrating and maddening, and can be very difficult to find. If you suspect a cable or a connector, try wiggling it to see if the problem goes away or gets worse. I once spent several hours trying to find the cause of a floppy disk problem. It turned out it was a loose wire in the connector. It was just barely touching the contact, and any slight vibration caused the disk drive to become erratic.

You might also try unplugging a cable or board and plugging it back in. Sometimes the pins might be slightly corroded or not seated properly. Recently I turned on one of my computers that hadn't been used for about a month. I got a message that the FDC had an error. This board also controls my hard drives so I was a bit concerned. I unplugged the controller board, cleaned the contacts, and plugged it back in. (The copper contacts on plug-in boards can become corroded. You can clean them with an ordinary pencil eraser.) I still got the FDC error message.

I got out another FDC and prepared to plug it in, but I had to change the setting of a shorting bar on the controller board. On a hunch, I slipped the shorting bar on and off my original controller a few times, then tried the board again. The floppy drives worked perfectly. The shorting bar and the pins had become corroded during the time it was not used.

The problem could be a dipswitch. Try turning it on and off a few times. CAUTION! Always write down the switch positions before touching them. Make a diagram of the wires, cables, and switch settings before you disturb them. It is easy to forget how they were plugged in or set before you moved them. You could end up making things worse. Make a pencil mark before turning a knob, variable coil, or capacitor so that it can be returned to the same setting when you find out it didn't help. Better yet, resist the temptation to reset these types of components. Most were set using highly sophisticated instruments. They don't usually change enough to cause a problem.

If too much current flows through a chip, it can get hot and fail. It might fail only at certain times when you are running a particular program. If you suspect a chip and it seems to be warmer than it should be, you might try using a hair dryer to heat it up. If it fails due to the extra heat, then you have found the problem. Be careful that you do not heat up a good chip and cause it to fail.

If a component seems too hot, you can spray a coolant on it. If the component works properly, you have found your defect.

Monitor problems

Monitors are usually rather long-lived and don't cause too many problems. If you are having monitor problems, check the switch settings on the motherboard. Some have dipswitches or shorting bars that must be set to configure the system to the type of monitor you are using, such as monochrome, CGA, EGA, or VGA. Most monitors also have fuses. You might check them. Also check the cables for proper connections.

Parallel ports

The parallel ports allow data to be input or output over a system of eight separate lines. It takes eight bits of data to make a character. With a parallel system one bit is transmitted on each of the eight lines, so a whole character is sent at one time. In a serial system, there is only a single line and a ground line, so data is sent one character at a time. Therefore, parallel systems are much faster than serial systems.

In the past, the parallel ports were used primarily for printers. Recently, several other devices have been designed to operate on the parallel ports. Several companies now offer such devices as hard disk drives and tape backup systems that can plug into a parallel port. (Some of these systems were discussed in chapter 5 and in chapter 9.) This makes it very easy to install these systems, because you don't have to remove the cover from your computer; all you do is plug them in.

Your computer is capable of supporting two parallel ports—LPT1 and LPT2. These ports are available on each of the plug-in slots. Ordinarily, a system has a plug-in board that has a DB25 female connector on the back panel.

Serial ports

Many printers today have both parallel and serial connectors. The IBM compatible ISA systems default to the parallel system. If at all possible, use the parallel port, as there are fewer problems with parallel as compared to serial. If you use the serial port, you have to use the DOS MODE command to change from the LPT port to the serial port. The commands might look something like this:

    MODE COM1:9600,N,8,P then MODE LPT1:=COM1.

In the command, the 9600 sets the baud rate, the N means no parity, the 8 means 8 bits, and the P means send the output to the printer. The printer has to be set to match these settings.

Every time the computer is booted up, it automatically defaults to the LPT port, so each time you want to use the serial port to print, you have to invoke the above commands. If you use the serial printer all the time, you can put the commands in your autoexec.bat file so they will be loaded each time you boot up. Most printers have a self test. It might run this test fine, then completely ignore any efforts to get it to respond to the computer if the cables, parity, and baud rate are not properly set.

Like the parallel ports, the serial ports are available on any of the plug-in slots. Most systems use a plug-in board with a connector on the back panel. The serial port might be a male DB25 connector with pins, or it might be a male DB9 connector. The original RS-232 specification called for 25 lines, but most systems only use four or five lines, so the DB9 connector is more than sufficient. Many of the mice sold today have DB9 connectors, and if your system has a DB25 connector, you will need to order an adapter. The adapter costs about $3.

The serial ports are most often used for mice or other pointing devices, modems, fax boards, plotters, scanners, and several other devices. DOS only supports two serial ports—COM1 and COM2. DOS has two interrupt request (IRQ) lines: IRQ4 for COM1 and IRQ3 for COM2. Some software communications programs, such as PRO-COMM, support COM3 and COM4. Because there are only two IRQ lines, IRQ4 is used for COM3 and IRQ3 is used for COM4. They can do this because it is not likely that all four IRQ lines will be used at the same time.

If two devices are set for the same COM port, it causes a serious conflict. Neither device will operate properly. When installing a mouse, modem, or fax board, the interface plug-in boards must be configured so none of the devices use the same port. If you have devices already installed on your system, you might not know which port they are set for. There are several programs that can help you determine which ports are being used. One of the better ones is a low-cost shareware program called Port Finder. It is available from mcTRONic Systems ((713) 462-7687) and sells for $13.95. I have spent countless hours of frustration trying to set up serial ports. I would gladly have paid 10 times more for a program like this, if it had been available. If you intend to add any kind of serial device to your system, and your time is worth anything at all, then you need this software.

Other programs are available that are very helpful when you are trying to configure your system. Norton Utilities 6.01 has a system info file that can search your system and give you a detailed report of everything you have in it. Of course, Norton Utilities has many other absolutely essential tools. Another good diagnostic program that can determine how your computer is configured is CheckIt-Pro from Touch-Stone Software ((714) 969-7746).

Computer hang up

Sometimes your computer will hang up. You or the software you're running might have told the computer to do something it cannot do. Because it is very obedient, the computer will try forever to do the task. You can usually do a warm reboot of the computer by pressing the Ctrl-Alt-Del. Of course, this wipes out any file in memory.

Occasionally the computer will not respond to a warm boot. You can pound on the keyboard all day long and it will ignore you. In this case, you have to switch off the main power, let it sit for a few seconds, then power it up again. Always wait for the hard disk to wind down and stop before turning the power on again.

Diagnostic and utility software

Most BIOS chips have many diagnostic routines and other utilities built in. These routines allow you to set the time and date, tell the computer what type of hard and floppy drives are installed, the amount of memory, the wait states, and several other functions. The AMI and DTK BIOS chips have a very comprehensive set of built-in diagnostics. They allow hard and floppy disk formatting, check the speed of rotation of the disk drives, do performance testing of hard drives, and several other tests. I mentioned some utility software programs in chapter 16. Many of them have a few diagnostics among the utilities.

Norton Utilities

Norton ((310) 453-2361) is now part of Symantec Corp. Norton Utilities includes several diagnostic and test programs such as Disk Doctor, Disk Test, Format Recover, Directory Sort, System Information, and many others. Norton Desktop for Windows is very good for those who use Windows.

Mace Utilities

Mace ((504) 291-7221) is now a part of Fifth Dimension. Mace Utilities does almost everything that Norton does. It has recover, defragment, diagnose, remedy, and several other very useful programs primarily for the hard disk.

PC Tools

PC Tools, from Central Point Software ((503) 690-8090), has several utilities much like Norton and Mace Utilities. It has a utility that can recover data from a disk that has been erased or reformatted. It has several other data recovery and DOS utilities, and can be used for hard disk backup. It also includes several utilities such as those found in SideKick.

SpinRite and Disk Technician

SpinRite, from Gibson Research ((714) 362-8000), and Disk Technician, from Prime Solutions ((619) 274-5000), are utilities that allow you to diagnose, analyze, and optimize your hard disk.

CheckIt-Pro

CheckIt-Pro, from TouchStone Software ((714) 969-7746), checks and reports on your computer configuration by letting "you look inside your PC without taking off the cover." It reports on the type of processor, checks the amount of RAM and each chip, and checks the video adapter, hard and floppy drives, parallel and serial ports, clock and calendar, keyboard, and mouse. It can also run a few benchmark speed tests.

Touchstone also has CheckIt Floppy Drive Testing System. If any of your floppy disk drives get out of alignment, you might not be able to read disks from other computers, and drives in other computers might not be able to read disks made from a defective drive. CheckIt measures how well the floppy drive is aligned, checks the rotation speed and its ability to read track 0, and several other tests. The system includes precise test disks in both 3½-inch and 5¼-inch formats. It is inexpensive, but it is a valuable tool. CheckIt LAN can check and diagnose network problems.

Micro-Scope

Micro-Scope, from Micro 2000 ((818) 547-0125), can check items in the CMOS setup, display the active IRQs, check interrupts, show the partition table of your hard disk, check the CPU and memory, and run floppy disk, hard disk, serial and parallel port, keyboard, and video tests. It also allows you to edit disk sectors, test and set optimum interleave on hard disks, and do low-level formatting of most hard disks (see Fig. 18-3). Several other diagnostic software and hardware tools are available. Check the ads in the computer magazines.

18-3   Micro-Scope, a diagnostic and utility software from Micro 2000.

Software problems

I have had far more trouble with software than I have had with hardware. Quite often it is my fault for not taking the time to completely read the manuals and instructions. For instance, I tried to install Charisma. It is a large program that works under

Windows. I kept getting errors and it would not load. I finally read the manual and found that it requires at least 500K of memory to install. I have several drivers, TSRs, and other things in my config.sys file that eat up a lot of RAM. I had to boot up with a basic disk with a very simple config.sys file that left me over 500K of RAM. I had no trouble after that. MS-DOS 5.0, DR DOS 6.0, DESQview, and several other programs can load drivers, TSRs, and other things into memory above 640K, leaving as much as 630K of free RAM.

There are thousands and thousands of other software problems that you will run into. Many vendors have support programs for their products. If something goes wrong, you can call them. A few of them offer toll-free numbers, but with most of them you have to pay for the call. Some companies charge for their support, and some have even installed 900 telephone numbers. You are charged a certain amount for the amount of time you are on the phone.

If you have a software problem, document everything that happens. Before you call, try to duplicate the problem. Carefully read the manual. When you call, it is best to be in front of your computer, with it turned on, and with the problem on the screen if possible. Also, before you call, have the serial number of your program handy. One of the first things they will ask for is your name and serial number. If you bought and registered the program, it will be in their computer.

There are still compatibility problems with updates and new releases. I had lots of problems trying to get the latest WordStar release to work with files I created with an early version. It was mostly my fault because I didn't take the time to read the manual. Like so many other updates and revisions, they make them bigger and better, and out of necessity, they change the way things are done.

Most software is reasonably bug-free. But there are millions of things that can go wrong if the exact instructions and procedures are not followed. In many cases, the exact instructions and procedures are not very explicit. The problem is most software manuals are written by people who know the software very well, and they forget that the person using it for the first time does not know it. You know that the manuals are bad when you see books written by third parties to supplement the original manuals. There are hundreds of books written to help you learn DOS, Lotus 1-2-3, Windows, WordPerfect, WordStar, and most of the other more-popular software. If the original manuals were done properly, there would be little need for supplemental books.

User groups

There is no way to list all of the possible software or hardware problems. Computers are dumb and very unforgiving. It is very easy to plug a cable in backwards or forget to set a switch. Thousands of things can go wrong. Sometimes it might be a combination of software and hardware. Often there is only one way to do something right, but ten thousand ways to do it wrong. Sometimes it is difficult to determine if it is a hardware problem caused by software or vice versa. There is no way that every problem can be addressed.

One of the best ways to find answers is to ask someone who has had the same problem. One of the best places to find these people is in a user group. If at all possible, join one and become friendly with all of the members. They can be one of your best sources for troubleshooting information. Most members have had similar problems and are glad to help. Many local computer magazines list user groups in their area. The nationally distributed *Computer Shipper* alternates a listing of bulletin boards one month and user groups the next.

Glossary

access time   The amount of time it takes the computer to find and read data from a disk or from memory. The average access time for a hard disk is based on the time it takes the head to seek and find the specified track, to lock onto it, and for the disk to spin around until the desired sector is beneath the head.

active partition   The partition on a hard disk that contains the boot and operating system. A single hard disk can be partitioned into several logical disks. This can be done at the initial formatting of the disk. Only one partition, usually drive C, contains the active partition.

adapter boards or cards   The plug-in boards needed to drive monitors. Monitor boards can be monochrome graphic adapters (MGAs), color graphic adapters (CGAs), enhanced graphic adapters (EGAs), or video graphic adapters (VGAs).

algorithm   A step-by-step procedure, scheme, formula, or method used to solve a problem or accomplish a task. Might be a subroutine in a software program.

alphanumeric   Data that has both number and letters.

analyst   A person who determines the computer needs to accomplish a given task. The job of an analyst is similar to that of a consultant. Note that there are no standard qualifications for either of these jobs. Anyone can call themselves an analyst or consultant. They should be experts in their field, but many are not.

ANSI   American National Standards Institute. A standard adopted by MS-DOS for cursor positioning. It is used in the ANSI.SYS file for device drivers.

ASCII   American Standard Code for Information Interchange. Binary numbers from 0 to 127 that represent the upper- and lowercase letters of the alphabet, the numbers 0 to 9, and the symbols found on a keyboard. A block of eight 0s and 1s are used to represent all of these characters. The first 32 characters, 0 to 31, are reserved for noncharacter functions of a keyboard, modem, printer, or other device. Number 32, or 0010 0000, represents the space, which is a character. The numeral 1 is represented by the binary number for 49, which is 0011 0001.

Text written in ASCII is displayed on the computer screen as standard text. Text written in other systems, such as WordStar, has other characters added and is very difficult to read. An additional 128 character representations were added to the original 128 for graphics and programming purposes.

assembly language   A low-level machine language made up of 0s and 1s.

asynchronous   A serial type of communication where one bit at a time is transmitted. The bits are usually sent in blocks of eight 0s and 1s.

attributes   The DOS ATTRIBUTE command allows files and subdirectories to be configured as read-only, hidden, system, or archive. If a file is read-only, it cannot be accidentally erased or changed. If it is hidden, it will not show up when you do a DIR request. The system files are those important files such as IO.SYS and IBMBIO.COM that cannot and should not be changed. The archive attribute is a flag that changes when a file is backed up. The ATTRIBUTE command can be used to change the attributes of files except for the system files.

AT-type systems   The 286, 386SX, 386DX, and 486 are all based on the original IBM AT-type 16-bit bus.

autoexec.bat   The autoexec.bat file is a file that is loaded when you boot up your computer. It tells the computer which files to load. You can change the autoexec.bat with any text editor, but the file must be in ASCII. It is a file you can configure to suit your own needs. It can load and run certain programs or configure your system.

baby motherboards   The AT-type motherboards that have been shrunk to the size of the XT motherboard by combining and integrating several of the chips.

.BAK files   Anytime you edit or change a file in some of the word processors and other software programs, they save the original file as a backup and append the extension .BAK to it.

BASIC   Beginners All Purpose Symbolic Instruction Code. A high-level language that was once very popular. There are still many programs and games that use it. BASIC programs usually have a .BAS extension.

batch   The batch command can be used to link commands and run them automatically. Batch commands can be made up by the user. They all have the extension .bat.

baud   A measurement of the speed or data transfer rate of a communications line between the computer and a printer, a modem, or another computer.

benchmark   A standard program against which similar programs are compared.

bidirectional   Both directions. Most printers print in both directions, thereby saving the time it takes to return to the other end of a line.

binary   Binary numbers are 0s and 1s.

BIOS   Basic Input/Output System. The BIOS is responsible for handling input and output operations.

bitmapped   The representation of a video image stored in the computer memory. Fonts for alphanumeric characters are usually stored as bitmaps. When the letter A is typed, the computer goes to its library and pulls out a preformed A and sends it to the monitor. If a different size A is needed, it requires another bitmap set. Graphic images can also be bitmapped. They consume an enormous amount of memory. Newer techniques allow different sizes and fonts to be scaled rather than bitmapped. *See* typeface.

bits   Binary digits.

boot or bootstrap   When a computer is turned on, all the memory and other internal operators have to be set or configured. A small amount of the program to do this is stored in ROM. Using this the computer pulls itself up by its bootstraps. A warm boot is sometimes necessary to get the computer out of an endless loop or if it is hung up for some reason. A warm boot can be done by pressing Ctrl-Alt-Del.

buffer   A buffer is usually some discrete amount of memory that is used to hold data. A computer can send data thousands of times faster than a printer or modem can utilize it. The data is input to a buffer, which can then feed the data into the printer as needed. The computer is then free to do other tasks.

bug, debug   The early computers were made with high-voltage vacuum tubes. It took rooms full of hot tubes to do the job that a credit card calculator can do today. One of the large systems went down one day. After several hours of troubleshooting, the technicians found a large bug that had crawled into the high-voltage wiring. It had been electrocuted and had shorted out the whole system. Since that time, any type of trouble in a piece of software or hardware is called a bug. To debug, of course, is to try to find all the errors or defects.

bulletin board service   A computer with a hard disk that can be accessed with a modem. Software and programs can be uploaded or left on the bulletin board by a caller, or a caller can scan the software that has been left there by others and download any that he likes. The bulletin boards often have help and message services. They are a great source of help for a beginner.

burst mode   The bus is taken over and a packet of data is sent as a single unit. During this time the bus cannot be accessed by other requests until the burst operation is completed. This allows as much as 33Mb per second or more to be transmitted over the bus.

bus   Wires or circuits that connect a number of devices together. It can also be a system. The configuration of the circuits that connect the 62 pins of the 8 slots together on the motherboard is a bus.

byte   A byte is eight bits, or a block of eight 0s and 1s. These eight bits can be arranged in 256 different ways—$2 \times 2 \times 2 \times 2 \times 2 \times 2 \times 2 \times 2$ or $2^8 = 256$. Therefore, one byte can be made to represent any one of the 256 characters in the ASCII character set. It takes one byte to make a single character.

cache memory   A disk cache or a high-speed memory cache. A high-speed buffer set up in memory can hold data that is being read from the hard disk. Often a program requests the same data from the disk over and over again. This can be quite time-consuming, depending on the access speed of the disk drive and the location of the data on the disk. If the requested data is cached in memory it can be accessed almost immediately. For some of the very fast 386 and 486 systems, the DRAM is too slow to keep up, so a cache of very fast RAM is installed for these systems.

carriage width   The width of a typewriter or printer. The two standard widths are 80 columns and 132 columns.

cell   A place for a single unit of data in memory, or an address in a spreadsheet.

Centronics parallel port   A system of eight-bit parallel transmission first used by Centronics. It has become a standard and is the default method of printer output on the IBM.

character   A letter, a number, or an eight-bit piece of data.

chip   An integrated circuit, usually made from a silicon wafer. It can be microscopically etched and have thousands of transistors and semiconductors in a very small area.

CISC   Complex Instruction Set Computing. This is the standard type of computer design, as opposed to the RISC (reduced instruction set computers) used in larger systems. It might require as many as six steps for a CISC system to carry out a command. An RISC system might need only two steps to perform a similar function.

clock   The operations of a computer are based on very critical timing, so they use a quartz crystal oscillator to control their internal clocks. The standard frequency for the PC and XT is 4.77 MHz. The 486 CPUs operate at 16 MHz to 66 MHz.

cluster   Each track of a disk is divided into sectors. Two or more sectors are called a cluster. This term has been replaced by the term *allocation units*. An allocation unit can be one or more sectors.

.COM   A .COM or .EXE extension on the end of a file name indicates that it is a program that runs commands to execute programs.

COM   Usually refers to serial ports COM1 or COM2. These ports are used for serial printers, modems, mice, plotters, and other serial devices.

COMDEX   Computer Dealers Exposition. The nation's largest computer exposition and show, usually held once in the spring in Atlanta or Chicago and once in the fall in Las Vegas.

COMMAND.COM   An essential command that must be present in order to boot and start the computer.

composite video   A less-expensive monitor that combines all the colors in a single input line.

console   In the early days, a monitor and keyboard were usually set up at a desk-like console. The term has stuck. A console is a computer. The command COPY CON allows you to use the keyboard as a typewriter. Type COPY CON PRN or COPY CON LPT1 and everything you type will be sent to the printer. At the end of your file, or letter, type Ctrl-Z or F6 to stop sending.

consultant   Someone who is supposed to be an expert who can advise and help you determine what your computer needs are. Similar to an analyst. There are no standard qualifications that must be met. Anyone can call themselves an analyst or consultant.

conventional memory   Also called *real memory*. The first 640K of RAM, the memory that DOS handles. The memory actually consists of 1Mb, but the 384K above the 640K is reserved for system use.

coprocessor   Usually an 8087, 80287, or 80387 that works in conjunction with the CPU and vastly speeds up some operations.

copy protection   A system that prevents a disk from being copied.

CPS   Characters Per Second. When referring to a printer, the speed it can print.

CPU   Central Processing Unit. The Intel 8088, 80286, 80386, or 80486.

CRT   Cathode-Ray Tube. The large tube that is the screen of computer monitors and TVs.

CSMA/CD   Carrier Sense Multiple Access with Collision Detection. A network system that controls the transmissions from several nodes. It detects if two stations try to send at the same time, and notifies the senders to try again at random times.

current directory   The directory of files that is in use at the time.

cursor   The blinking spot on the screen that indicates where the next character will be input.

daisywheel   A round printer or typewriter wheel with flexible fingers that have the alphabet and other formed characters. A solenoid-driven hammer hits the assigned character and presses it against a ribbon onto the paper. Daisywheel printers provide excellent letter-quality type, but they are very slow.

database   A collection of data, usually related in some way.

DATE command   The date is displayed anytime DATE is typed at the prompt sign.

daughterboard   An additional board, such as a modem or extra memory, that is plugged into a board that is plugged into a motherboard.

DES   Data Encryption Standard. First developed by IBM. It can be used to encrypt data so that it is almost impossible to decode it.

DIP   Dual In-line Package. Refers to the two rows of pins on the sides of most integrated circuit chips.

disk controller   A plug-in board that is used to control the hard and/or floppy disk drives. All of the read and write signals go through the controller.

DMA   Direct Memory Access. Some parts of the computer, such as the disk drives, can exchange data directly with the RAM without having to go through the CPU.

DPMI   DOS Protected Mode Interface. A proposed specification to govern the interaction of large applications with each other, DOS, and OS/2.

documentation   Manuals, instructions, or specifications for a system, hardware, or software.

DOS   Disk Operating System. Software that allows programs to interact and run on a computer.

dot matrix   A type of printer that uses a matrix of thin wires or pins to make up the print head. Electronic solenoids push the pins out to form letters out of dots. The dots are made when the pins are pushed against the ribbon and paper.

double density   At one time, most disks were single-sided and had a capacity of 80K to 100K. The technology has advanced so that disks can be recorded on both sides with up to 200K per side. The 5¼-inch, 360K and the 3½-inch, 720K disks are double-sided, double-density. The 1.2Mb and 1.44Mb disks are high-density.

DRAM   Dynamic Random-Access Memory. This is the usual type of memory found in personal computers. It is the least expensive of the memory types.

DTP   Desktop Publishing. A rather loose term that can be applied to a small personal computer and a printer, as well as to high-powered sophisticated systems.

dumb terminal   A terminal that is tied to a mainframe or one that does not have its own microprocessor.

duplex   A characteristic of a communications channel that enables data to be transmitted in both directions. Full-duplex allows the information to be transmitted in both directions simultaneously. In half-duplex, it can be transmitted in both directions, but not at the same time.

EATA   Enhanced AT Attachment. A standard proposed by the Common Access Method (CAM) committee. Their proposal defines a standard interface for connecting controllers to PCs. It defines a standard software protocol and hardware interface for disk controllers, SCSI host adapters, and for other intelligent chip-embedded controllers.

echo   A command that causes information to be displayed on the screen from a .bat or other file. Echo can be turned on or off.

EEPROM   Electrically Erasable Programmable Read-Only Memory.

EGA   Enhanced Graphics Adapter. A board used for high-resolution monitors.

E-mail   Electronic mail. A system that allows messages to be sent through LANs or by modem over telephone lines.

EMS   Expanded Memory Specification. A specification for adding expanded memory put forth by Lotus, Intel, and Microsoft (LIM EMS).

EPROM   Erasable Programmable Read-Only Memory.

ergonomics   The study and science of how the human body can be the most productive in working with machinery. This includes the study of the effects of things like the type of monitor, the type of chair, lighting, and other environmental and physical factors.

errors   DOS displays several error messages if it receives bad commands or there are problems of some sort.

ESDI   Enhanced System Device Interface. A hard disk interface that allows data to be transferred to and from the disk at a rate of 10 megabits per second. The older standard, ST506, allowed only 5 megabits per second.

.EXE   A file with this extension indicates that it is an executable file that can run and execute the program. It is similar to .COM files.

expanded memory   Memory that can be added to a PC, XT, or AT. It can only be accessed through special software.

expansion boards   Boards that are plugged into one of the eight slots on the motherboard to add memory or other functions.

extended memory   RAM that can be added to a 286, 386, or 486.

external commands   DOS commands that are not loaded into memory when the computer is booted.

FAT   File Allocation Table. This is a table on the disk that DOS uses to keep track of all of the parts of a file. A file might be placed in sector 3 of track 1, sectors 5 and 6 of track 10, and sector 4 of track 20. The FAT keeps track of where the parts are located and directs the read or record head to those areas when requested to do so.

fax   A shortened form of the word facsimile and X for transmission. A fax machine scans an image or textual document and digitizes it in a graphic form. As it scans an image, a 0 or 1 is generated depending on the presence or absence of darkness (ink). The 0s and 1s are transmitted over the telephone line as voltages. *See* modem.

fonts   The different types of print characters such as Gothic, Courier, Helvetica, and others. Each is a collection of unique characters and symbols. A typeface becomes a font when associated with a specific size.

format   The process of preparing a disk so that it can be recorded. The formatting process lays down tracks and sectors so that data can be written anywhere on a disk and recovered easily.

fragmentation If a disk has records that have been changed several times, bits of the files will be on several different tracks and sectors. This slows down writing and reading of the files because the head has to move back and forth to the various tracks. If these files are copied to a newly formatted disk, each file will be written to clean tracks that are contiguous. This decreases the access time of the hard disk.

friction feed A printer that uses a roller or platen to pull the paper through.

game port An input/output port for joysticks, trackballs, paddles, and other devices.

gigabyte One billion bytes. This will be a common memory size in a very short time.

glitch An unexpected electrical spike or static disturbance that can cause a loss of data.

global A character or something that appears throughout an entire document or program.

googol 1 followed by 100 zeros.

GUI Graphical User Interface. It usually makes use of a mouse, icons, and windows such as those used by the Macintosh.

handshaking A protocol or routine between systems, usually the printer and the computer, to indicate a readiness to communicate with each other.

hardware The physical parts that make up a computer system such as disk drives, keyboards, monitors, etc.

Hayes compatible Hayes was one of the first modem manufacturers. Like IBM, they created a set of standards that most others have adopted.

hexadecimal A system that uses the base 16. The binary system is based on 2, the decimal system is based on 10. The hexadecimal system is 00, 01, 02, 03, 04, 05, 06, 07, 08, 09, 0A, 0B, 0C, 0D, 0E, 0F. Most of the computer's memory locations are in hexadecimal notation.

hidden files The files that do not show up in a normal directory display, such as the DOS files that are necessary to boot a computer. They are hidden so they will not be accidentally erased. They can be changed with the ATTRIBUTE command.

high-level language A language such as BASIC, Pascal, or C. These program languages are fairly easy to read and understand.

ICs Integrated Circuits. The first integrated circuit was the placing of two transistors in a single can early in the 1960s. Then ways were found to put several semiconductors in a package. This was called small-scale integration (SSI). Then came large-scale integration (LSI), then very large-scale integration (VLSI). Today there is very high-scale integrated circuits (VHSIC).

IDE Integrated Disk Electronics. Western Digital and other companies are manufacturing hard drives with most of the controller circuitry on the disk assembly. They still need an interface of some sort to connect to the computer. They are somewhat similar to SCSI.

interface A piece of hardware or a set of rules that allows communications between two systems.

internal commands Those commands that are loaded into memory when DOS boots.

interpreter A program that translates a high-level language into machine readable code.

I/O Input/Output. The computer's system of accepting data or sending it out.

IRQ Interrupt Request. The PC might have up to 16 IRQ lines that communicate with the CPU. When a device such as a modem or printer needs to become active, it requests the attention of the CPU over one of the IRQ lines.

ISDN Integrated Services Digital Network. A standard for telephone communications for transmission of voice, data, and images.

jumper A shorting bar or clip that can be placed over a set of pins to connect them. Jumpers can be used on motherboards and plug-in boards to configure them for a particular purpose.

kilobyte 1000 bytes. More exactly, it is 1024 bytes, 2^{10}.

LAN Local Area Network. Several computers tied together or tied to a central server.

laser printer A type of printer that uses the same type of "engine" used in copy machines. An electronically controlled laser beam sweeps across a drum. The beam leaves a static charge on the drum with an image of the letters or graphics that is to be printed. The charged areas of the drum then pick up toner particles and deposit them on the page. The page is routed through a heat process that fuses the toner particles to the page.

LIM-EMS Lotus-Intel-Microsoft Expanded Memory Specification.

low-level format Most hard disks must have a preliminary low-level format performed on them before they can be formatted for DOS. Low-level formatting is sometimes called initializing.

low-level language A machine-level language, usually in binary digits, that is very difficult for the ordinary person to understand.

LQ Letter Quality. The type from a daisywheel or formed-type printer.

LUN Logical Unit Number. A number given to a device attached to a SCSI bus.

macro A series of keystrokes that can be recorded, somewhat like a batch file, and typed back when one or more keys are pressed. For instance, I can type my entire address with just two keystrokes.

magneto-optical recording A method of recording on a disk using a laser beam to heat and change tiny segments of magnetic media. This results in very high-density recording.

mainframe A large computer that serves several users.

MCA Micro Channel Architecture. Used in high-end PS/2 products.

megabyte 1,000,000 bytes. More precisely, it is 2^{20}, or 1,048,576 bytes. It takes a minimum of 20 data lines to address 1Mb, a minimum of 24 lines (2^{24}) to address 16Mb, and a minimum of 25 lines (2^{25}) to address 32Mb.

menu A list of choices or options. A menu-driven system makes it very easy for beginners to choose what they want.

micro A prefix meaning one-millionth, such as a microsecond.

milli A prefix meaning one-thousandth, such as a millisecond.

MIPS Million Instructions Per Second.

MFM Modified Frequency Modulation. The scheme for the standard method of recording on hard disks. This method is now obsolete.

MHz Megahertz. A million cycles per second. A few years ago, a committee decided to honor Heinrich Rudolf Hertz (1857–1894) for his early work in electromagnetism, so they changed the cycles per second to hertz.

modem   MOdulator-DEModulator. A device that allows data to be sent over telephone lines. A modem creates digital voltages that are changed or modulated to analog voltages so they can be transmitted over the telephone lines. They are then demodulated by the receiving modem.

mouse   A small pointing device that controls a cursor and moves it anywhere on the screen. It usually has two or three buttons that are assigned various functions.

MTBF   Mean Time Before Failure. Purists say that it should indicate mean time between failures, usually used in describing a hard disk or other component. Purists say the acronym MTTF should be used for new products to indicate the mean time to failure.

multitasking   The ability of the computer to perform more than one task at a time. Many computers have this capability when used with the proper software.

multiuser   A computer that is capable of providing service to more than one user, such as a server for a LAN.

NEAT chipset   New Enhanced AT chipset. Chips and Technology combined the functions of several chips found on the original IBM motherboard into just a few VLSI circuits. These chips are used on the vast majority of clone boards.

NLQ   Near Letter Quality. The better formed characters from a dot matrix printer.

NTSC   National Television Standards Committee. They set the standards for television and video playback in the United States. Europe and other countries use different systems.

null modem cable   A cable with certain pairs of wires that are crossed. If the computer sends data from pin 2, the modem receives it on pin 3. The modem sends data back to the computer from its pin 2 and it is received by the computer on pin 3. Several other wires might also be crossed.

OCR   Optical Character Reader. Used by scanners and other devices to read and convert type into digital data.

OOP   Object-Oriented Programs. A type of programming that utilizes parts of existing programs to provide new applications.

OS/2 2.0   A 32-bit high-end operating system from IBM. It includes DOS 5.0 and Windows.

oscillator   Computers must have very accurate timing pulses. They use quartz crystals that vibrate at accurate frequencies when a voltage is applied to create the precise clock timing signals.

parallel   A system that uses eight lines to send eight bits at a time, or one byte.

parity checking   In the computer memory system, it is an error-detection technique that verifies the integrity of the RAM contents. This is the function of the ninth chip in a memory bank. Parity checking systems are also used in other areas such as verifying the integrity of data transmitted by a modem.

pixel   A picture element, also called a pel. The smallest element of a screen that forms an image.

platter   A magnetic-coated disk used in a hard disk system. A hard disk can have several platters.

plotter   An *X-Y* writing device that can be used for charts, graphics, and other functions that most printers can't do.

pointing device A device such as a mouse, a trackball, or a light pen.

port A plug or socket that allows a peripheral device, such as a printer, to be connected to the computer. It might also be accessible through the slots of the motherboard for items such as plug-in modems, fax boards, or a mouse.

prompt The > sign that shows that DOS is waiting for an entry. The PROMPT command can be programmed to display almost anything you want it to. If you place the command PROMPT PG in your autoexec.bat file, it causes the current drive letter and current directory to be displayed.

protocol The rules and methods by which computers and modems communicate with each other.

QIC Quarter-Inch Cartridge. A width of tape used in tape backup systems.

RAM Random-Access Memory. This is computer memory that is used to temporarily hold files and data as they are being worked on or changed. It can be written to and read from. It is volatile memory. Any data stored in it is lost when the power is turned off.

real mode The only mode available for the 8088 and 80286 systems. It is the lower 1Mb that can be addressed by all systems.

resolution In reference to monitors, it is the number of pixels displayed on the screen. The smaller the dot pitch—the distance between the pixels—the greater the resolution. A dot pitch of 0.31 mm is good, but 0.28 mm or 0.24 mm is better.

RGB Red, Green, and Blue. The three primary colors used in color monitors and TVs. Each color has its own electron gun that shoots streams of electrons to the back of the monitor display causing it to light up in the various colors.

RISC Reduced Instruction Set Computing. A design that allows a computer to operate with fewer instructions, allowing it to run much faster.

RLL Run Length Limited. A scheme of hard disk recording that allows 50 percent more data to be recorded on a hard disk than with the standard MFM scheme. The MFM system divides each track into 17 sectors of 512 bytes each. The RLL format divides the tracks into 26 sectors with 512 bytes each.

ROM Read-Only Memory. It does not change when the power is turned off. The primary use of ROM is in the system BIOS and on some plug-in boards.

scalable typeface Unlike bitmapped systems where each font has one size and characteristic, scalable systems allow typefaces to be shrunk or enlarged to different sizes to meet specific needs. This allows much more flexibility and uses less memory. There are also scalable graphic systems.

SCSI Small Computer System Interface. Pronounced scuzzy. A fast parallel hard disk interface system developed by Shugart Associates and adopted by the ANSI. The SCSI system allows multiple drives to be connected. It supports a parallel transfer rate of 1.2Mb per second. The ESDI serial system can send 10 megabits per second, one bit at a time. It takes eight bits to make a byte, so the ESDI and SCSI systems have about the same speed.

sector A section of a track on a disk. A sector ordinarily holds 512 bytes. A 360K disk has 40 tracks per side. Each track is divided into nine sectors.

serial The transmission of one bit at a time over a single line.

shadow ROM A technology provided on some motherboards that allows the option to copy system ROM BIOS into unused portions of high memory. Because RAM is faster than ROM, it can speed up the system somewhat.

SIMM Single In-line Memory Module. An array of memory chips on a small plug-in board.

SIP Single In-line Package. A memory module that has pins. Many small resistor packs and integrated circuits have a single line of pins.

source diskette When using the DISKCOPY command, it is the original disk to be copied from.

SPARC Scalable Processor Architecture. A RISC system developed by Sun Microsystems for workstations.

spool Simultaneous Peripheral Operations Online. A spooler acts as a storage buffer for data that is then fed to a printer or other device. In the meantime, the computer can be used for other tasks.

SRAM Static RAM. A type of RAM that can be much faster than DRAM. SRAM is made up of actual transistors that are turned on or off and will maintain their state without constant refreshing, such as needed in DRAM. SRAM is considerably more expensive and requires more space than DRAM.

target disk When using the DISKCOPY command, it is the disk to be copied to.

time stamp The record of the time and date that is recorded in the directory when a file is created or changed.

tractor A printer device with sprockets or spikes that pulls the computer paper with the holes in the margins through the printer at a very precise feed rate. A friction feed platen might allow the paper to slip, move to one side or the other, and not be precise in the spacing between the lines.

Trojan horse A harmful piece of code or software that is usually hidden in a software package. It is unlike a virus in that it does not grow and spread.

TSOP Thin Small Outline Packages. A new standard proposed for memory cards such as those used in laptops. It is about the size of a credit card.

TSR Terminate and Stay Resident. When a program such as Sidekick is loaded in memory, it normally stays there until the computer is booted up again. If several TSR programs are loaded in memory, there might not be enough room left to run some programs.

turbo Usually means a computer with a faster-than-normal speed.

UMB Upper Memory Block. Refers to the memory above 640K. With DOS versions higher than 5.0 and other memory managers such as DESQview, this area can be used for such things as TSRs and device drivers. This frees more space in the lower 640K.

user friendly Easy to learn, use, understand, or deal with. Usually means bigger and more expensive.

user groups A club or group of people who use computers. Often the club is devoted to users of a certain type of computer, but in most clubs anyone is welcome to join.

vaporware Products that are announced, usually with great fanfare, but are not yet ready for market.

virtual Something that might be essentially present, but not in actual fact. If you have a single disk drive, it is drive A, but you also have a virtual drive B. If you want to copy a file from one floppy disk to another on your single drive, you can use the command COPY A:filename B:filename (filename is the name of the file you want to copy).

virus   Destructive code that is placed or embedded in a computer program. A virus is usually self-replicating and will often copy itself onto other programs. It might lie dormant for some time, then completely erase your hard disk.

volatile   Refers to memory units such as RAM that lose stored information when power is removed. Nonvolatile memory is similar to that of ROM or a hard disk.

VRAM   Video RAM. A type of RAM used on video or monitor adapters. The better adapters have more memory so that they can retain full-screen high-resolution images.

windows   Many new software packages are now loaded into memory. They stay in the background until they are called for, then they pop up on the screen in a window.

Windows 3.1   The excellent GUI program from Microsoft. It provides an operating environment for programs that makes them easier to use.

XGA   eXtended Graphics Array. A system first introduced by IBM, it supports better resolution than VGA or Super VGA.

Y-connector   A connector that is split so that two devices or two signals can be attached to one cable or one connector.

ZIF   Zero Insertion Force. A type of connector now being used on many motherboards that can have the processor upgraded. Some CPUs and other VLSI chips have up to 169 pins, making them quite difficult to remove and replace. A ZIF connector has a lever that opens the socket so the chips can be easily inserted or removed.

Zmodem   A protocol used on most high-speed modems. It has a high degree of error checking and several other improved features that make it a better choice for high-speed transmissions.

Index

printers, 7, 23
  bar code, 193
  bubblejet, 167
  daisywheel, 167
  dot-matrix, 165-167
  HP DeskJet Plus, 167
  inkjet color, 167-168
  installing, 174
  laser, 168-173
  plotters, 173-174
  sharing, 174-175
  upgrading, 165-175
programmed option select (POS),
  55
protected mode, 74
protocols, 157

R
radio frequency identification
  (RFID), 193
random-access memory (RAM),
  63-64
read-only memory (ROM), 63
  BIOS, 4, 77-83
real mode, 74
repairing (*see* troubleshooting and
  repairing)
run length limited (RLL), 102, 105

S
scan rates, 134-135
scanners, 6, 151, 164
  sources, 151
sectors, 93, 118
serial ports, 223-224
single in-line memory module
  (SIMM), 65
single in-line package (SIP), 65
small computer system interface
  (SCSI), 102-103
software, 7, 23, 177-188
  backup, 128
  CAD, 186-187
  communications, 157
  data compression, 90-91
  database, 182-183
  desktop publishing, 198-199
  diagnostic, 225-226
  directory/disk management
    programs, 185-186
  grammar checkers, 182
  miscellaneous applications, 187
  monitor testing, 144
  operating systems, 74-75, 178-181
  problems with, 226-227

public domain, 209
shareware, 209
spreadsheets, 183-184
tax programs, 190-191
unerase, 123-124
utilities (*see* utilities)
word processing, 181-182
spreadsheet programs, 183-184
  Excel, 183
  Lotus 1-2-3, 183
  Quattro, 184
  SuperCalc5, 184
static electricity, 15, 72, 221
static RAM (SRAM), 43, 68-69
Super VGA, 5, 133
swap meets, 200
switches
  DIP, 27
  fax/phone, 159
  LAN, 197
  setting, 26

T
tape backup, 60
taxes
  deducting computer cost, 189
  deduction for donating
    computer, 154
  electronic filing, 191
  home business preparation, 190
  IRS rules, 189-190
  software programs, 190-191
telecommunications, 6, 22-23,
  155-164
  CCITT standards, 160
  combination units, 164
  sources, 161
  technology advances, 162
telecommuting, 164
tools, 11-13, 220-221
trackballs, 6, 150
  keyboard combination, 150-151
tracks, 93, 118
tracks per inch, 94
troubleshooting and repairing,
  211-228
  AUTOEXEC.BAT, 212-213
  batteries, 220
  business opportunity, 10
  chips, 222-223
  common problems, 220-221
  components, 216-217
  computer lock-up, 224-225
  CONFIG.SYS, 212-213
  dead computer, 212-216

do-it-yourself benefits, 8-9
documentation, 211, 217
DOS error messages, 217-218
electricity, 216-217
instruments/tools, 220-221
intermittent problems, 222-223
monitors, 223
parallel ports, 223
power on self-test (POST), 213-
  216
power supply, 218-220
PS/1 and PS/2 systems, 62
serial ports, 223-224
software, 226-227
swapping spare parts, 221-222
user groups, 227-228

U
uninterruptible power supply
  (UPS), 35
upgrading, 25-35
  286 to 386, 43
  286 to 486, 43
  386 to 486, 43
  alternatives, 9
  AT BIOS, 81
  cost, xv
  determining necessity of, xiv
  new computers, 9
  PC to 286, 42
  PC to 386DX, 43
  PC to 386SX, 42-43
  PC to XT turbo, 41-42
  PC XT to 286, 42
  PC XT to 386DX, 43
  PC XT to 386SX, 42-43
  PC XT to 486, 43
  PC XT to XT turbo, 41-42
  printers, 165-175
  PS/1, 53-62
  PS/2, 53-62
  PS/2 BIOS, 81
  reasons to, xv
  ROM BIOS, 77-83
  software, 177-188
  tools needed, 11-13
  tools, 220-221
  XT BIOS, 81
user groups, 227-228
utilities, 23
  BIOS, 78-79
  built-in motherboard, 53
  CheckIt, 185, 225-226
  defragmentation, 119
  Disk Technician, 185, 225